MEDIAEVAL ORVIETO

Prince Consort Prize Essay
1950

ORVIETO
General View from the South

MEDIAEVAL ORVIETO

The
Political History of an Italian City-State
1157–1334

BY

DANIEL WALEY

FELLOW OF KING'S COLLEGE, CAMBRIDGE
LECTURER IN MEDIAEVAL HISTORY AT THE
LONDON SCHOOL OF ECONOMICS
AND POLITICAL SCIENCE

CAMBRIDGE
AT THE UNIVERSITY PRESS
1952

CAMBRIDGE UNIVERSITY PRESS
Cambridge, New York, Melbourne, Madrid, Cape Town,
Singapore, São Paulo, Delhi, Mexico City

Cambridge University Press
The Edinburgh Building, Cambridge CB2 8RU, UK

Published in the United States of America by Cambridge University Press, New York

www.cambridge.org
Information on this title: www.cambridge.org/9781107621725

© Cambridge University Press 1952

First published 1952
First paperback edition 2013

A catalogue record for this publication is available from the British Library

ISBN 978-1-107-62172-5 Paperback

TO
MY WIFE

CONTENTS

CONTENTS

LIST OF ILLUSTRATIONS

PLATES

MAP

GENEALOGICAL TABLES

Available for download at www.cambridge.org/9781107621725

ix

PREFACE

THE history of Orvieto was suggested to me as a topic for research by the late Dr C. W. Previté-Orton and my debt of gratitude to him is very great. I should like to thank Mr John Saltmarsh for valuable suggestions concerning the presentation of this work. I am indebted most of all to my wife, who has aided me constantly with wise advice and criticism.

My thanks are due to the authorities of the archives in which I have worked and particularly to those of the Archivio Comunale, the Archivio Vescovile and the Biblioteca Comunale at Orvieto. Professore Arch. Renato Bonelli and Signorina Elena Bonelli have been most kind in obtaining photographs for me.

Part of Chapter X has appeared in the *Transactions of the Royal Historical Society*, 4th. series, Vol. XXXII (1950) and I am grateful to the Council of the Society for permission to reproduce it here.

I wish to acknowledge gratefully the financial assistance I have received from King's College and from the Ministry of Education (through a Further Education and Training grant), which has enabled me to undertake this work.

The four plates are from photographs by the Ditta Raffaelli-Armoni-Moretti, Orvieto, and are reproduced by their permission.

D.W.

LONDON
October 1950

ABBREVIATIONS

(See also BIBLIOGRAPHY, p. 159)

ARCHIVES

ACO	=	Archivio Comunale, Orvieto.
AVO	=	Archivio Vescovile, Orvieto.
Arch. Vat.	=	Archivio del Vaticano.
ASS	=	Archivio di Stato, Siena.
ASF	=	Archivio di Stato, Florence.
ACT	=	Archivio Comunale, Todi.
ACP	=	Archivio Comunale, Perugia.

DOCUMENTS IN ARCHIVIO COMUNALE, ORVIETO

Rif.	=	Riformagioni (minutes of Council meetings).
Lib. Don.	=	Liber Donationum.
Lib. Cond.	=	Liber Condemnationum (records of cases tried in the Potestà's Court).

PUBLICATIONS

ASI	=	*Archivio Storico Italiano,* Florence.
ASRSP	=	*Archivio della Società Romana di Storia Patria,* Rome.
BRDSPU	=	*Bollettino della Reale Deputazione di Storia Patria per l'Umbria,* Perugia.
MGH	=	*Monumenta Germaniae Historica (Scriptores),* Hanover, 1820–88.
P.L.	=	*Patrologiae Cursus Completus,* Series I (Latin), Paris, 1844–64.
RIS, O.S.	=	*Rerum Italicarum Scriptores,* ed. L. A. Muratori, Milan, 1723–51.
RIS, N.S.	=	Ditto, ed. G. Carducci and V. Fiorini, Città di Castello, 1900–.

INTRODUCTION

ORVIETO is a small town in central Italy, celebrated for its cathedral and its wine. It is situated almost exactly half-way between Rome and Florence. Perched on an isolated mass of volcanic rock, it dominates the bridge where the road between these two cities crosses the river Paglia. Just above this point the Paglia has been joined by the Chiana, and five miles to the east the two flow into the Tiber; the bridge is not a very long one, but it is the longest on the Val di Chiana-Arezzo route from Rome to Florence. The corresponding bridge on the Rome-Siena road lies a dozen miles west of Orvieto, below the town of Acquapendente. Orvieto is a mile from the bridge as the crow flies, and is more than six hundred feet above it. The town dominates each of its approaches, to the north the valley of the Paglia and the junction with the Chiana, to the south the road to Bolsena and Rome.

Orvieto's own impregnability sets the seal on its strategic importance. From every side it can only be reached by ascending a rocky slope that is at first steep and finally almost sheer. The site has been inhabited since early times, and excavations suggest that it was among the most important of Etruscan towns. It was a fortress which required few man-made defences, and history records no successful assault on it against a united garrison since Belisarius drove out the Goths in the sixth century.

Of the town's history in the early Middle Ages almost nothing is known, but from the twelfth century until the fourteenth it was an independent republic within the States of the Church, and thereafter it fell under the sway of a succession of tyrants, some of them local, others from neighbouring towns, others papal Vicars; it continued to form part of the Patrimony of St Peter until the unification of Italy in 1860. The chapters following are a study of Orvieto's history as a commune, or democratic city-state, from 1157, when the papacy recognized the town's self-governing status, until 1334, the year in which power was assumed by its first Signore, or tyrant, Ermanno Monaldeschi.

The sources for the political history of the town in this period contain serious gaps, but sufficient material is available to make it worth while undertaking what has not previously been attempted, a full-length historical study of the commune.[1] The municipal archive is rich in diplomatic documents, especially from the thirteenth century onwards, and where evidence is lacking from these sources it is often provided by the episcopal archive, which is particularly informative about the last decade of the twelfth century. Chroniclers do much to reveal the events that underlie the bare terms of treaties and submissions, especially in the thirteenth century and later. Incomparably the most valuable source for the commune's history, however, are the minutes of Council meetings, or 'Riformagioni', which are extant with very few breaks from 1295. Thirty-six volumes, of an average length of five hundred pages each, contain the Council minutes for the years 1295-1334, and thanks to them it becomes possible to glimpse between the lines something of the reality of Orvieto's political scene. Like a procession moving forward out of the shadows into a sunlit patch, the town's history shows gradually more clearly throughout the thirteenth century and near its end is suddenly fully illumined. This study is concerned with the commune in its prime rather than with its ill-documented origins and growth.

Most of the valuable diplomatic documents in the Orvieto archive are printed or summarized in Fumi's *Codice Diplomatico della Città d'Orvieto*, and the same scholar edited several Orvietan chronicles under the title *Ephemerides Urbevetanae* in the new edition of Muratori's *Rerum Italicarum Scriptores*. The value of the *Codice Diplomatico* is unfortunately greatly impaired by the hundreds of careless—but occasionally important—errors contained in it.[2] The volume is nevertheless indispensable to the student of

---

[1] The only works that deal generally with the history of the commune in the Middle Ages are Fumi's fragmentary and popular *Orvieto. Note storiche e biografiche* and Rondoni's short review of the *Codice Diplomatico* in the *ASI*.

[2] Many addenda and corrigenda to the *Codice Diplomatico* are incorporated in my article in the *Bollettino dell'Istituto Storico-Artistico Orvietano*, a. IV, fasc. 2 (July-December, 1948) ('Contributo alle Fonti della Storia Medioevale di Orvieto').

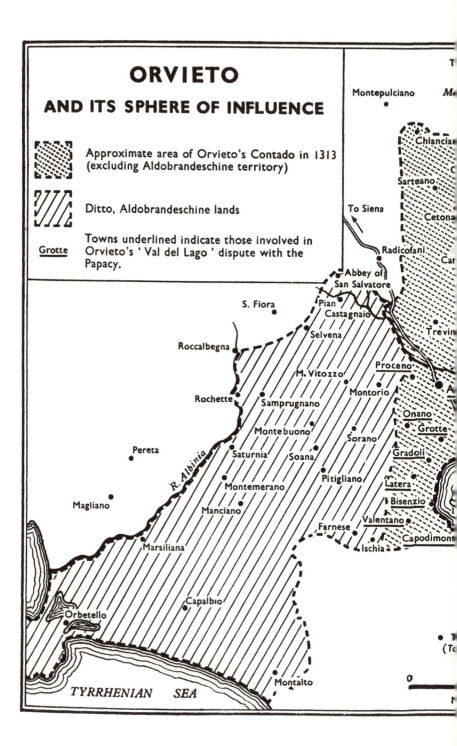

ORVIETO

AND ITS SPHERE OF INFLUENCE

Approximate area of Orvieto's Contado in 1313 (excluding Aldobrandeschine territory)

Ditto, Aldobrandeschine lands

Grotte Towns underlined indicate those involved in Orvieto's 'Val del Lago' dispute with the Papacy.

Montepulciano

Chiancia

Sarteano

To Siena

Cetona

Radicofani

Abbey of
San Salvatore

S. Fiora

Pian
Castagnaio

Trevin

Selvena

Roccalbegna

Proceno

M. Vitozzo

Montorio

Rochette

Onano

Samprugnano

Grotte

Montebuono

Sorano

Gradoli

Pereta

Saturnia

Soana

Pitigliano

Latera

Montemerano

Magliano

Bisenzio

Manciano

Valentano

Farnese

Capodimon

Marsiliana

Ischia

Capalbio

Orbetello

R. Albinia

Montalto

TYRRHENIAN SEA

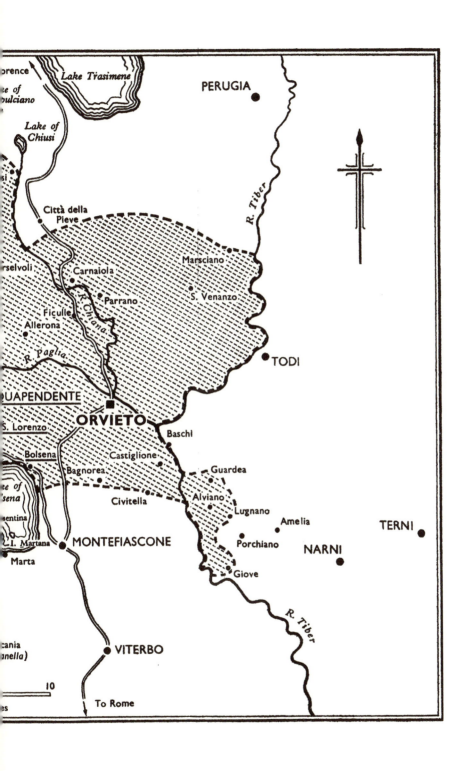

orence

e of
ulciano

Lake Trasimene

PERUGIA

Lake of
Chiusi

Città della
Pieve

R. Tiber

rselvoli

Carnaiola

Marsciano

Parrano

S. Venanzo

Ficulle

R. Chiana

Allerona

R. Paglia

TODI

UAPENDENTE

ORVIETO

Baschi

S. Lorenzo

Bolsena

Castiglione

Bagnorea

Guardea

sena

Civitella

Alviano

sentina

Lugnano

I. Martana

MONTEFIASCONE

Amelia

Marta

Porchiano

NARNI

TERNI

Giove

R. Tiber

cania
nella)

VITERBO

10

To Rome

es

Orvieto's history, and without it and the same editor's *Ephemerides*, a history of the commune in the Middle Ages would be the work of a lifetime, instead of one of a few years. Other useful printed sources are the Orvietan continuation of Martin of Troppau's chronicle, the chronicles of Bishop Ranieri and of the Dominican Caccia, and Pardi's summary of the census of 1292. The few secondary works that exist are so unreliable and inadequate that this study is based almost entirely upon primary authorities, printed and in manuscript.

Historians have not neglected the Italian city-states, but they have studied Venice and Genoa and the great republics of Tuscany and Lombardy, while the independent communes of the Papal States have attracted little attention. Consequently the history of central Italian politics in the Middle Ages is almost unknown in one of its aspects, while an equally important side of papal administration has likewise been overlooked.

After 1157, when Adrian IV visited Orvieto and reached an agreement clarifying the town's status within the Patrimony, it was constantly affected—sometimes favourably, sometimes unfavourably—by its subordination to the papacy. In the next two hundred years the degree of influence exerted by the popes over the commune varied continually and in these variations is echoed the whole frenzied history of Italy during the period. The relations between the communes of the Patrimony and the popes are fundamental to an understanding of the papacy's more spectacular struggles with the Empire. The wealth and peacefulness of the popes' possessions were one of the chief sources of their strength, while the fluctuations of their fortunes in the greater contest in turn affected the reality of their grip on the Patrimony.

Nothing is more typical of the popes than their policy with regard to the communes of the States of the Church. The first years of the thirteenth century saw Innocent III intervening firmly and successfully in the affairs of Orvieto, and its close saw Boniface VIII scheming ineffectually to achieve the same end. How accurately these episodes mirror in little the actions of these popes in wider spheres! Documents in Orvieto's municipal archive reveal in startling detail a lengthy and characteristic intrigue of

Boniface VIII on behalf of his family, while the whole involved tale of Italy in the intervening century is reflected in the gains and losses in papal power over the commune. Innocent succeeded after the long decades of strife with Barbarossa, and at Orvieto—as in Paris and Westminster—the papacy was again a force to be reckoned with.[1] While Innocent's successors were preoccupied with the struggle against Frederick II, Orvieto could almost forget their existence. After a breathing-space for the papacy a new menace arose in Manfred and later Conradin, and the popes continued to have greater affairs than Orvieto on their hands. They called in foreign aid, and when victory came it was a French one, with its concomitant of French authority and French garrisons in the Patrimony. But the popes were free again to concern themselves with their central Italian possessions, and the close of the century brought a crisis in Orvieto's relations with the papacy which was ended only by the Curia's removal beyond the Alps. Unfortunately the few writers to concern themselves with this fascinating study in the theme of *de facto* and *de jure* have been lawyers rather than historians, and have constantly sought evidence on the former only to dogmatize unhistorically about the latter.[2]

Economically as well as politically Orvieto is typical of a kind of commune that has been extremely little studied. Historians have in the main been content to investigate the great trading and manufacturing towns, while the smaller communes, those agglomerations of farmers and shopkeepers that were so peculiarly characteristic of Italy, have scarcely been touched upon. There were hundreds of communes throughout Italy of a similar size to Orvieto, though few had so impregnable a site. The town

[1] It was also Innocent who subdivided the States of the Church; thenceforth Orvieto was part of the Patrimony of St Peter in Tuscany, an area administered from Viterbo (later Montefiascone), the boundaries of which were marked approximately by Civita Castellana in the south, Toscanella and Castro in the west, Orvieto and Todi in the north, and Narni in the east.

[2] *V.* (for example) C. Calisse, 'La Costituzione del Patrimonio di S. Pietro in Tuscia' and the works of Ermini cited in the Bibliography. These writers summon evidence from widely separated periods to reach—quite inaccurate—conclusions about the 'rights' of the papacy in the Patrimony. None of the books dealing with single towns of the Patrimony —even such reputable works as Guardabassi's on Perugia, Ceci's on Todi, and Pinzi's on Viterbo—treats the subject at all adequately.

xvi

probably numbered over twenty thousand inhabitants at the end
of the thirteenth century. It was thus of a fair size, though only
about a quarter as large as Florence.[1]

A high proportion of its people were shopkeepers and small
artisans (the occasional presence of the Curia tided them over hard
periods) and many of these also owned land. Some employed a
few labourers, others tilled the soil themselves and tended the
animals which usually shared their houses.[2] Figures unfortunately
are available only for the town and the zone immediately adjacent
to it, but these show that there were over three thousand persons
possessing land in this area. The small number of noble families
(twenty-seven in 1322) precludes the possibility of most of these
landowners being nobles, and the census of 1292 records the trade
of two hundred and fifty of the three thousand landowners.
These artisan-smallholders usually owned plots of land valued at
between one hundred and five hundred lire (the value of any
buildings is specifically excluded), though nine of them had
large holdings worth over a thousand lire, while a number had
very small plots worth as little as five lire. A petition from some
'debiles et impotentes et populares homines' owning land in the
contado suggests that many of Orvieto's small tradesmen also
farmed areas beyond the boundaries of the town.[3]

These land-owning artisans and shopkeepers tended to be a
conservative element, and the division of the land among so many
lent a stability to the commune that was constantly sapped by
divisions among the nobles. From the second half of the thirteenth century, and particularly after 1280, the artisans were
engaged in a struggle to increase their own power at the expense
of the nobility, but after 1284 that contest never led to fighting,
in complete contrast to the quarrels within the nobility. Though
popular officers governed the commune officially after 1292, the
share of power exerted by them and by the nobles actually

[1] For this figure and the statistics on which the discussion of the ownership of land by
shopkeepers is based, v. Pardi, Catasto, passim.
[2] Many of the mediaeval buildings surviving in Orvieto still house horses and donkeys,
but it has recently been made illegal to keep cows in dwellings used by humans.
[3] ACO, Rif. 1304, fos. 221-4v. In 1312 (Rif., fo. 264) one hears of a 'popolano' who
owns nine pigs at Pitigliano, in the contado.

fluctuated until both were submerged by the dictatorship of one noble. That this process was in the main a peaceable one is largely attributable to the numerous class of wealthy artisans, whose interests and traditions linked them with the nobility rather than with their fellow guild-members. This unreliable element played an important rôle during the period of the Popolo's decadence and the popular organization paid dearly for the heterogeneity of its membership.

It has often been remarked that the Italian city-states were one of the great nursing-grounds of Europe's political maturity, because here for the first time in the modern world all the citizens played their part in the affairs of the community, and thereby acquired both experience in politics and a sense of political responsibility. In this respect the Italian school was more valuable than the Flemish one, since republics governing subordinate towns and great areas of countryside gave a richer experience in diplomacy and external affairs than the communes of the Low Countries whose territory comprised only the city.[1] Certainly the government was not democratic in the modern sense, for even under the popular régime only members of Guilds shared in it; the exclusion of journeymen and apprentices, as well as those who exercised no trade, meant that less than half of the adult male population was concerned in the politics of the commune. Yet the participation of even this restricted element in the town's public affairs marks an important contribution to the political education of Europe.

The politics of the Italian communes are also the earliest politics that we are able to study in their day-to-day transactions over a long period, owing to the survival of the minutes of thirteenth-century Council meetings in many municipal archives. Thanks to these volumes it is possible to visualize the meetings of the city-fathers and to catch something of the 'flavour' of communal politics. There is somehow a two-dimensional character about these figures, for we have no Clarendon or Creevey to tell us what

[1] The area ruled by Orvieto in its heyday was approximately the size of the modern duchy of Luxemburg, i.e. about 1,000 sq. miles. There is of course one notable exception to this generalization about the Flemish towns—the position of Ghent under Jacob van Artevelde.

sort of men they were outside the Council-chamber, but towards
the end of the century they begin to acquire more substance; the
first chronicle to depict vividly the events and personalities in the
government of an Italian commune is that of Dino Compagni,
who describes Florence between 1280 and 1312. It is thanks to
Compagni, even more than to Dante or Villani, that the history
of Florence in these years lives with such extraordinary clarity.
The importance of the Ordinamenti della Giustizia has been
exaggerated through our acquaintance with their originator Giano
della Bella, the 'uomo virile e di grande animo', who 'era tanto
ardito, che difendeva quelle cose che altri abandonava, e parlava
quelle che altri taceva, e tutto in favore della giustizia contro a'
colpevoli',[1] while the demagogy of the time comes to life in the
description of Pecora 'the mighty butcher', 'uomo di poca verità,
seguitatore di male, lusinghiero . . . grande era di corpo, ardito,
e sfacciato, e gran ciarlatore'.[2]

The politics described by Compagni would certainly differ in
feeling from the politics of Orvieto, for they are those of a large
town possessing a very important cloth industry, and with a
completely different tradition and personality. The real fascination
of communal history lies in the distinctive character of each city,
the subtle product of the interplay of historical and topographical
factors. Institutions might be copied from other cities, but funda-
mentally it was the men of each city who made it politically as
well as architecturally, building up a tradition which gradually
conferred upon the town its own personality. When Dante speaks
of a town it is immediately apparent that to him it is a character,
almost a person, certainly not a 'place' in the modern sense. When
his Pia says 'Siena mi fe' ', she means that it is Siena with its whole
history, its organization and its outlook that has shaped her, not
just that she was born at the place called Siena. Again and again
the Divina Commedia hits off in a phrase the personality of a town.
Pistoia is a fit lair for the wild beast Vanni .Fucci, Cesena lives

[1] 'A strong man and one great in spirit; he was so daring that he defended the causes
that others abandoned and spoke out about the things that others hushed up, and always
on the side of justice against the guilty.'
[2] 'A man of little truth, a follower of evil, a flatterer . . . large of body, daring, shame-
less, and a great talker.'

between tyranny and liberty just as she is situated between the mountains and the plain.[1]

Orvieto has no Dino Compagni and the reports of Council meetings, which do provide a picture of the politics of the commune, suffer in comparison both by their formal nature and by being written in Latin. This tends to make them yet more impersonal, for their Latin lacks the spontaneity of the vernacular in which the notaries actually thought. Nor has Dante characterized Orvieto in a line, though he makes a reference to the town in the *Divina Commedia*, when he quotes the Monaldeschi and Filippeschi, the great Guelf and the great Ghibelline family, as typical of the factions that rent every Italian city.[2]

Yet one can trace some of the ingredients that were important in the formation of Orvieto as an entity. First of all must come its isolated position, its natural impregnability, and its strategic importance; these factors gave the town a status that it would not otherwise have attained and strongly influenced the character of its inhabitants. The social composition of the town, with its big class of artisan-farmers, has already been discussed. As early as the middle of the twelfth century a series of political factors begins to work upon these 'natural' ones. The earliest and perhaps the most important is the town's long connection with the papacy. Orvieto gave hospitality to ten popes between 1156 and 1297, and in the thirty-five years after 1262, when Urban IV came there to seek refuge from Manfred, the town was the seat of the Curia for a total period of ten years. The presence of this enormous colony of ecclesiastics, with their guards and servants, must have had an important economic effect; they provided a market for the town's produce as well as many forms of employment for its inhabitants. But Orvieto was far from being the ideally pro-papal town. From the late twelfth century onwards it had an acrimonious dispute with the papacy over the possession of Acquapendente and the Val del Lago di Bolsena, a fertile area comprising the northern shore of Lake Bolsena and the towns of S. Lorenzo, Grotte,

---

[1] *Purgatorio*, v., 133-6 ('Siena made me'); *Inferno*, XXIV, 124-6; *ibid*.., XXVII, 52-4.

[2] 'Vieni a veder Montecchi e Cappelletti,
Monaldi e Filippeschi, uom senza cura:
color già tristi, e costor con sospetti'   (*Purgatorio*, VI, 106-8). (See p. 92.)

Gradoli and Latera on the ridge dominating it.[1] Relations between Orvieto and the popes were constantly embittered by this long-drawn-out controversy.

The grain-producing Val di Chiana in the north and the Val del Lago in the south early came within the commune's sphere of influence, but the vast expanses of the Aldobrandeschine contado in the west were the primary field of Orvieto's ambitions and she exercised her greatest powers in their retention. As early as 1216 the city obtained the submission of a huge area stretching from the river Albegna in the north to Montalto in the south and including the valuable port of Orbetello, sixty miles from Orvieto. The attempt to hold and govern this enormous territory was the republic's paramount concern for the rest of its existence.

Dating back almost as far as this submission was the alliance with Florence, which arose from the mutual enmity of the two towns with Siena, Orvieto's northern neighbour and her constant rival for the control of the Aldobrandeschine lands and the fortresses of Chiusi, Sarteano and Chianciano in the Val di Chiana.

One more factor specially characteristic of Orvieto was the domination of each of the great factions by one family. This was particularly true of the Monaldeschi, the town's most powerful family from the early thirteenth century and the undisputed leaders of the Guelfs; the Filippeschi, though they never attained a position approximating to that of the Monaldeschi, were by far the most important of the Ghibelline families.

All the above were elements in Orvieto's special tradition. There are some factors common to the politics of all the communes, factors which were dependent on the general structure of the city-states and their institutions, and can be examined in Orvieto as well as in the more intricate politics of a great town like Florence. The first impression made by a study of the communes is their extraordinary informality. There is a quite special flavour about their dealings that at once appears strange and almost mystifying to those accustomed to the clear-cut distinctions and rules of modern European governments. Each matter with which the Council deals is tackled on its own merits without reference

[1] See Map.

to any theoretical justification for the course of action decided upon. Principles are never stated, instead constitutions and political organs grow up through a series of *ad hoc* solutions to specific problems. As a result of this informality or unselfconsciousness it is very rarely possible to find a clear-cut answer to a question such as 'What powers had such a political body in such a year?' The powers actually exerted by that body depended not on any written code but on its own strength and assertiveness at the time—which might either shrink or grow drastically in the following year. In Orvieto, for example, the principal position within the commune was gradually usurped by the officers of the Popolo—the body of non-noble artisans—the process beginning before 1250 and gaining momentum in the 1280s and 1290s, but it was never complete and was never specifically recognized or defined in any constitutional document.

One aspect of this constitutional elasticity was the extraordinarily experimental nature of communal legislation, which made Dante call Florence, 'thou who makest provisions so fine that the threads thou spinnest in October do not last to mid-November'.[1] Perhaps the most characteristic organ of the commune is the Balia, an *ad hoc* committee usually appointed by Councils to advise on the action to be taken in a specific matter. Whenever a military campaign, an important piece of diplomatic business, or any other negotiation became necessary, a Balia was at once set up to deal with it. The principal advantage of the Balia was that it handled points of detail, thus enabling the Councils to concentrate on the more general aspects of policy. After the Popolo took control it was also valuable as a device whereby the aristocracy, excluded from the other organs of government, could give much-needed advice on military and diplomatic affairs.

Equally characteristic of the city-state was the existence of several 'States within the State' or what an Italian scholar has termed the *regime accentuato*. In many ways this is analogous to the Party-State of a Fascist or Communist type, for bodies existing

[1] . . . te che fai tanto sottili
provvedimenti, che a mezzo novembre
non giunge quel che tu d'ottobre fili'
(*Purgatorio*, VI, 142-4.)

within the State and independently of it had their own organization of officers and councils and their powers were extended to include much that in any other type of government would be the business of the State. The existence side by side of a Potestà and a Capitano del Popolo in Orvieto and most other Italian cities from the middle of the thirteenth century onwards is typical both of this régime and of the undefined powers of all communal institutions. The Potestà as the head of the greater, all-embracing body, the commune, was in theory the superior officer, but in practice his powers became almost exclusively judicial, while those of the Capitano were far wider.

At Orvieto the great *imperium in imperio* was the Popolo, the organization of the members of Arti, or guilds. It is not possible to follow in detail the steps whereby the Popolo usurped the powers of the commune, but the process was well under way by the 1280s, when the popular party derived much strength from its opposition to the pro-French policy of the Guelf nobles, and the installation of the régime of the Seven Consuls of the Seven Arti in 1292 marks the fundamental stage in the triumph of the Popolo. But the communal *regime accentuato* differs from the modern party-state in that several party-organizations, instead of one only, existed within the State and performed what would elsewhere be considered as State functions. Thus in Orvieto the Guelf party attained a certain degree of political power, though it never reached the status that it had, for instance, in Florence between 1267 and 1280. It existed quite independently of the Popolo, of which it was not even a rival, for the Guelfs included *popolani*, though they were mainly directed by the nobility.

It is also typical of the city-republic that two conflicting principles appear to have governed the methods of election to offices and councils. One of these was the strictly democratic principle of choice by lot, the other that of indirect election. Each had its advantages, for the former counteracted the tendency for certain individuals to acquire undue power (a danger to which the commune was always alert[1]), while the latter ensured some

---

[1] Its suspicions ought, however, to have been directed against cliques and families rather than individuals (see pp. 120-1).

continuity, since even if the *mediani*, chosen by the first electors, differed from their predecessors it was probable that the secondary election would leave some of the previous office-holders in place.

Within this extraordinarily elastic framework raged the two great struggles of the commune's history, between the Guelf Monaldeschi and the Ghibelline Filippeschi, and between the artisans and the hereditary nobility, who were represented in the last phase by the victors of the former contest, the Monaldeschi.

The division between nobles and Popolo was clear-cut institutionally, but it corresponded with no distinct economic or social dichotomy, and the Popolo's cause suffered constantly from the only tepidly anti-noble sentiments of most of its prominent personalities. Orvieto's social structure, with its lack of big industrialists and its extensive class of landowners, helps to explain this phenomenon, but a recent historian of Florence has observed an analogous situation in that city in the thirteenth century.[1] The Popolo as an institution was an importation, but it drew its strength from the reaction of the bulk of the artisans to the exorbitant power of the nobility. Through the Popolo's opposition to the Guelf nobles, who were in alliance with the hated Angevin garrison and the French popes, its cause acquired a certain idealological content, and as it grew in self-awareness it evolved a programme. The large part it played in the ambitious foreign policy of the last decade of the thirteenth century secured for the Popolo an ever greater share of power, and by the close of the century its officers governed the city. Yet its fight against the temporarily united aristocracy, conducted vigorously between 1303 and 1310, was unsuccessful, and the Popolo seems to have played little part in the decisive victory over the Ghibellines in 1313 or during the first phases of the Guelf régime that followed. From 1316 until 1322 it was engaged in its final struggle under the competent generalship of Poncello Orsini, but its own heterogeneity and the constitutional compulsion to find its leaders outside Orvieto were fatal to the

[1] 'The governing class of the Guelf commune is closely related to that of the First Popolo; in other words, it consists of members of Florence's business and trading world and can virtually be identified with the rulers of the First Popolo, which was substantially, though not formally, Guelf' (N. Ottokar, *Studi Comunali e Fiorentini*, Florence, 1948, p. 81).

Popolo, and it never recovered from its defeat by the Monaldeschi in the latter year.

The Monaldeschi, who had grown up under the commune, were the agents of its destruction. From small beginnings in the twelfth century they steadily increased their power, gaining with every crisis. The expulsion of the heretics in 1199 gave them Rocca Sberna, their first country seat, and probably much else. In the first half of the thirteenth century they forged ahead of every other Orvietan family, producing a number of outstanding men and filling scores of municipal offices. Around 1240 they fell out with their closest rivals, the Filippeschi, probably over some quite trivial question; Villani has often been ridiculed for his attribution of the quarrel between Guelf and Ghibelline in Florence to a personal feud over a broken marriage engagement,[1] but it is old scores such as these which, recalled for decade after decade, build up a tradition of revenge and harden rivalry into hatred. From the 1260s the Monaldeschi threw in their weight with the Angevin cause, which was destined to be the successful one, though it was not generally popular in Orvieto. They exceeded every other family in their devotion to the French, and their complete identification with the Guelf party in Orvieto probably dates from this time. Their feud with the Filippeschi can be traced without interruption from the same period, though it was temporarily laid aside between 1293 and 1303 on behalf of the higher interests of the city. But the Monaldeschi never receded from their leading position within the commune. In 1313 they won the decisive victory over the Filippeschi and less than ten years later they sealed the doom of the Popolo.

That a Monaldeschi tyranny was postponed until 1334 was due only to divisions within the family. The Monaldeschi had come far since Pietro di Cittadino—the great-great-grandfather of Manno, the Signore of 1334—farmed a small patch of land by the Paglia.

---

[1] G. Villani, *Cronica*, lib. v, cap. 38.

CHAPTER I

THE COMMUNE'S ORIGINS AND THE FIRST EXTENSION OF ITS RULE (1157-98)

As PART of Lombard Tuscany, Orvieto is included by name in the imperial Donations of 817, 962 and 1020,[1] but little is known of the history of the town before 1024 (the date of the earliest deed preserved in the episcopal archive) and the evidence of local chroniclers and documentary material in the municipal archive relates only to a period beginning with the second half of the twelfth century.

The early episcopal documents are valuable for their references to Orvieto's diocese, for this was the town's subject-territory, or 'contado', in embryo. As early as 1024 places lying within the diocese were described as within the 'comitatus'. Since Orvieto had no Count of its own (though there were several in the neighbourhood) it is clear that 'comitatus', which is once amplified as 'territorio et comitatu de Urbeveto',[2] had already taken on the meaning of 'territorium urbis' (Ducange). Thus the bishopric was the link that connected Orvieto with the surrounding territory, and the growth of the commune's rule in the contado is largely the history of its gradual absorption of episcopal rights. But the evidence concerning this process is both scanty and indecisive, and Orvieto can provide little ammunition to the combatants in the great academic war over municipal origins.

The first mention of a commune of Orvieto occurs in a document of 1137 whereby a local Count made a donation to the Bishop of Orvieto including that part of 'Vangno' (probably the village of Vaiano, eight miles south of Orvieto) not already granted to the 'commune civitatis'.[3] This isolated reference, revealing the existence of a property-owning commune, in the fourth decade of the twelfth century, is followed by a silence of twenty years.

[1] *Liber Censuum*, pp. 363-73.   [2] *C.D.*, I.   [3] *C.D.*, xxvII.

I

Deeds of this period are extant in the episcopal archive, but none of them relate to transactions in which the nascent commune was concerned.

Between 1155 and 1157 Orvieto suddenly takes a place of importance among the towns of the Patrimony of St Peter, thanks to the recognition by Adrian IV, the Englishman, of its advantages as a stronghold. In the latter year its commune was recognized by the pope and thenceforth its history is much more fully documented.

Pope Adrian was a much-travelled ecclesiastic and he had probably passed through Orvieto more than once on his journeys and noted its immensely strong site. In the summer of 1155 he planned to visit the town, which had never previously entertained a pope, and to await there the arrival of Frederick Barbarossa, but the Emperor arrived sooner than expected, and Adrian met him further south, at Civita Castellana.[1] In the autumn of the following year, however, the pope came to Orvieto and stayed there for a period of at least two, and possibly as much as twelve weeks.[2] While at Orvieto the pope confirmed the privileges and possessions of its Chapter, but it was not until after his return to Rome that he signed the agreement with the commune that regulated its relations with the papacy and marks the beginning of its history.

In this convention, which is dated February 1157, the 'populus urbevetanus' was represented by the provost of the chapter (the bishopric being vacant) and by two Consuls and two nobles.[3] So important are its terms that it is necessary to give them at length. Firstly, the Consuls declare themselves to be the liege men of the pope, swearing fealty to him and to his successors 'secundum tenorem iuramenti quod faciunt ei alii fideles sui de Regalibus', and the 'populus' owes the same fealty 'secundum consuetudinem

---

[1] Cardinal Boson's Life of Adrian IV in *Lib. Pont.*, II, 390.

[2] The minimum length of the stay is from 28 September to 15 October (Jaffé, nos. 10205-9). In August the pope was at Narni, and he was back in Rome on 12 November, having stayed some time at Viterbo on the way. The visit is mentioned by several chroniclers (Boson, p. 395; Bernard Gui in RIS, O.S., III, 1, col. 440; Amalricus Angerius, *ibid.*, 2, col. 372; Ptolemy of Lucca in *Cronache dei Sec. XIII e XIV*, Florence, 1876, p. 54).

[3] *C.D.*, p. 26; also in *Liber Censuum*, ed. P. Fabre, Paris, 1905, doc. CVI.

aliarum Civitatum domini Papae'. The Consuls are to renew the oath when requested (a renewal is always to be accompanied by the payment of ten lire) and are responsible for its observance by the 'populus'. Orvieto is to give military aid to the pope when requested, within the limits of Tintinnano to the north and Sutri to the south.[1] When the pope visits the town, it is to be responsible for his safety and that of his companions during their stay and on their journey to and from Orvieto. In return the pope was to pay Orvieto a sum of 300 lire on receipt of the town's oath; he was also to help bring about an agreement between Orvieto and Acquapendente should the citizens of the latter town renew their submission to him.

It is impossible to trace the precise significance of the opening clauses of this agreement,[2] for the terms of the oath taken by the communes of the Patrimony have not survived, and there seems to be no more explicit deed relating to any other town.[3] The importance of the document therefore greatly transcends its interest for the history of Orvieto. In the latter context, however, it represents the logical starting-point for this study, not merely because it provides the background against which must be seen the long and involved history of Orvieto's relations with the popes, but because it illustrates the organization of the primitive commune and in it the 'populus' receives its first official recognition by an external institution—a recognition that must have enormously enhanced its prestige.

From the papal point of view the agreement with Orvieto was part of a policy aimed at securing a real hold over the Tuscan Patrimony. Adrian IV made several purchases in the area from the Counts of Calmaniare, among them a half-share in Proceno, a strong position near Acquapendente; property at Bolsena; and

---

[1] Sutri is some thirty miles south of Orvieto on the main road, and Tintinnano a similar distance to the north-west. The latter is Rocca di Tintinnano in Val d'Orcia.

[2] When Muratori wished to exemplify the status of the communes of the Papal States he could find no document more explicit than this one, which is transcribed in his 'Dissertatio', no. 45 (vol. IV, p. 36 of the 1741 edition).

[3] The formula was still more vague when in 1210 Perugia's municipal institutions were confirmed by the pope and in exchange the town's officers 'juraverunt precettum Domini Pape Innocentii III . . . eiusque Catholicorum successorum . . . obedire et observare' in the area between Rome and Perugia (BRDSPU, I, pp. 149-50).

Ripesena, whose village lies perched below the craggy summit of a volcanic rock which rises out of the plain some three miles from Orvieto. Other measures included the purchase of a half-share in Castiglione Teverina and the re-fortification of Radicofani.[1]

By 1157, then, the commune of Orvieto was an entity capable of possessing property and of waging war. The greatest Italian authority on the communes has said of them that their formation is one process with their first acquisitions of territory in the contado,[2] and the successful subjugation of several neighbouring towns and feudatories is certainly the most important feature of Orvieto's activity in the second half of the twelfth century. Throughout central Italy this was the great period of municipal expansion, the towns rapidly extending their rule now that their desirability as allies and unwelcomeness as foes was coming to outweigh the disadvantages of reduced liberty. Some of these submissions represented solid conquests, others were the result of ephemeral victories and were never fully implemented.

The earliest form of submission to a town was through an oath to its archbishop or bishop. As early as 1118 Parrano was leased to its Count by the Bishop of Orvieto[3] on terms that foreshadow later submissions to the commune, though the military clause is much narrower, since the Count had only to defend Parrano itself, whereas subjects of the commune were normally held to 'facere bellum' wherever and whenever requested.

The earliest extant submission to the commune of Orvieto is that of Count Ranieri of Montorio, made in 1168.[4] The lands of this Count, sometimes known as the 'terra Guiniccesca', comprised the south-eastern corner of the Aldobrandeschine estates; they lay to the west of Lake Bolsena, running approximately from Montorio in the north to Farnese in the south, and such was their

---

[1] *Liber Censuum*, docs. CIII-CV, CXII, CXV; also the chroniclers cited above (p. 2, n. 2). Castiglione Teverina is six miles south-east of Orvieto.

[2] G. Volpe, *Medio Evo Italiano* (1928 edn.), p. 19.

[3] *C.D.*, XV (Parrano is about eight miles north of Orvieto). Dr Previté-Orton has observed (*Cambridge Medieval History*, V, 225) that bishops held an undisputed position in the legal chain which conferred on these deeds a legality in the eyes of feudal law that was inaccessible to the unrecognized organ of the commune.

[4] *C.D.*, XXXIX; Chr. Pot. 2 (*Ephemerides*, p. 141).

distance from Orvieto that it seems unlikely that the commune was able at this stage of its development to hold the Count to the conditions agreed upon. Nevertheless the submission is an interesting clue to Orvieto's early aspirations, and it represents an attempt to encircle the ever-defiant Acquapendente.

The terms of this deed are typical of the many submissions that followed. By them the Count promised to submit ('tradere') his lands to the commune of Orvieto, to declare war and make peace at the request of the commune (war against the pope, the Emperor, and his own tenants being excepted), to give hospitality twice yearly to Orvieto's Consuls or Potestà, to live at Orvieto for a part of each year, and to pay the commune a sum of ten lire. When fighting on behalf of Orvieto, he was to do so at his own risk and expense, and to pay 24 lire towards the general expenses of the campaign. In return for this the Consuls and 'populus' of Orvieto promised to defend and support the Count and his family against all men (with the same exceptions), and their military assistance would also be given at their own peril and expense, the Count however being liable to pay part of the commune's forces in certain circumstances.

Three years later, in 1171, there were two further submissions to Orvieto, by the people of Città della Pieve and by the Counts Bovacciani.[1] Città della Pieve occupies a strong position on the Rome-Florence road some twenty-five miles north of Orvieto. It already possessed its own 'populus', and this rather puzzling submission should probably be ascribed to the desire of the Pievesi to escape the firmer rule of Perugia, a more powerful commune then Orvieto; they even promised to exact no tolls of Orvietans and to pay 100 soldi whenever Orvieto raised a tax, but their plan failed, for in 1188 the Count of Parrano submitted Città della Pieve to Perugia, thereby annulling the previous submission to Orvieto.

The Counts Bovacciani, who submitted on similar terms,[2] were big landowners in the area immediately to the south and south-east

[1] C.D., XLI and XLII.
[2] Their taxation was fixed at the sum of that paid by Orvieto's two most highly taxed citizens.

of Orvieto. These are the last extant twelfth-century submissions to the commune. Probably, others have been lost; it is noteworthy that the submission of Chiusi in 1200[1] speaks of the town as having been subject to Orvieto for over thirty years.

The renewal in 1172 of the lease of Parrano from the Bishop of Orvieto is no less interesting than these submissions for the evidence it provides concerning the expanding power of the commune.[2] Consular representatives of the commune were now present and associated themselves with the bishop in granting tenure of Parrano to the Count,[3] though the terms of the lease itself were almost unaltered. The occasion symbolized the gradual absorption by the commune of the bishop's power in the contado.

Thus within fifteen years of the convention with Adrian IV the commune had stretched its tentacles in every direction. Its advance towards the west and north had been particularly striking, though some of its gains were to prove short-lived. Such expansion was only possible to the newly-constituted commune through the alliance of its neighbours. There is nothing really paradoxical in the fact that Siena, which was to be Orvieto's great enemy, was her first ally. So long as the principal preoccupation of each town was the subjugation of its own contado, its interest was to give support to its neighbour in maintaining pressure on the intervening territory; only when the contado had been conquered and neighbouring towns had truly common frontiers did the Italian municipal system of alliances assume its characteristic chequered pattern. Between Siena and Orvieto lay the vast feudal estates of the Aldobrandeschi, the greatest holding in Tuscany that was still subject to no commune. The mutual interest of the two towns in co-operating to subjugate this area explains sufficiently Orvieto's participation on the Sienese side in the war against Florence of 1174-6[4] and Siena's intervention on Orvieto's behalf at Acquapendente in 1198.[5]

---

[1] *C.D.*, LXX.   [2] *C.D.*, XLV. For the lease of Parrano in 1118 see p. 4.
[3] The deed is described as a 'carta convenentie et trasactionis que facta est inter R. Urbevetanum episcopum et R. comitem . . . de Castro Parrani et misterio eius', and the Bishop grants the Count Parrano 'una cum consulibus civitatis, scilicet . . . et populo eiusdem civitatis'.
[4] R. Davidsohn, *Geschichte von Florenz*, 1, 542-3.   [5] See p. 12.

6

At the same time as the commune was forming its earliest alliances its political personality was being moulded in the opening stages of that long struggle for the control of Acquapendente which was to extend all through the town's existence as a free commune. In the twelfth-century this entailed opposition to the mighty but distant powers of Empire and papacy.

Acquapendente was considered to lie within Orvieto's 'comitatus' as early as the eleventh century,[1] but she was a sturdy neighbour, probably almost equal to Orvieto in size and strength, and in 1157 seems to have recognized the suzerainty neither of pope nor commune. The first of her many wars with Orvieto probably dates from about this period,[2] but she only continued to exchange one master for another and after 1161 was under imperial domination for most of the remainder of the century. In that year Barbarossa ruled all the Papal State from Acquapendente to Ceprano, and though local tradition tells of a successful rising against the Empire in 1166, the town was still a centre of imperial administration in 1177.[3] A number of feudal barons of the area, among them the lords of Montorio and the Counts Aldobrandeschi and Manenti (of Val di Chiana),[4] gave powerful assistance to the imperial cause and against such a combination Orvieto was impotent.

The period of Alexander III's struggle with Barbarossa was a chaotic one in central Italy and the existence of a number of schismatic bishops, recognized by the Emperor but not by the pope, was an additional complication. Out of a predicament of this sort there arose a boundary dispute between the dioceses of Orvieto and Soana which in the 1190s culminated in a lawsuit.[5]

---

[1] *C.D.*, I.

[2] See p. 3 . There were two wars between Orvieto and Acquapendente before 1194 (*C.D.*, LXII). Chr. Ant. and Chr. Pot. 2 (*Ephemerides*, pp. 125 and 141) relate that peace was made between the two towns in 1161, but this assertion may be founded on two forged deeds printed in *C.D.*, XLIII-IV.

[3] Boson's Life of Alexander III in *Lib. Pont.*, II, pp. 403-4; N. Costantini, *Memorie Storiche di Acquapendente*, pp. 34-5; *ibid.*, doc. IX. Henry VI paid a visit to Acquapendente in 1187 (T. Toeche, *Kaiser Heinrich VI*, Leipzig, 1867, p. 641), and nine years later Proceno was formally claimed for the Empire (*Liber Censuum*, ed. Fabre, pp. 553-5).

[4] Toeche, p. 650; Stumpf, *Die Reichskanzler* (Innsbruck, 1865-), I, 380; Ciacci, doc. CCXII.

[5] *C.D.*, LXI-III; Ciacci, docs. CCXXXIV and CCXXXVI; Chr. Ranieri, p. 6.

7

The claims put forward by the Bishop of Soana to Grotte and several other parishes south of Acquapendente were connected with Acquapendente's aspirations to civil and ecclesiastical independence,[1] and this quarrel likewise added momentum to the growth of the commune's political tradition and its self-awareness.

There were two wars between Orvieto and Acquapendente before 1194 and a third before 1198,[2] but by far the most important episode for Orvieto in this long contest of the second half of the twelfth century was the imperialist siege of Orvieto in 1186. In a sense this siege was an extension of the struggle for Acquapendente, for it represents an attempt to secure possession of the positions dominating the Paglia river-crossing on both the main routes from Tuscany to Rome. 1186 was the year of Henry VI's great offensive against the Italian communes, when he attempted to deprive them by legislation of their contadi, and routed the Sienese, who had resisted this measure. In June Henry marched south from Siena and laid siege to Orvieto. Three royal deeds, the earliest on June 24th and the latest on July 6th are dated 'in obsidione Urbis veteris'.[3] Since Henry was at Siena early in June and at Gubbio by August 7th, he cannot have been present himself at the siege for more than two months. It is improbable that the siege continued longer, although the Orvietan chroniclers describe it as lasting for several years.[4] The outcome of this siege is as uncertain as its duration. By a deed of 3 April 1189 Henry VI restored to Pope Clement III 'omnem possessionem quam habuit papa Lucius in civitate Urbevetana' and absolved from their oaths such Orvietans as had previously sworn fealty to the pope and later 'magestati nostre juraverunt';[5] this document led Davidsohn to state that Henry conquered ('besiegt') Orvieto,

---

[1] The Abbey of S. Sepolcro at Acquapendente claimed exemption from the authority of the Bishop of Orvieto (Della Valle, p. 20) and the parish of Grotte lay within the jurisdiction of this Abbey (see p. 23).

[2] *C.D.*, p. 43 (see pp. 12-13).　　　　　　　　　　　　　　　　　[3] Toeche, p. 638.

[4] One chronicle says three years, another as much as seven (*Ephemerides*, pp. 126, 141 275-6): this may indicate that the siege was renewed in the succeeding summers, but there is no confirmation.

[5] *C.D.*, LVIII. For the controversy over the outcome of the siege v. Davidsohn, *Geschichte von Florenz*, I, 581, and Fumi's reply in BRDSPU, XXII (1916), the latter asserting patriotically that no German had captured Orvieto or would ever do so.

but his conclusion has been challenged. It does indeed seem probable that the vague wording of the deed is intentional, and that those 'qui juraverunt' were not the undisputed officers of the town. Possibly the phrase refers to nobles of the Orvietan contado or to representatives of the commune the validity of whose appointment was questionable (such as leaders of a pro-imperial faction). Evidently Henry did not abandon the siege empty-handed, but it seems improbable that he brought it to a completely victorious conclusion.

The chronicles at least make it evident that this episode was remembered as an important and glorious one in the history of the commune. Like the contado submissions and the struggle for Acquapendente, King Henry's siege was both a symptom and a factor in the growth of the commune's strength.

The sole evidence for the constitution of the commune during the period of its earliest expansion is that which can be deduced from formulae employed in the convention and deeds described above. No municipal constitution of the twelfth century has survived, nor is it likely that much more would be known of the political machinery of the primitive commune if a 'constitutum' of this period was extant; for the one referred to in a deed of c.1200 apparently concerned only the judicature, while the 'statutes' of 1209 and 1220 are of little interest.[1]

The most striking characteristic of the twelfth-century commune is its fluidity. Not even the title of the municipal body remains consistent. We first meet it as the *commune*, but by 1157 it is the *populus*, and for the remainder of the century the two names alternate, while *communitas* and *civitas* appear to be further synonyms. It is possible that the word 'populus' excludes the noble element, but analogies with other towns suggest that this is not so.[2] A deed of 1170[3] throws some light on this point and at the same time affords an interesting parallel with the commune's

---

[1] *C.D.*, LXXI (see p. 20).

[2] The use of 'populus' as a synonym for 'commune' is found in the twelfth century at Florence (P. Villari, *I Primi Due Secoli della Storia di Firenze* (3rd edn.), p. 115; at Viterbo (C. Pinzi, *Storia di Viterbo*, I, 142, 175, 190); and at Siena (L. Zdekauer, *Il Constituto di Siena dell'anno 1262*, Milan, 1897, p. XLII). [3] *C.D.*, XL.

participation in the bishop's lease of Parrano two years later; the document concerns the upkeep of the bridge over the Paglia and it shows that decisions concerning this traditionally ecclesiastical matter were by then reached by the Consuls and 'universus populus', in conjunction with the bishop and clergy.

The 'universus populus' of 1170 was the 'parlamentum' or 'arenga' of all the citizens, the characteristic legislative body of the primitive commune. It is evident that had a smaller body existed it could have dealt with so unimportant a matter, but the first reference to a Council of one hundred members does not occur till about the year 1200;[1] there is very little evidence concerning the intervening decades and the appearance of the first Council must be placed vaguely 'within the last thirty years of the twelfth century'.

Fluidity also characterized the titles and numbers of the commune's office-holders. In 1157 there were two Consuls, in 1168 five, in 1170 and 1172 four, and in 1194-7 (except perhaps 1196) two again.[2] The two Consuls of 1157 did not represent the nobles, who had two representatives of their own, and this suggests that when the number of Consuls was increased to four, nobles and non-nobles each had two representatives.

By the close of the century the Consuls were paid servants of the commune,[3] but already the office was being superseded by that of the individual 'Potestas' or 'Rector'. The first 'orvetane civitatis rector' was one Guglielmo in 1171, and there was again a Rector in 1177, in 1181, and perhaps in 1196.[4] The innovation is typical of the period; Viterbo is first known to have had a Rector in 1170 and Perugia in 1174.[5] In Orvieto, as elsewhere, in the late twelfth century a Rector was chosen in some years, while in others the consulate was the supreme authority; the two never existed side by side. It was only in the first years of the thirteenth century that the former office ousted the latter definitively. Until then the word 'potestas' was used in deeds to describe either, rather like

[1] C.D., LXXI, which mentions a Council of 100 'bonorum virorum simul coadunatorum de nobilibus et popularibus'.
[2] C.D., XXXIX, XL, XLV; *Ephemerides*, pp. 137-8.   [3] C.D., LXXI.
[4] C.D., XLI, XLII, XLIX; MGH, XIV, p. 89; *Ephemerides*, p. 138.
[5] C. Pinzi, *Storia di Viterbo*, I, 175; F. Guardabassi, *Storia di Perugia*, I, 128.

10

the modern 'powers that be'.[1] Their position was identical, for they took the same oath on assuming office. The form of oath taken in about 1200[2] reveals that they were held to rule ('regere') Orvieto and to be responsible for the preservation of the commune's property, and that they had certain judicial powers (though there was also a municipal judge to advise them on legal matters).

The chronology of the growth of Orvieto's commune is closely parallel to that of her neighbours; the Perugian commune is first mentioned in the year 1139, that of Viterbo in 1148, and of Todi in 1171.[3] Furthermore the communes of Orvieto and Perugia made their first appearances in Italian diplomacy on the same occasion, the negotiations preceding the Treaty of Venice in 1177, when each town was represented by its Rector.[4] Twelfth-century Orvieto was, however, exceptional in the strength of its heretical faction. Catharism flourished in the troubled soil of Italy throughout the period with which this chapter is concerned, but Orvieto was particularly noted as a centre of heresy; in the next chapter the strength of Orvieto's heretics will be found combining with the commune's aspirations to rule Acquapendente to bring it into conflict with the papacy.

---

[1] This observation is made by P. Villari, *I Primi Due Secoli della Storia di Firenze* (3rd edn.), pp. 146-7. There is an analogy with the French 'poestatz' (= 'feudal magnates').

[2] *C.D.*, LXXI.

[3] Guardabassi, I, 88; Pinzi, I, 141; G. Ceci, *Todi nel Medio Evo*, p. 63.

[4] MGH, XIV, pp. 88-9.

CHAPTER II

FURTHER EXPANSION AND AN INTERNAL CRISIS (1198-1216)

THE pontificate of Innocent III coincides almost precisely with the period between the premature death of Henry VI and Frederick II's coming-of-age. It was natural that the papacy should take advantage of this *détente* to strengthen its hold on the Patrimony; here, as in other fields, Innocent seems to have received praise for pursuing a programme that some equally competent but less fortunate predecessors could have carried out with the same degree of success.

Innocent first turned his attention to the northern fringe of the Papal State and in the first year of his papacy he compelled a number of communes to recognize his sovereignty, among them Perugia, Spoleto, Todi and Orvieto.[1]

The bone of contention between Orvieto and Innocent was Acquapendente; the imperial claimant having temporarily disappeared, there was now a straightforward contest for control of this strategic stronghold. In about 1196 Acquapendente had revolted against Orvieto and on his accession Innocent placed the latter town under an interdict for usurping jurisdiction over Acquapendente.[2] The Orvietans reacted to this threat by calling in as arbiters between themselves and Acquapendente the Consuls of Siena, who in November 1198 announced the exhaustive terms of their decision, which was strongly in favour of Orvieto.[3] The claim that this arbitration was undertaken 'contra voluntatem hominum Acquapendentis et per vim' seems superfluous. Orvieto

---

[1] 'Gesta Innocentii III', chs. 9-12, in P.L., vol. 214.

[2] *Ephemerides*, p. 278; *Parenzo*, § 3.

[3] Acquapendente was to swear to make war and peace at the request of the Consuls of Orvieto, to destroy part of her fortifications and to make Orvieto an annual payment of twenty soldi in token of submission; furthermore she was to pay Orvieto taxes, including 150 lire arrears, but she could not exact tolls from Orvietans (*C.D.*, LXVIII). The protest quoted was made many years later: it is in Theiner, doc. CCLXXIII.

EXPANSION AND CRISIS (1198-1216)

and Siena were already allies and only four years thence were to initiate the division of the vast Aldobrandeschine contado which separated the two towns; this situation explains adequately Siena's good offices to Orvieto.

Within Orvieto itself Innocent III's interdict set in motion a most dramatic chain of events. The existence of a strong heretical faction in the town has already been mentioned. Heresy entered Orvieto during the last three decades of the twelfth century, probably from Florence, for many of its earliest preachers were Florentines[1]. At this time Catharist beliefs were current throughout central Italy, and particularly in the area between Florence and Viterbo, where Innocent III was compelled to conduct a struggle less spectacular but scarcely less momentous than that against the Albigenses in Languedoc. Orvieto was a vital point in this struggle and the murder and posthumous victory of a papal Rector who was later canonized mark a critical stage in the triumph of orthodoxy.

The history of Orvieto's heretics is recounted in the contemporary 'Legend' of St Pier Parenzo, one of the most detailed and vivid sources for the study of Catharist heresy. The earlier and most important part of this Legend was written, probably in 1200, by a certain 'Magister Ioannes' who was a resident of Orvieto and perhaps a Canon there.[2]

The Legend names one Ermannino of Parma as the first to bring Catharism to Orvieto. In about 1170 he was followed by two other preachers, one of them a Florentine. Thanks to the pre-occupation of Bishop Rustico (1168-76) with an anti-bishop recognized by Barbarossa, the heretical community flourished and rapidly increased in numbers; they also drew much of their strength from Ghibelline feeling.[3] Their persecution only began under Bishop Richard (1178-1202), who secured the exile of some and the condemnation to death of others.

The author of the Legend mentions the following heretical tenets of the Orvietan Cathars: they denied the Real Presence of

---

[1] *Parenzo* (which is the authority for all the following passage), § 2.

[2] 'Magister Ioannes' is probably the Canon of that name who is mentioned in several Orvietan deeds of the late twelfth century (e.g. *C.D.*, pp. 33-7; Ciacci, doc. ccxxxvi). The author of the Legend displays a close acquaintanceship with the topography of Orvieto and with local personalities.   [3] *Chr. Ranieri*, pp. 6 and 15.

Christ's Body in the Eucharist and the utility of Catholic baptism and prayers for the dead; they believed that all the popes since Saint Sylvester (the supposed recipient of the Donation of Constantine) were damned, that there was no difference of degree between the joys of all the blessed in Heaven nor between the sufferings of all the damned in Hell, and finally 'omnia visibilia esse a diabolo facta et eius subdita potestati'. The last doctrine contains the dualism fundamental to the Catharan heresy.

Innocent III's quarrel with Orvieto over Acquapendente and the interdict he subsequently laid on the town provided the heretics with the opportunity to reorganize their forces. In the absence of the bishop (whom the pope kept at Rome for nine months) they were able to preach publicly and even to hold a Council of Cathars from neighbouring towns under the presidency of a Viterbese heretic who called himself 'Peter Lombard'. The heretics even spoke, says the Legend, of throwing all the Catholics out of Orvieto and of making the impregnable town a stronghold for their fellow-believers 'ex omnibus mundi partibus'.[1]

On learning of this plan the orthodox decided in consternation to send a deputation to Rome to find a Rector for Orvieto and to seek reconciliation with the pope. The choice of these representatives fell upon a young Roman noble, Pier Parenzo, whose nomination as Rector was approved by Innocent. Parenzo took up his office in February 1199. After consulting the bishop and others, he announced a date by which all heretics were to make their submission to the Church; those doing so would receive clement treatment, but those who did not would be punished strictly, in accordance with the law. Many submitted and were passed by the bishop to the secular arm; some of these, on Parenzo's orders, were whipped, others were fined, while more serious offenders were exiled and their houses destroyed.

At Easter (April 18th) Parenzo visited Rome and during his absence the heretical party formed a plot with the object of compelling him to abandon his office. His punitive measures

---

[1] The Cathars of Southern France, the Albigenses, were actually to conduct such a last defence at Montségur in 1242-4 (*v.* G. Belperron, *La Croisade contre les Albigeois*, Paris, n. d., pp. 427-33). Montségur is an isolated rocky feature very similar to that on which Orvieto stands.

against the heretics continued after his return on May 1st, and on the 20th of that month the plot came to a head. Parenzo was captured, with the complicity of a treacherous servant who admitted the conspirators to his house by night, and taken to a hut on the outskirts of the town;[1] his captors then demanded that he should give up his office, promise to cease persecuting heretics, and return the guarantees paid him. He refused to do any of these, whereupon he was attacked and put to death. His body was found the following morning by monks on their way to the mill, and it is an interesting commentary on the perils of trade in this period that they at first failed to identify the corpse, taking it for 'some merchant who had been killed by robbers'.

Probably indignation at the murder aroused many who had previously been apathetic, and was responsible for the reaction that set in against the heretics. Some of these fled, but others were lynched by the mob. A series of trials followed and many heretics were condemned to lose their property by confiscation.[2]

The Legend describes at length the miracles associated with Parenzo's body and the rapid growth of his cult, which was doubtless fostered as an aid to the revival of orthodoxy in Orvieto. In the very year following the murder its anniversary was regarded as an important local feast, for the Bishop of Chiusi agreed in 1200 to give Orvieto a candle annually, either at Assumption or 'in festivitate beati Petri martiris'.[3]

By that year Orvieto was again a faithful and orthodox subject of the papacy. From 1200 till 1203 the Potestà was Parenzo di Parenzo, brother of the martyr of 1199, and in 1200 Innocent III even gave his approval to the appointment of an Orvietan as Rector of Acquapendente.[4] Though he died in accomplishing it, Parenzo's mission had been fully successful.

---

[1] One party among the conspirators had apparently wished to take Parenzo to the castle of Rispampani, west of Viterbo. This castle was in revolt against the pope ('Gesta Innocentii III', ch. 16) and some of those found guilty of Parenzo's murder later fled there (see also App. III, p. 152).

[2] C.D., LXXI. Bishop Ranieri (Chr., p. 11) mentions 'tres quaterni paterenorum'. These probably recorded the trials that followed the murder; unfortunately they have been lost.

[3] C.D., LXX. The martyrdom of the more famous S. Peter Martyr O.P. did not occur until 1252.   [4] C.D., pp. 49-53: P.L., vol. 214, l. v, n. CXXXVIII.

The most striking demonstration of the pope's determination to make his rule in the Patrimony a reality was the Parliament held at Viterbo in 1207, at which Orvietan representatives were present.[1] Innocent called to this meeting the bishops, abbots, feudal nobility and municipal representatives of the northern belt of the Patrimony, in order to confirm their subjection to him, to legislate for them, and to hear petitions.

His conduct towards Orvieto continued to be firm. In 1203 he again intervened at Acquapendente to forbid a certain noble (this time a Viterbese) to hold the rectorate there,[2] and in 1209 there was once more serious trouble with Orvieto. The origin of this appears to have been a renewed Orvietan claim to control Acquapendente and the surrounding area, for in a typically eloquent letter Innocent wished the commune 'salutem et spiritum consilii sanioris' and allowed it two weeks within which to relinquish the property it had stolen and to cease molesting Acquapendente: after that time he would be compelled to have recourse to 'ferrum vel ignem', to place an interdict on the town and excommunicate the municipal officers, to fine Orvieto four thousand marks, and to call in the secular arm![3] With this bull the fragmentary evidence concerning Innocent's troubles with Orvieto over Acquapendente comes to an end; there is no reference to a new interdict, which suggests that Orvieto withdrew in face of these papal threats.

Innocent's interventions in the affairs of Orvieto were not all to the detriment of the commune; in 1210, for example, he instigated the peace negotiations between Orvieto and Todi.[4] The Orvietans seem to have learnt at the last that not even an eagle's nest (as Luchaire calls their city[5]) was adequate protection from the wrath of the great pope, and a few months before his death Innocent paid them a friendly visit, preaching the crusade and consecrating the church of S. Giovanni.[6]

---

[1] For this Parliament, v. P.L., vol. 215, 'Gesta Inn. III', cols. XXVIII-IX and CLXI-II, and l. X, nos. 131-2.

[2] P.L., vol. 214, l. V, n. CXXXVIII. The pope would only give his approbation to one who was both 'indigena . . . et vassalus noster'.

[3] C.D., LXXXIII (where the date is given wrongly as 1210); P.L., vol. 216, l. XII, n. 80.

[4] C.D., LXXXII.   [5] Innocent III, Rome et l'Italie, p. 85.

[6] Chr. Ant. and Chr. Pot. 2 (Ephemerides, pp. 126 and 142) and Parenzo, § 42. Bulls are dated from Orvieto on 5-7 May 1216 (Potthast, nos. 5104-6).

Apart from the stormy interlude of Pier Parenzo's rectorate, the commune's struggle against Innocent for the control of Acquapendente had been a paper war. The physical strength of the growing town was expended in other enterprises, and above all in a spectacular expansion to the west, far beyond Acquapendente.

A most important factor in this expansion was the continued friendship of Siena. In 1202 a formal military and economic alliance was signed between the two communes. The treaty was to last twenty years, during which period each town was to treat the citizens of the other on a parity with its own and to raise a force of 200 cavalry and 500 infantry twice a year, should it be needed in defence of the other.[1]

It is at least highly probable that this alliance contained a secret clause defining the Sienese and Orvietan 'spheres of influence' within the Aldobrandeschine lands, for in the following year the partition of this territory was begun. Siena at first approached Count Aldobrandino as a friend, and signed a military alliance with him in January 1203.[2] But in addition to provisions for mutual assistance in war the treaty contained terms giving the Count a status very similar to that of the commune's subjects.[3] The agreement had Orvieto's consent and only five months later the Count signed a treaty with Orvieto whereby he was to become a citizen of Orvieto, to pay an annual tribute of 130 lire, and provide hospitality for the commune's officers three times a year. There was a certain ambiguity about the Count's situation *vis-à-vis* Siena and Orvieto, but the two communes agreed to this arrangement and it at least served to secure the Count to their cause while also preparing his complete subjugation.

Siena's most immediate need was an ally against her northern neighbour, Florence. In 1202 the Florentines had made an alliance with Montepulciano,[4] a small but powerfully situated town south of Siena, in an attempt to surround the Sienese and check their southerly expansion. Both the alliance with Orvieto and the pseudo-alliance with Count Aldobrandino were part of Siena's

[1] *C.D.*, LXXIII; *Calef. Vecch.*, I, 71-81.
[2] *C.D.*, LXXIV; *Calef. Vecch.*, I, 81-6.
[3] The Count was to buy property in Siena and live there for at least one month each year. [4] Davidsohn, I, 639-40.

diplomatic counter-offensive,[1] and in 1205 war broke out between the two rival systems of alliance. This war continued spasmodically until 1208,[2] the only major engagement being that fought near Asciano in 1207, in which the Florentines were victorious and Orvieto suffered very heavily. On the whole the war went well for the Florentines, and the peace-terms of 1208 were slightly in their favour, for they gained Poggibonsi. Siena had failed to win over Montepulciano, but had lost none of her southern territory.

This war was followed by two decades of uneasy peace during which Orvieto and Siena set to work to strengthen their hold on their respective spheres of influence in the Aldobrandeschine contado. The old Count Aldobrandino died in 1208 (or soon afterwards),[3] leaving four sons, between whom he ordered his lands to be divided. The brothers failed to agree and Orvieto was able to use their dissensions to its own advantage. The commune was the natural arbiter between the brothers and thus the power whose favour was sought by them all. This situation it exploited with great persistence and success.

As early as 1213 the eldest brother, Aldobrandino 'Maggiore', permitted the town of Soana to submit to Orvieto.[4] This was probably by way of a preliminary bribe, for in 1216 the quarrel between the brothers came to a head and Orvieto was duly called in to arbitrate. The arbitration appears to have been made in the early summer of that year, but by June it was clear that it had failed, and Orvieto came to terms with Aldobrandino 'Maggiore'; the commune undertook to support him in his claims against his brothers and he in return was to submit to Orvieto his expected share in the contado.[5] The territory thus subjected to Orvieto comprised the whole of the Aldobrandeschine lands south of the

---

[1] She also made an alliance with the Counts Manenti and Scialenghi (*Calef. Vecch.*, 1, 78-81).

[2] For this war and the subsequent peace negotiations, *v.* 'Annales Senenses' in MGH, XIX, p. 227; 'Sanzanomis Gesta Florentinorum', in O. Hartwig, *Quellen und Forschungen zur ältesten Geschichte der Stadt Florenz*, p. 16; Ciacci, doc. CCLXVIII; Davidsohn, I, 654-5.

[3] His will is dated 22 October 1208 (Ciacci, I, 61-7 and II, doc. CCLXIX). There was certainly a new Count Aldobrandino in 1212 (*C.D.*, XC).

[4] *C.D.*, XCVI. The town does not appear to have submitted until 1216 (*ibid.*, CV).

[5] *C.D.*, CV-CVII. Aldobrandino Maggiore's claim to this area was based on a previous arbitration made by the Pannocchieschi (Ciacci, doc. CCLXXIX).

river Albegna; its eastern boundary was the Rome-Siena road, its southern one the contadi of Orvieto, Toscanella and Viterbo, while to the west it was bounded by the sea. The extent of this acquisition was equal to the whole area previously subject to the commune.

The promise to support Aldobrandino involved Orvieto in a siege of Pitigliano,[1] but in October the younger brothers decided again to have recourse to the arbitration of the commune, 'tanquam ad propriam matrem'. Orvieto's division of the contado between the four brothers was then accepted by them all. Not all the estates south of the Albegna went to the eldest, but the commune safeguarded its recent acquisitions by the insertion of a clause providing that the lands 'ab Albigna citra' allotted to the younger brothers were to be held of Aldobrandino 'Maggiore', whose submission of them to Orvieto still held. This settlement proved to be a lasting one, and the brothers were probably grateful to an arbiter which had not even simulated unselfish motives.

Altogether the area subject to Orvieto must have been nearly trebled between 1198 and 1216, for the Aldobrandeschine lands were only the most spectacular gain among many. Except to the east and north-east, where Todi was a powerful and jealous neighbour[2] and the Tiber a natural boundary, the commune expanded in every direction. Lugnano, to the south-east (and beyond the Tiber), was conquered in a short campaign in 1204.[3] In 1215 the Viscount of Campiglia submitted his lands, some of which lay between Lake Bolsena and the Aldobrandeschine country, while others adjoined the commune's extreme north-western possessions, towards Siena.[4] In the latter year the commune purchased Bisenzio, a powerful fortress on the western shore of Bolsena.[5] Chiusi was probably subject to Orvieto in the twelfth century, but its earliest extant submission also dates from this period.[6]

---

[1] C.D., CVII (clause 16); Ephemerides, p. 99.
[2] The first of many wars between Todi and Orvieto was fought in 1207-10: C.D., LXXXII and C; Chr. Pot. 2 and L. Manente (Ephemerides, pp. 141 and 285-6).
[3] C.D., LXXVIII.   [4] Ibid., CI-II.
[5] Ibid., XCIX; Viterbese chronicle of Fr. Francesco d'Andrea in ASRSP, XXIV (1901), p. 236.   [6] C.D., LXX.

In two decades the commune had secured the formal submission of a vast territory extending from the Tiber to the Tyrrhenian and from Monte Amiata to Lake Bolsena. So small a town as Orvieto can hardly have dreamt of further expansion. Thenceforward even the most ambitious policy could only aim at the retention and thorough domination of the area already subject to the commune.

Material relating to the commune's constitution is almost as scarce for the early thirteenth century as for the twelfth.

After Parenzo's rectorate the Consuls began to be replaced by Potestà or Rectors drawn from outside Orvieto. In the first decade of the new century there was a Rector every year, though in 1203 both offices seem to have functioned. Between 1210 and 1215 the consulate was apparently revived and existed on its own, but after the latter year it is found only in conjunction with a Potestà, and that during the two brief periods of 1218-21 and 1240-2.[1] The consulate fell entirely into desuetude after 1242, but for a quarter of a century before this the 'stranger' Potestà elected annually had superseded the Consuls as head of the commune. This change was taking place in almost all the Italian communes at the turn of the century. It seems to represent the end of the commune's struggle for recognition; the social elements whence the Consuls were drawn had stood together to achieve this, but as soon as victory had been won, their differences came to the fore. The only solution to the problem of dissensions within the consular class was the importation of rulers from outside.

The 'brevi', or forms of oath, sworn by the municipal officers in about 1200 have survived, as have some statutes carved in stone, the latter dating from 1209 and 1220.[2] Both these sources afford some incidental information concerning the functioning of the commune at this time, but they are disappointingly non-committal. The 'brevi' reveal the existence of a municipal treasurer and judge, and refer to a written 'constitutum', though the latter may have been nothing more than a table of punishments prescribed for

[1] C.D., pp. 52-3, 58-69, 88-92, 166-170; *Ephemerides*, pp. 139-44.
[2] C.D., LXXI; Gualterio, II, doc. VI.

given offences.[1] The statutes on stone relate only to taxation, the payment of salaries to municipal officers, and the system whereby each of the wealthier citizens maintained a horse for the commune's cavalry. They serve to illustrate, however inadequately, that increasingly elaborate organization which was both a cause and a result of the commune's expansion during this period.

---

[1] The only reference to the 'constitution' is in the promise of the Consuls or Potestà to award no greater punishment for any offence than 'in constituto scripta erant et infra statuentur' (*C.D.*, LXXI).

CHAPTER III

CONSOLIDATION: THE LAST YEARS OF THE SIENESE ALLIANCE (1216-29)

THE major theme of the years after 1216 is consolidation in the face of opposition from the papacy and from components of the contado itself, the most prominent among the latter being members of the Aldobrandeschi family. Later, as Siena's power increased and her ambitions began to threaten Orvieto's share of the Aldobrandeschine plunder, there was a third menace.

The opposition from the papacy was weak and, above all, spasmodic. At the height of the contest with Frederick II and his descendants the popes could devote little of their time and resources to affairs within the Patrimony; occasionally a protest would be uttered against some usurpation of papal rights, but effective intervention ended with Frederick's rupture with Honorius III in 1226 and was not resumed until the second half of the century.

The first challenge to Orvieto's newly won authority came in August 1217, when Honorius III warned the commune that Count Aldobrandino's submission of his lands was illegal, since they were held by him of the monastery of S. Anastasio.[1] Orvieto was also charged not to molest the people of these parts with 'indebitis exactionibus'. The mild, almost apologetic, tone of the bull suggests that this ineffective protest was made at the request of the monastery, which had long since lost any real power in the area.

When Honorius intervened again it was once more at the request of a threatened party. In 1219 the lords of Bisenzio appealed to the pope against Orvieto's attempts to secure the judicial submission of their castle, which the commune had purchased four years before.[2] Honorius directed Orvieto to pay a fine and to send a

---

[1] *Reg. Hon. III*, n. 750.
[2] C.D., CXXIX-CXXXII and CXXXV-VI. For the commune's purchase of Bisenzio, see p. 19.

representative to receive a reprimand, but his action merely delayed the submission of Bisenzio by one year.

There is a greater air of reality about Honorius' dealings with Orvieto when they relate to the disputed suzerainty of Acquapendente and Proceno, for here the rights at issue were those of the papacy itself. In 1220 the pope was at Orvieto from June till October, and in that year he seems to have wrested control of the two highly prized fortresses from the commune, though at Proceno his authority was disputed by a German governor appointed by Frederick II. The pope's rule did not long survive his departure, for in June 1222 the Consuls of Acquapendente renewed their oath of submission to Orvieto and Proceno followed suit the next year.[1] After this solitary intervention the papal claim seems to have lapsed by default.

Meanwhile the struggle for lay control of Acquapendente was complicated by the claim of the Abbot of S. Sepolcro to be exempt from the diocesan authority of Orvieto's bishop. The appointment of a series of arbiters failed to put an end to this long-standing controversy, in which ecclesiastical authority on either side received municipal support.[2]

At the same time Orvieto was engaged in combating a much more serious threat in the newly conquered Aldobrandeschine territory. The first sign of unrest in that area came in 1219 when one of the brothers, Count Boniface, perpetrated a large-scale cattle robbery at the expense of some Orvietan citizens; the commune, however, successfully imposed terms whereby the Count restored such cattle as could be traced and paid compensation for the rest.[3] His other debts to the commune were to be paid off at the rate of 1,500 lire annually, after an initial payment of 1,500 lire; the nature of these debts is not revealed.

In 1222 the Aldobrandeschi brothers and some of the towns lying within Orvieto's Aldobrandeschine territory renewed their submissions.[4] In the light of subsequent events and of a reference to arrears in payment of taxes to Orvieto by the brothers, it is

[1] *C.D.*, CLI and CLXVI-II.   [2] *Reg. Hon. III*, n. 6283; Costantini, p. 22.
[3] *C.D.*, CXX and CXXII.
[4] *C.D.*, CXLIX and CLII; and documents mentioned in 'Registro degli Atti' (1339) in *Ephemerides*, p. 100.

probable that this renewal was an extraordinary one made at the request of the commune. Its insincerity was soon apparent. A mysterious dispute concerning a certain Andrea da Morrano and the Counts' continued failure to pay taxes seem to have been the occasion of the war which followed. The details of the campaign are unknown, but the Aldobrandeschi, after capturing Castiglione, appear to have suffered a heavy defeat at the hands of the Orvietans, who were reinforced by troops from the Val del Lago. The three elder Aldobrandeschi brothers were captured and in February 1223 they began peace negotiations.[1]

The settlement of April 1223 was anything but vindictive. The Counts were released after promising to pay an indemnity of 5,000 lire. They also provided many guarantors and securities for their future behaviour, and Orvieto held Pitigliano and Vitozzo until the indemnity was paid in full. The moderation of Orvieto's policy towards the Counts can doubtless be attributed to her own weak situation, but it proved to be wise, for this was their last revolt against the authority of the commune. Before the end of 1223 Orvieto resumed possession of all the Aldobrandeschine territory south of the Albegna.[2]

Orvieto's alliance with Siena was renewed in 1221,[3] but later in the same decade several factors combined to alter the foreign policy of the commune. It has been suggested above that once each city-state had obtained a real control of its subject territory, its neighbour ceased to be its natural friend and became its natural foe. Both Siena and Orvieto were attaining this degree of mastery during the period after 1223. Siena's first appearance in the rôle of a potentially aggressive neighbour was in 1224, when the Sienese drove south to conquer Grosseto, and in the course of the campaign captured Count Guglielmo Aldobrandeschi.[4] Grosseto was not within the area subject to Orvieto, but it lay well to the south of

---

[1] C.D., CLVIII, CLXI and CLXV; ACO, Tit. A, fo. 46; 'Reg. degli Atti' (Ephemerides, p. 103).

[2] C.D., CLXVIII; 'Reg. degli Atti' (Ephemerides, pp. 101 and 122-3).

[3] C.D., CXLI-V.

[4] Ciacci, I, 83 ff. There had been trouble between Orvieto and Siena in 1226 (Entr. & Usc. Siena, I, 14-78); it was probably nothing but a commercial dispute, but it may not have been without some influence on the future relations of the two communes.

the territory originally submitted to Siena, and the move might presage further advances at the expense of Orvieto itself.

The more immediate cause of Orvieto's rupture with Siena was the knowledge that Florence was preparing to take the field against her old enemy. Without Florentine support Orvieto was too weak to defy Siena, but Florence was a formidable ally and she had probably made overtures to Orvieto sometime before the crisis came in the summer of 1229. It seems likely that Orvieto was promised territorial gains in the event of the alliance wresting from Siena some of her southerly possessions.

The year 1229 opened with a Sienese attempt to win over Montepulciano, Florence's former ally in the south. Some nobles of Montepulciano had been exiled and in March Siena made an alliance with them;[1] a papal warning to the Counts Aldobrandeschi not to 'molest' the Sienese was doubtless the outcome of Siena's fear of the Counts taking Florence's side. However, the Sienese attempt to force Montepulciano into submission ended in failure.[2]

Matters came to a head in June. On the 8th of that month four Sienese ambassadors informed the Orvietan Council that their commune was at war with Montepulciano; they asked Orvieto to raise an army to fight on her behalf, in accordance with the terms of the alliance of 1221.[3] The Orvietans refused the Sienese offer to produce the treaty involving them in this obligation, 'dicentes quod bene sciebant quid in eo continebatur', and the Potestà promised on behalf of the commune to raise the force requested. The Sienese were probably aware of Orvieto's unreliability and their doubts can hardly have been allayed by this promise. If the Sienese had any illusions they were rapidly compelled to shed them, for only two days later an agreement was signed between Montepulciano and Orvieto, whereby each promised to make war upon the enemies of the other. Orvieto at once sent two hundred cavalry to strengthen Montepulciano's garrison. Three days later, on June 13th, the treaty was ratified by Montepulciano.[4]

---

[1] *Calef. Vecch.*, I, 394-400. Villari (p. 171) wrongly ascribes this treaty to 1228; the date is Sienese style.

[2] Ciacci, docs. CCCXLVI-CCCLII; Sienese document in ASI, 3rd s., IV, 2, p. 17 n. The Pope feared the Counts as potential powerful allies of Frederick II.   [3] *C.D.*, CXCI.

[4] *C.D.*, CXCII; ASI, 3rd s., IV, 2, p. 17 n.; Chr. Pot. 2 (*Ephemerides*, p. 143).

The presence of a Florentine judge as a witness to the earlier deed is suggestive of the part played by Florence in these negotiations.

The *volte-face* of June 1229 marks a permanent change in the alignment of the commune. On June 27th, a military alliance was signed with Florence,[1] and at once war broke out against Siena. Thenceforward the Florentine alliance was the very foundation of Orvieto's foreign policy. In the course of time the growth of the tradition of friendship with Florence and enmity with Siena was to be abetted by Orvieto's and Florence's Guelfism and Siena's Ghibellinism—but these principles in turn were conditioned by the diplomatic alignment of the towns.

[1] *C.D.*, CXCIII.

CHAPTER IV

THE FIRST SIENESE WAR (1229-40)

THE initial phase of the war went greatly in Siena's favour.[1] An Orvietan incursion into the Sienese contado was repulsed, and the defeated army retired to the strong fortress of Sarteano in Val di Chiana, which they hoped to hold with a large garrison. But the Sienese stormed and captured the keep, taking prisoner more than three hundred Orvietan knights. Among the killed was the Florentine Potestà of Orvieto, who with his officials had accompanied the army. Immediately after this defeat the Counts of Sarteano and Chianciano deserted to Siena's cause,[2] and only a Florentine expedition which harried the country almost to the gates of Siena saved Orvieto from being entirely crushed.

The following year, 1230, was a bad one for Siena, for in June a raiding force of Florentines and Orvietans again reached the gates of the city, only to retreat on account of a Pisan threat to Florence.[3] After this the war began to assume a pattern; each year there were incursions into the contadi, but the main forces avoided contact. The only notable departure from these tactics was a Sienese attempt at chemical warfare; a courier was despatched to scatter 'a certain powder' in the streets of Orvieto.[4]

The principal aim of Florence and Orvieto was the retention of Montepulciano (which now had an Orvietan Potestà) and Montalcino. In 1232 Siena achieved a great diplomatic victory, winning over both Montalcino and Chiusi (which lies astride the main route from Orvieto to Montepulciano), and that October she at

[1] The Orvietan authority for the campaign is Chr. Pot. 2, (*Ephemerides*, p. 143), the Sienese the chronicles in RIS, N.S., xv, 6, pp. 28 and 38, and in RIS, O.S., xv, col. 24.

[2] *C.D.*, cxcv; *Calef. Vecch.*, I, 401-3; *Entr. & Usc. Siena*, III, 147, 206, 212, 216 (Sienese bribes to the Counts of Sarteano and Chianciano).

[3] Villari, p. 172; *Entr. & Usc. Siena*, IV, XXVI-XXXIV; Ciacci, II, 134.

[4] *Entr. & Usc. Siena*, II, 179 ('pro remuneramento servitis que fecit quando ivit ad Urbemveterem et seminavit quadam pulverem per civitatem istam').

last captured Montepulciano.[1] Meanwhile the pope had intervened and both Orvieto and Florence had earned themselves a sentence of excommunication by their refusal to accept his arbitration.[2] The summer campaign of 1233, however, was the last of the war. Siena defeated Campiglia, a new enemy, but she lost the support of Chiusi and the raid by Florentine and Orvietan troops in the Sienese countryside was particularly successful that year; before winter Siena agreed to open peace negotiations.[3]

In March 1234 both sides accepted the arbitration of a papal nominee, a Franciscan. Orvieto was absolved from excommunication, and peace was concluded in June 1235, the terms providing for a return to the frontiers prevailing before the war.[4] Siena was thus obliged to restore Chianciano, with some other minor gains, to Orvieto. Not only had the Sienese nothing to show for a long war in which they had appeared at times to be on the verge of conclusive victory, but they were compelled to pay in full for the rebuilding of Montepulciano's defences; this item cost them eight thousand lire.

In July 1235, while Siena was fulfilling the terms of the peace, the Florentines and Orvietans confirmed their alliance of 1229. It had already been strengthened by the addition of several new clauses, and during the six years of war Florence had provided Orvieto with a Potestà in every year but one.[5] No doubt both parties were satisfied with an agreement which had tided them over a most critical period of Sienese aggression.

The first war with Siena dominates the Orvietan scene in the fourth decade of the century. Another theme that runs through the period is the papacy's constantly reiterated claim to the Val del Lago, but for a long time to come this claim was to lack substantial backing. Gregory IX's first protest against Orvieto's pretensions to the area was made in 1230; he commanded the commune to

---

[1] *Calef. Vecch.*, I, 504-13. [2] *C.D.*, CCII and notes.
[3] *Calef. Vecch.*, I, 400-1, 403-7, 513-6; Villari, p. 173: *C.D.*, CCVII; Chr. Pot. 3 (*Ephemerides*, p. 149); Sienese chronicles in MGH, XIX, p. 229 and RIS, N.S., xv, 6, p. 38 (*ad* 1233, in error).
[4] *C.D.*, CCVIII and notes (arbitration); CCXI (absolution); CCXIII-CCXIX; *Calef. Vecch.*, II, 434-6 and 445-50; Fumi, *Chianciano*, docs. IV-XI (the peace).
[5] *C.D.*, CLXXXIX (dated 1229, in error for 1230) and CCXX; Chr. Pot. 2 (*Ephemerides*, pp. 143-4.)

return this part of the Patrimony to the papacy, on pain of being fined and compelled to refund the revenue received from the Val del Lago during its illegal retention.[1] The Bull went unheeded, as did another four years later which forbade the alienation of certain Patrimonial property, including Acquapendente, Proceno and Bolsena 'cum tota Valle Laci'.[2] An Orvietan chronicler notes gleefully that when a papal chaplain visited Bolsena in 1236, to claim the Val del Lago for the Church, the tails of his horses were cut off and he was ejected from the town.[3] If Orvieto was considered the more desirable of the two claimants at the time, this was probably an indication rather of the ineffectiveness than of the popularity of her rule.

In 1230 Gregory IX had instructed the bishop of Orvieto to exhort the commune to obey his commands concerning the Val del Lago. This was a singularly optimistic measure, since the bishop was as interested as the commune in the retention of the Val del Lago. Bolsena was the original seat of the bishopric, and most of its property was situated near that town. Bishop Ranieri (1228-39) was careful to hold an enquiry into his rights at Bolsena when he collected tenths there in 1229 and he caused the due collection of tenths to be recorded annually.[4] Meanwhile the commune gave its full support to the bishop. When (as in the case of Orvieto) a town had not been the seat of a Count, its claim to its contado was based upon the area of the diocese, for the so-called 'right of the Italic cities' equated the area ruled by the city with the diocese of its bishop.[5] The commune too had possessions near Bolsena, and it co-operated fully with the bishop in his territorial claims.[6]

By 1240 the commune had weathered successfully the persistent

---

[1] C.D., cxcvi = Reg. G. IX, n. 514.

[2] Reg. G. IX, nos. 1715 and 2056.

[3] Chr. Pot. 3 (Ephemerides, p. 149). The pope retaliated by ordering the Sienese not to pay their debts to Orvieto (C.D., p. 152).

[4] Dottarelli, p. 80; AVO, Cod. B, fos. 59-65, 118 and 125.

[5] For Orvieto's use of this 'right' to support her claim to the Val del Lago, v. C.D., DLXX.

[6] For communal property at Grotte, San Lorenzo, etc. v. ACO, 'Comunalie Communis Urbisveteris a. 1244' in Instrumentari, Sottop. I. An analogous case was the Bishop of Todi's claim in 1250 (on behalf of the commune of that town) that the disputed castle of Montemarte was part of Todi's 'comitatu . . . et episcopatu et . . . districtu' (Gualterio, II, doc. 9).

but ineffectual protests of the papacy against its acquisitions and
had carried on a lengthy war against its most powerful neighbour
and rival. The latter was by far the more important of these
achievements, for it had shown that Orvieto could hold its own
in the greater world of city diplomacy and city strife. In the next
decade the commune was to be confronted by a yet more formidable
antagonist, the Emperor Frederick II.

CHAPTER V

A DECADE OF IMPERIAL ASCENDANCY
(1240-50)

DURING the fifth decade of the thirteenth century Orvieto found itself engulfed in the great struggle between Empire and papacy. Between such powers the commune could only follow a cautious policy and hope to survive the troubled period by guile rather than by its own strength.

In 1240 Frederick II undertook a campaign of which the object was the conquest of all central Italy. The Emperor himself marched on Rome from Siena early in the year and after abandoning the capture of the capital he entered the Regno. Meanwhile fighting between imperialist and papal forces had flared up in the Romagna and Tuscany. Almost the whole of Tuscany was occupied and placed under an imperial Vicar-General, while the Patrimony was assigned to a second Vicar-General.

Most of Orvieto's contado was overrun by the imperialists, Selvena and Soana in the Aldobrandeschine country only falling after each had undergone a full-scale siege.[1] Acquapendente, which never lost an opportunity of eluding Orvietan rule, again became an imperialist strong-point after half a century, and took the opportunity to obtain a privilege from the Emperor whereby he recognized the town's customs and liberties and took its inhabitants under his protection.[2] This charter might not signify much, but it could serve as legal ammunition in future struggles with Orvieto.

Meanwhile Orvieto was faced with a critical situation. As the tide of imperial strength flowed strongly round its ramparts, its

---

[1] Chr. Pot. 3 (*Ephemerides*, p. 150); Ciacci, docs. 389 and 390.

[2] Costantini, doc. XII; Huillard-Bréholles, *Hist. Dipl. Frederici II*, VI, 166 (for Frederick's presence at Acquapendente in 1244).

survival depended upon a capacity for remaining inconspicuous and adjusting its policy rapidly in accordance with changing circumstances. Unfortunately the extant sources are inadequate for an assessment of the strength of pro- and anti-imperial feeling in the town during this period. The chroniclers speak of a 'magnum prelium inter omnes urbevetanos' and of 'magna bella inter nobiles', but they never specify the outcome of these disturbances.[1] Of their origin there can be little doubt, though again the chronicles are silent; they must have revolved around the question of the commune's attitude to Frederick. These troubles make their appearance in 1240, when the Empire first threatened Orvieto; that year was characterized by a spectacular outbreak of the heresy which had probably lain smouldering since Parenzo's martyrdom in 1199. It is noteworthy that some heretics who set upon the Dominican inquisitor and beat him included a former Consul and Chamberlain of the commune.[2] 1241 and 1242 were the years of serious internal dissensions; there is some evidence that a coalition between pro- and anti-imperialists was attempted in 1241, but that in the next year the leading members of each faction were sent into exile.[3]

By 1243 Orvieto had apparently committed itself to support of the papal cause, for in that year the commune gave assistance to Viterbo (which was undergoing a Ghibelline siege) and housed imperialist prisoners.[4] Yet this may not indicate a decisive alignment on the papal side, for the Potestà in 1244, Rainaldo Migliorelli, was a member of a Florentine Ghibelline family, while a letter from Frederick II to the commune (written probably in 1247) seems to be addressed to an ally, and exhorts the Orvietans

---

[1] Chr. Pot. 3 (*Ephemerides*, p. 150).

[2] Chr. Pot. 3 and L. Manente (*Ephemerides*, pp. 150 and 297); *C.D.*, ccccxv, ccccxxxvi and pp. 161-6 and 170.

[3] At a later period (*v.* Ch. vIII ff.) the Monaldeschi were the leading Guelf family and the Filippeschi the leading Ghibellines: the two Consuls in June 1241 were Buonconte Monaldeschi and Enrico Filippeschi (*C.D.*, p. 170). L. Manente (*Ephemerides*, p. 298) gives a list of four Filippeschi and five Monaldeschi who were exiled in 1242; the names are slightly confused but they bear every sign of having been copied—with characteristic carelessness—from a document now lost. In May 1241 the pope had appealed to Orvieto to resist Frederick (MGH, *Epistolae Selectae Sec. XIII*, I, 716-7).

[4] Chr. Pot. 3 (*Ephemerides*, p. 150); Theiner, p. 116.

to rejoice over the latest imperial victory.[1] Not only is evidence for this period deficient, but what little exists is puzzling and apparently contradictory. All that can be definitely ascertained is that the commune was torn by factions which respectively favoured the papal and the imperialist causes and that it followed a policy which secured its survival throughout the years of imperial ascendancy. There is no mention of Orvieto itself being attacked by Frederick, yet its passive anti-imperialist rôle was sufficient to earn the praise of Innocent IV because 'ab eius (sc. Romane Ecclesie) fidelitate nullis persuasionum temptationibus avelli potuerint tempore tempestatis'.[2] This combination is a compliment to the sagacity of the commune's rulers during the period, if not to their plain dealing.

---

[1] R. Davidsohn, *Forschungen zur älteren Geschichte von Florenz*, Berlin, 1896, IV, 560; Pardi, 'Podestà, Capitani, Vicari', p. 50; *C.D.*, CCLXV = Huillard-Bréholles, *Hist. Dipl. Frederici II*, VI, pt. 2, 919.

[2] *C.D.*, LXXX (wrongly ascribed to 1208 instead of 1252; this error is corrected by Böhmer's *Regesta Imperii*, ed. Ficker and Winkelmann, V, 2, n. 8502).

CHAPTER VI

THE SECOND SIENESE WAR AND THE EMERGENCE OF THE POPOLO (1250-60)

THE dissolution of Frederick II's central Italian dominion on his death in December 1250 marks not so much a new phase in the commune's development as a return to the conditions prevalent before the imperialist intervention in 1240. With the subsidence of the great powers of Empire and papacy the city-states again came into their own, resuming control of their subject territory and taking up the old alliances and rivalries.

The period immediately following the Emperor's sudden death was a critical one, for all central Italy was in the melting-pot. Frederick had ruled the Aldobrandeschine contado and the Maremma through a Vicar, Manfred Lancia, a relative and later a supporter of King Manfred. On receiving news of the Emperor's death both Lancia and the neighbouring cities acted with great rapidity. Within a fortnight Siena had been offered the Aldo-brandeschine lands by the imperial Vicar and a week later provisional terms were reached between the Vicar and Orvieto.[1] By virtue of this agreement Orvieto resumed possession of Pitigliano and the other principal castles in the part of the Aldobrandeschine lands formerly subject to her, while in return Lancia received the pro-tection and citizenship of the commune; the settlement was so favourable to Lancia that it is not surprising to hear that Orvieto's Captain was fined for accepting a bribe from him. The formal re-submission of the Counts Aldobrandeschi and the towns of the contado followed in the spring and summer of 1251, and in the same period the Val del Lago towns renewed their allegiance.[2] As usual Acquapendente's re-submission was unwilling and was

---

[1] Ciacci, doc. 426; *C.D.*, CCLXXXIV. It is not clear whether Siena was offered Orvieto's former territory; if so, this part of the plan was abortive.

[2] Chr. Pot. 3 (*Ephemerides*, p. 151); *C.D.*, CCXCIII-IV, CCXCVI-VII, CCCII-VIII.

accompanied by disturbances; after the town had taken the oath the Orvietans destroyed part of its walls, whereupon the inhabitants again rose in revolt. The rising was soon suppressed and new terms were imposed which increased the degree of Acquapendente's subjection to her neighbour. Meanwhile these reconquests had earned for Orvieto the imposition of an interdict by Innocent IV.[1]

The collapse of imperialist rule was followed by the reconstruction of the system of Patrimonial and Tuscan Guelf alliances. A local league was formed between Orvieto, Perugia, Narni, Assisi and Spoleto, and in the autumn the long-standing alliance with Florence was again renewed.[2] With the removal of the immediate threat from imperialist power, Orvieto could turn to the pro-Guelf policy that her friendship with Florence implied but which caution had compelled her to abandon (or at least to disguise) during the previous decade.

The struggle with Siena was resumed almost at once, and again the *casus belli* was the Aldobrandeschine contado, where the situation had become fluid as a result of the break-up of Frederick II's dominion. The rivalry of Siena and Orvieto became entangled with the internecine quarrels of the Aldobrandeschi family; Count Guglielmo took the side of Orvieto while his nephew Aldobrandino, who feared that his two cousins might inherit the whole estates, showed his enmity for his uncle by befriending Siena. In May 1251 Aldobrandino reached a secret agreement with Siena to fight Orvieto on behalf of that commune if requested, and during the summer he received a loan from Siena and built a house in the city.[3] Meanwhile Florence had designs on the parts of the Sienese Maremma and in April she signed a commercial agreement with Orvieto's ally Count Guglielmo whereby she acquired the use of Port' Ercole and Talamone;[4] this action was a direct defiance of Siena.

Thus the stage was set for a new episode in the long struggle

---

[1] *C.D.*, cccxliii. The pope only attacked Orvieto's renewed claim to the Val del Lago; the commune's resumption of the other lands previously occupied by Frederick II was recognized by a Bull of 1 August 1252 (*C.D.*, lxxx; for the correct date of this Bull, see p. 33, n. 2).
[2] *C.D.*, ccxcii, ccxciv-v, cccx-xii.   [3] *C.D.*, ccxcix-ccc; Ciacci, docs. 447 and 448.
[4] *C.D.*, ccxcviii.

E

35

between Siena and her northern and southern neighbours. It will be noted that not once did Orvieto attempt to wage war on Siena without the aid of Florence, and indeed the relative strength of the towns was such that the undertaking would certainly have ended in disaster for Orvieto. But Siena was always compelled to exert her greatest efforts in the contest with Florence, not only because defeat in this might have brought about her complete downfall, but also because the territory at stake—the rich Chianti country— was of far greater value than the barren Aldobrandeschine uplands which divided her from Orvieto.

Fighting broke out late in the summer of 1251, and again Orvieto's main task was the defence of Montepulciano and Montalcino.[1] The year 1252 saw a successful Orvietan raid into the Sienese contado and a Sienese siege of Montalcino which was ended in November by a great victory for Florence and Orvieto. The following year, however, Siena won over Montalcino and there was again fighting for this town in 1254. In the summer of 1254 papal intervention brought about a temporary pacification, Siena again being compelled to renounce her projects against Montepulciano and Montalcino; another long war had brought no change in the balance of power in south-western Tuscany.[2] Later in the year the Aldobrandeschine lands were divided a second time, on the death of Count Guglielmo; Aldobrandino, Siena's ally, received a share though he failed to oust his cousins.[3]

Although this peace was followed by a treaty of alliance between Florence and Siena, signed in 1255, its life was even shorter than that of its predecessors. In the same year Siena sought revenge by attacking Pian Castagnaio, a town which had given support to Count Guglielmo. By 1256 Florence and Lucca were at war with Pisa and Siena, and in September a hundred Orvietan knights fought on the Florentine side in an engagement on the Serchio.[4] The commune was probably prevented from sparing more troops

[1] For this war v. Chr. Pot. 3 (Ephemerides, pp. 151-2) and Ann. Sen. in MGH, XIX, p. 230; also Ciacci, doc. 645 and C.D., cccxiv.

[2] Ciacci, doc. 467; C.D., cccxxi; Calef. Vecch., II, 777-9.

[3] Ciacci, I, 128; Bruscalupi, Monografia . . . di Pitigliano, pp. 115-6. The peace-terms of that summer had compelled Siena to restore to Count Guglielmo all his previous possessions (Calef. Vecch., II, 775).

[4] Ciacci, I, 128; Chr. Pot. 2 (ad 1257, in error) and 4 (Ephemerides, pp. 145 and 154).

by a fresh series of disputes with Acquapendente. That town had sought aid against Orvieto from Siena in 1251: the war had delayed Orvieto's punitive expedition until 1255, when Acquapendente was compelled to renew its submission and to present its statutes for Orvietan approbation, but the pope soon afterwards instructed the Rector of the Patrimony to absolve Acquapendente from this oath and to force Orvieto to relinquish the Val del Lago.[1] Again Acquapendente's triumph was short-lived, for in August 1256 the town confirmed its subjection to the Orvietans, who once more destroyed part of its walls.[2]

Thus the constant themes of Orvieto's foreign policy, the Sienese threat and revolt in the western contado, again alternate, complicated in this decade by papal claims to the Val del Lago as in the previous one by the renaissance of imperial power, but still surviving as the basic problems with which the commune's rulers were faced and varying only slightly in each generation according to the balance of political forces in central Italy.

After the supersession of the Consuls by a 'foreign' Potestà the first half of the thirteenth century had seen no important changes in the constitutional organization of the city, but in 1250-1 there was a sudden and spectacular increase in the powers of Orvieto's Popolo.

Since many of the remaining chapters of this study will be concerned with the rivalry of nobles and 'popolani', it is necessary to digress briefly in order to attempt a definition of the two classes into which the commune's citizens were divided. There is almost no evidence directly relevant to the composition of Orvieto's nobility, so that it can only be guessed at by analogy with other Italian cities. Within this class itself it is possible to distinguish two categories, the old feudal nobility or 'nobilitas persone', whose aristocratic status dated from before the formation of the commune (such nobles were often inhabitants of the contado), and the new 'nobilitas divitiarum'[3] who had acquired nobility during the

---

[1] Jordan, p. 152 n. ; C.D., cccxxiii-v; Theiner, doc. cclxxiii; Reg. Alex. IV, n. 557; Chr. Pot. 4 (Ephemerides, p. 154).   [2] ACO, Cod. Galluzzi, fo. 3; Chr. Pot. 4 (ut sup.).

[3] The distinction between 'nobilitas persone' and 'nobilitas divitiarum' is made in the Sienese constitution of 1262 (edited by L. Zdekauer, Milan, 1897).

municipal régime and indeed had usually received their knight-hoods from the commune. It was Orvieto's feudal nobility which had claimed separate representation from the 'populus' in the convention with Adrian IV in 1157,[1] but the communes were already ennobling their own citizens in the twelfth century (as Otto of Freising had noted with snobbish disgust[2]) and Orvieto's Monaldeschi, whose origins were non-noble, were 'nobiles viri' by the turn of the century.[3] Such promotion, while usually due to the recipient's own city, might be accomplished by an outside power, such as the Count Caetani who knighted sixty-four Orvietans in 1303; sometimes it was the reward for an exceptionally successful tenure of office, as in the case of the Capitano del Popolo, a Perugian, whom Orvieto knighted after the truces of 1330.[4] In Florence any person in whose family there had been a knight in the preceding twenty years was considered to be a noble,[5] and everywhere nobility seems to have been regarded as a status involving families rather than single individuals.

The earliest extant list of Orvieto's noble families dates from 1322,[6] when they numbered forty-eight, of which twenty-seven were probably permanently resident within the city (the remainder being nobles of the contado); there is no indication of the size of these families. In general these nobles may be described as com-prising the more wealthy inhabitants of the town, but it is possible to amplify and modify this extremely vague definition in one or two respects. Firstly, there was an emphasis on 'old' families, as is indeed obvious by the nature of the institution, since one or two generations must normally have elapsed between a family's attaining wealth and its ennoblement. Secondly, a sort of negative definition is afforded by the organization of the Popolo, which in one of its aspects consisted of the artisans, or guild-members, of the town. Noblemen could not be members of guilds. This does not appear to have meant that in no case could they exercise a trade (the Monaldeschi had a 'fundicus' and were clearly merchants[7]), but the ownership of land was the main source of revenue of the

[1] C.D., p. 26.
[2] *De Gestis Friderici*, lib. II, cap. 13.
[3] See App. III.
[4] L. Manente (*Ephemerides*, pp. 337-8).
[5] G. Salvemini, *Magnati e Popolani in Firenze*, Florence, 1899, p. 27.
[6] See p. 108.
[7] See App. III.

38

nobility. Yet in this respect they again defy clear-cut classifications, for not all big land-owners were nobles; one of the richest owners of property in the Orvietan contado was a lawyer and a 'popolano'.[1] The lack of any distinct social or economic boundary between nobles and 'popolani' is discussed at length below,[2] in connection with a period when the composition of the nobility had become almost static. The first half of the thirteenth century, the age of the Potestà, was the period during which the outlines of the commune's social and political pattern were becoming more sharply defined; the principal families were emerging and securing recognition as nobles at the same time as the Popolo's first institutions made their appearance. The Orvietan nobility, then, as it existed when it first clashed with the Popolo in the last third of the thirteenth century, consisted of descendants of the feudal aristocracy (which was certainly not a large class) together with those families which had acquired wealth and prominence within—very approximately— the first century of the commune's existence.

The composition of the Popolo is far easier to determine, since it comprised all the non-noble citizens of the commune.[3] It had, however, a complicated organization, which was two-fold, topographical and corporative. In its topographical aspect, the Popolo was the sum of Orvieto's twenty-one 'rioni', or districts, while in its corporative aspect it comprehended all the guilds or 'Arti', thus including (as mentioned above) the entire artisan population of the town.

An organization of non-noble elements in the commune had existed in rudimentary form since quite early in the thirteenth century. A guild of merchants is recorded as early as 1212, and by 1214 there were also guilds of inn-keepers and hosiers, each of which had an officer, known as the Consul.[4] By 1229 every 'rione' had its representatives (known as 'anterioni'),[5] elected by the votes of its own non-noble citizens. The first reference to an organization

---

[1] See p. 115. [2] Pp. 113-15.

[3] It should be noted that to be a citizen it was necessary to be not merely a male and of age, but to be a native of Orvieto. Probably not more than one quarter of the town's inhabitants were citizens. The artisans who enjoyed membership of the Arti were also of course only the master-craftsmen.

[4] *C.D.*, LXXXV and XCVII. [5] *Ibid.*, CXCIII.

of all the guilds occurs in 1235, when some were known as 'Arti' and others (probably the minor guilds) as 'Società'; their officers were then described (apparently indiscriminately) as Rettori, Signori, or Capitudini.[1] Nine years later the two elements had coalesced and the popular body had secured the title and the organization that it was to maintain from thenceforth. The Popolo's officers were now called its 'Rettori' and by 1247 it had two Councils, of one hundred and of two hundred popolani respectively, the members of which were chosen by the 'rioni'; each of these Councils was supplemented by twenty-four representatives of the Arti and Società.[2] The Popolo's 'Carta', or written constitution, is also first mentioned in 1247.[3]

Thus popular institutions had been gradually growing in strength throughout the first half of the century. By 1247 the Council of the Popolo was concerning itself with municipal finance and a commercial dispute with another commune, Todi.[4] But the most significant development in the Popolo's organization and juris-diction occurs only in the years 1250-1 and is clearly connected with the special political situation of those years and in particular with Orvieto's reconquest of its contado.

In 1250 the Popolo was for the first time headed by a Captain, who was moreover a stranger to the town.[5] This innovation is analogous to the replacement of the Consuls by a Potestà in the government of the commune fifty years before. In both cases the change is symptomatic of that point in an institution's development at which it has acquired sufficient power and sufficient complexity for the fissures inherent in its structure to have become apparent. Hence the need to import a 'foreigner' to override the internal factions that were enfeebling first the commune and later the Popolo. Like the Potestà-ship, the new office was not at first permanent, though the body of two or four Rectors of the Popolo is not found after 1251. Between 1255 and 1259 the captaincy existed in a modified form, known as the Priorate of the Popolo or of the Arti and Società, which was usually held by a native of

---

[1] C.D., CCXIII and CCXV-XVI.
[3] Ibid., CCLXIV.
[5] Ibid., CCLXXXIV.

[2] Ibid., CCLX, CCLXIV, CCLXXIII.
[4] Ibid., CCLXIV, CCLXVI, CCLXXIII.

Orvieto.[1] Thereafter, except during brief periods of crisis, the Captain of the Popolo was a stranger.

The Popolo's earliest intervention in the external affairs of the commune (excepting the purely commercial dispute of 1247) coincides exactly with the advent of the Captain. When Orvieto came to terms with the imperial Vicar in the Aldobrandeschine contado on 7 January 1251 the contracting party was described as the 'Captain, Consuls, and Rectors of the Popolo, and the Commune and Popolo' of Orvieto.[2] The entire negotiations for the resubmission of the Aldobrandeschine contado were conducted by the popular authorities in conjunction with those of the commune. Thereafter the Popolo normally—but not invariably—is associated in acts involving Orvieto's relations with external powers.[3] It is clear that from January 1251 the Popolo had achieved recognition by the commune and secured a share in the determination of Orvieto's foreign policy.

The Popolo acquired its new powers in the same month that saw the collapse of Frederick II's hegemony, and it has already been suggested that this development is connected with the commune's recovery of its subject-territory. The precise nature of this connection is not clear, but it seems probable that the Popolo claimed constitutional concessions as a reward for its share in the military reconquest of the contado. It may indeed have refused to co-operate until such concessions were promised.

A further factor in the rise of the Popolo was the example of Florence, Orvieto's great ally. The commune tended to model itself on any city with which it had diplomatic relations, for in such negotiations it was convenient for the contracting parties to have the same, or at least analogous, constitutional organs and offices. But the most important influence was that of Florence,

---

[1] C.D., pp. 206 ff.; Ephemerides, p. 145, n. 8.

[2] ACO, Istr. B, fo. 5v (summarized in C.D., CCLXXXIV). The Vicar had sought terms 'a domino Roffino dei gratia capitaneo urbevetanae civitatis et a consulibus et Rectoribus populi dicte civitatis et a communi et popolo civitatis eiusdem'.

[3] The renewal of the Florentine alliance in 1251 and the peace with Todi six years later were negotiated by the Populo and commune, and both organizations are mentioned in the submissions of Valentano and Castel Pero in 1257 and of Bisenzio in 1259—yet the submission of Capodimonte, which also occurred in 1257, was made to the commune alone (C.D., CCCX, CCCXXXIX–CCCXLII, CCCLIX–LX).

where the new régime of the Primo Popolo, incorporating a 'foreign' Captain and giving the greatest share in political power to the Popolo, had come into being in October 1250. The political circumstances of that winter facilitated Orvieto's own constitutional revolution, but the form that it took must have been largely determined by the example of her powerful ally.

Thus the second half of the thirteenth century opens with the commune resuming the old threads of its foreign policy, both in the contado and in its relations with the Tuscan cities. Its internal affairs acquire a new complexity with the emergence of the constitutional dichotomy of commune and Popolo, the framework within which a long battle was to be fought which ended almost a century later in a personal tyranny. The formative period of Orvieto's republic was over; after the appearance of the Captain of the Popolo there was no important alteration in the constitutional organization of the commune.

CHAPTER VII

A SECOND PERIOD OF
GHIBELLINE PREDOMINANCE (1260-6)

THE recrudescence of fighting between Florence and Orvieto on one hand and Siena on the other reached its climax in 1260. Two years before this, Manfred, the illegitimate son of Frederick II, had assumed the regal title. In 1259 it became evident that his ambitions were spreading to Tuscany; Siena recognized him as King of the Romans and accepted his overlordship, while the Florentines took the precaution of negotiating a new Guelf alliance. The new threat from the Hohenstaufen caused Orvieto and Florence to draw closer to each other, and Florence chose an Orvietan Potestà, Buonconte Monaldeschi, for the year 1260.[1]

Yet such were the disasters of that year for the Guelfs that Monaldeschi was fated never to assume office. By the spring Siena had received powerful reinforcements of German cavalry from Manfred, and the stage was set for the new Ghibelline resurgence in Tuscany. The waverers were already preparing to desert the Guelfs, and Perugia, normally a reliable ally, refused Orvieto aid against Siena. In May the Guelfs even achieved a victory (a narrow one) at Santa Petronilla, near Siena. Orvietan troops were engaged in this battle, as they were in the disastrous defeat at Montaperti on 4 September, 'che fece l'Arbia colorata in rosso'.[2] Orvieto's losses at Montaperti were particularly severe; Villani recounts that many of her troops were among the infantry who fled to the keep, shut themselves up there, and were massacred when the castle fell to the Ghibellines.[3] One source talks of sixty Orvietan knights who were killed and of seventy who were taken prisoner; another chronicle puts the total of Orvietan prisoners at

---

[1] Degli Azzi, I, 255.
[2] *Reg. Per.*, pp. 190-2; *Inferno*, x, 85-6
[3] G. Villani, *Cronica*, lib. vi, cap. LXXIX-LXXX.

1,350,[1] so that if the proportion of killed to prisoners was the same for the foot-soldiers as for the cavalry—though judging from Villani's story it was probably higher—Orvieto's infantry must have suffered well over a thousand casualties in killed alone. It was a tremendous loss for a town whose total population was then probably less than twenty thousand persons.

The terms of the subsequent peace allotted Montalcino and Montepulciano to the Sienese, whose third war against Orvieto thus brought them a long-postponed triumph. Manfred and the Ghibellines now ruled all Tuscany and Guelf Orvieto could only bow her head before the storm, as she had done in similar circumstances twenty years before.

This time, however, she was destined to play a less inconspicuous rôle; in 1262 Orvieto was called upon to give hospitality to the pope, Urban IV.[2] No doubt the town's impregnable site and its Guelf record were the reasons for Urban's choice. The visit lasted two years and inaugurated a tradition; popes had stayed at Orvieto before—not since 1220, however—but never for so long a period.

The presence of the pope and Curia further identified Orvieto with the Guelf cause and ensured the acquiescence of the local Ghibellines.[3] Nevertheless relations between the Curia and commune were unfriendly from the first. The grievance felt by the papacy over Orvieto's defiant retention of the Val del Lago was redoubled now that the disputed area lay so close at hand. Urban was determined to insist on his rights within the Patrimony and in the summer of 1262, when at Montefiascone, he reclaimed Marta —on Lake Bolsena—from Giacomo di Bisenzio and the Prefetti di Vico.[4] In the autumn he moved to Orvieto and before long took a similar step in freeing one of the islands (the Martana) from

---

[1] L. Manente (Ephemerides, pp. 306-7); 'Annales Senenses' in RIS, N.S., xv, 6, p. 219.

[2] The principal source for the events of the Pope's stay in Orvieto is Thierri de Vaucouleurs' 'Vita Metrica Urbani IV', in RIS, O.S., III, pt. 1, cols. 411-9; for its duration, Reg. Urb. IV, nos. 147-2805.

[3] The Orvietan Ghibellines were sufficiently strong in 1262 to attempt to secure the election of a Potestà favourable to themselves (v. Pflugk-Harttung, Iter Italicum, pp. 676-7). Moreover one near relative and supporter of Manfred held the neighbouring town of Pitigliano (Caccia, pp. 121-2) and another owned much property in Orvieto (see p. 34).

[4] Dottarelli, p. 109. The pope had quarrelled with Giacomo di Bisenzio over the submission of a castle to Toscanella (Theiner, CCLXIX), and he now put him in prison (Pflugk-Harttung, p. 676).

its obligations to the same Giacomo and to Orvieto. Despite
Orvieto's protests he proceeded to capture this island and another,
on which he built a castle.[1] The following summer the pope
quashed in similar terms the submission to Orvieto of Valentano,
in the same area, which town he purchased outright.[2] What was
even more serious for the commune, he re-opened the question of
Acquapendente; in April 1263 he instructed the vicarial Rector of
the Patrimony to hold an enquiry into the rights of the Church in
that town.[3] The enquiry produced voluminous evidence of the
Church's executive, judicial and fiscal rights in Acquapendente,
but Urban never acted upon it. Perhaps it was only intended as a
threat; it certainly provoked great alarm, and despite the financial
and spiritual advantages of the pope's sojourn Orvieto must have
regretted the days of Innocent IV and Alexander IV, when papal
intervention over the Val del Lago had been spasmodic and
ineffective.

The year 1264 saw the lowest ebb of the Guelf-papal cause.
Manfred's campaign north of Rome that summer was aimed at
the capture of Orvieto and the pope himself and his victory near
Vetralla in June seemed to make this possible of achievement. In
July the pope wrote that Orvieto was threatened with a siege if
Manfred effected a junction with his forces in Tuscany, and he
ordered the preaching of a regular Crusade.[4]

In the same year the lords of Bisenzio took a bitter revenge on
Urban by murdering Guiscard of Pietrasanta, Rector of the Tuscan
Patrimony.[5] This crime was an indication of the unchallenged
strength of Ghibellinism in the northern Patrimony, and the
situation grew more serious when Orvieto refused to yield Bisenzio
and Capodimonte to the pope. A little later the Orvietan garrison

---

[1] *C.D.*, CCCLXXVII-VIII; Theiner, CCLXX. The second of these islands, previously known
as the Isola Bisantina, was re-named 'Isola Urbana'.

[2] *Reg. Urb. IV*, n. 307; *C.D.*, XCI (Valentano's submission to Orvieto in 1212) and
CCCXLII.

[3] Theiner, CCLXXII. The evidence is more plentiful than convincing. The witnesses show
an amazingly accurate memory of the events of sixty-five years before, and in their answers
one seems often to detect the anxiety of a puzzled yokel to satisfy his learned interrogator.

[4] *Reg. Urb. IV*, nos. 853-60, 870, etc.; papal letter in Martène and Durand, *Thesaurus
Novus Anecdotorum*, Paris, 1717, II, cols. 82-6; Jordan, pp. 331 and 500.

[5] *Reg. Urb. IV*, nos. 757 and 764; *C.D.*, CCCLXXXIII; Chr. Ant. and Chr. Pot 2
(*Ephemerides*, pp. 129 and 155).

of Bisenzio surrendered the town to its lords with suspicious rapidity—Urban's biographer says that the Popolo was content to support the pope, but the nobles wished to secure Bisenzio for the commune—and though Orvieto condemned to death the murderers of Guiscard of Pietrasanta, the sentence was never carried out. By the autumn the danger from Manfred had passed and the aged pope left Orvieto in disgust, transferring his residence to Todi.[1]

Meanwhile the Sienese had begun an attempt to enlarge their dominions at the expense of Orvieto. Manfred's Vicar in Tuscany, Count Guido Novello, officially announced his support of this undertaking in 1264, and in the same year Siena achieved several successes, among them the capture of Campiglia, an important Orvietan outpost.[2] The following summer Orvieto signed a treaty of alliance with Siena's exiled Guelfs, and the war began in earnest.[3] The Sienese attacked in August, capturing S. Salvatore (on Monte Amiata) and Sarteano. Thence they proceeded to Chianciano, but at this critical moment there occurred the first intervention of the saviour of the Guelfs; the Orvietan army (which had already been reinforced by two hundred Perugians and fifty mercenaries) was joined by a thousand knights sent by Charles d'Anjou, who had recently arrived in Italy. A year before Benevento, Tuscany was granted an advance view of Manfred's overthrow by the Angevin, for when these reinforcements reached the Orvietans the Ghibelline army abandoned the siege, and fled by night leaving its baggage, 'tanquam debellatus'.

Orvieto followed up this success with an incursion into the Sienese contado as far as Buonconvento, terminating in a successful engagement near Montepulciano; meanwhile the towns lost in August had renewed their submission to the commune.

---

[1] Dottarelli, p. 112. The condemnation of the lords of Bisenzio is C.D., CCCLXXXIV, but they were still alive almost twenty years later (ibid., DXXIII).

[2] Chr. Ant. and Chr. Pot. 4 (Ephemerides, pp. 130-1 and 156) and 'Ann. Sen.' in MGH, XIX, p. 231 (Campiglia); Fumi, Chianciano, doc. XIV; C.D., CCCLXXXVIII-CCCXCI (Guido Novello); Potthast, n. 19033 (cardinals' bull of 2 November 1264, reproving Siena for attacking Orvieto).

[3] C.D., CCCC. For the fighting of 1265, v. Chr. Ant. and Chr. Pot. 4 (loc. cit.) and Sienese chronicle in RIS, O.S., XV, p. 34: also C.D., CCCCI-II and especially Potthast, n. 19323 (Clement IV describes the campaign in a letter to Cardinal Ottobono).

The following spring, however, the succession of victories ended suddenly and disastrously. An anti-Sienese rising at Grosseto was organized and supported by Orvieto, Count Aldobrandino, and the Visconte di Campiglia. This rebellion was crushed by the Sienese in a battle in which the Orvietans suffered heavy casualties. Among the many prisoners was a French follower of Charles d'Anjou who had been made Potestà of Orvieto: his appointment is strikingly indicative of the speed and totality of the process whereby the leadership of the Guelf cause throughout Italy had passed to the Angevin.

Peace negotiations began in May 1266, but dragged on until August, when at last a papal Nuncio persuaded both sides to agree to terms which determined practically nothing except the mutual release of prisoners.[1] The wars of Tuscany were now nothing more than a side-show, for the event of the battle fought in February near Benevento was decisive for the fate of the whole peninsula.

---

[1] For the Grosseto rising and this peace, Chr. Ant., Chr. Pot. 2, Chr. Pot. 4 (*Ephemerides*, pp. 131, 146 and 156-7), and Sienese chronicles in RIS, O.S., xv, col. 35, and MGH, xix, p. 231; Ciacci, doc. 545 and II, 225-7; C.D., ccccv-viii; *Reg. Cl. IV*, n. 111; *Ephemerides*, p. 146 n. (Charles d'Anjou pleads for the release of the captured Potestà).

CHAPTER VIII

THE ANGEVIN DOMINATION (1266-80)

THE victory of Charles d'Anjou over Manfred at Benevento in 1266 put an end to the period of Ghibelline supremacy. The Angevins and the pro-French papacy now became the supreme power in Tuscany and Central Italy, and save during the brief episode of Conradin's ill-fated expedition they retained their position for twenty years.

Henceforward Orvieto was an important centre of Angevin power. Urban IV had set the example by his stay in 1262-4 and his successors appreciated that the town had great advantages, among them its impregnability, its central position midway between Rome and Florence, and its proved fidelity to the Guelf cause.[1] The Curia or the Angevin Court (and often both) resided at Orvieto during twelve of the twenty-six years following the battle of Benevento. Clement IV was there in 1266, Charles d'Anjou in 1268, and Gregory X in 1272 and 1273 (accompanied for part of this time by Charles and his Court). Martin IV (with a French garrison and sometimes with Charles) stayed at Orvieto, but for one short absence, from the spring of 1281 till the summer of 1284; there was another Angevin visit in 1289, and Nicholas IV was at Orvieto in 1290 and 1291.[2] During this period the frequent presence of the papal Curia and of a foreign Court and garrison is the most important factor in the politics of the commune.

Orvieto had been a steadfast supporter of the Guelf-Angevin cause but it did not follow that she was prepared to receive the Angevin Court with enthusiasm. Siena had been Orvieto's great enemy for forty years and Florence her close ally for the same time, and the respective political traditions of these two cities were

---

[1] According to current Italian tradition the popes' choice of residences outside Rome was largely determined by the excellence of the local vintages.

[2] *Ephemerides*, pp. 131-3, 157-9, 162, 309-10 and 314 n.

the most important cause of Orvieto's Guelfism. Certainly the Angevins were welcome allies against Siena, especially when their reinforcements arrived as opportunely as they had done at Chianciano in 1265, but the popularity of an allied garrison, rarely great during a war, has never been known to survive it. Moreover the Angevin troops were for the most part French, and national feeling was strong enough for this to make them yet more unpopular ('Death to the Frenchmen!' was the cry of the rioters in 1281, as it was in Sicily a year later).[1] The popes were not a great deal more welcome, particularly because their visits tended to coincide with challenges to the commune's authority in the Val del Lago; Urban IV had fallen out with Orvieto in 1264 over this, and Clement IV's stay in 1266 was immediately followed by an attempt to reclaim the disputed area through the Captain of the Tuscan Patrimony.[2]

The suspicion with which Charles d'Anjou was regarded by Orvieto is shown by the commune's attitude to his first visit, in 1268. A debate took place in which the possibility of opposing with arms the King's entry was discussed at length. The Guelfs themselves at first closed the city gates against their ally, while they besought the Ghibellines to remain in the town and preserve its solidarity. Eventually the decision went against armed opposition and Charles entered Orvieto 'magna cum pace', but the episode is most significant.[3] It will be seen later than the presence of the Angevin Court always led to increased tension in the political atmosphere.

Orvieto's Ghibellines seem to have enjoyed a brief period of power after the town's disastrous defeat by the Sienese at Grosseto in 1266 (they provided the Capitano del Popolo that summer),[4] but this did not outlast the peace settlement of August. In 1268 there was a campaign against heresy in Orvieto which led to some hundred condemnations and it is clear that political motives were involved as well as religious ones: not only did those convicted include members of leading Ghibelline families, but the charges

---

[1] See pp. 44-6.   [2] Chr. Ant. and Chr. Pot. 4 (Ephemerides, pp. 131 and 157).
[3] Chr. Pot. 4 (Ephemerides, p. 157).
[4] The Capitano was Oderico di Ranieri Filippeschi (C.D., p. 252). It is possible that Ghibelline officers were considered to have better hopes of obtaining easy terms from the victorious Sienese.

were often slender ones of having had social contact with heretics.[1]

Meanwhile the leading Guelf family, the Monaldeschi,[2] had whole-heartedly identified themselves with the Angevin cause. The political programme of Orvieto's Guelfs at this period is vividly illustrated by a sort of mascot which no doubt graced one of the Guelf households; this is an earthenware plate representing a siren (the symbol of Naples) and three shields, two of them bearing the arms of the Monaldeschi and the third the Angevin lilies.[3] A Monaldeschi was appointed to be a judge in the papal lawcourt, while others held municipal offices such as that of Difensore del Comune in 1277 and Capitano del Popolo in 1283-4.[4] This political ascendance shows also in the dating of a number of official deeds 'in palatio Monaldescorum', and at the same time one of the family made a large loan to the commune.[5] Other Monaldeschi, to judge by the important offices they filled, were among the most competent members of the sort of pool of nobles who specialized in holding captaincies and Potestà-ships in the Guelf communes.[6] But the family's thorough-going adherence to a temporarily victorious cause and their high prestige in Guelf circles exposed them all the more to local animosity against supporters of the hated foreigner.

In the spring of 1272 anti-Guelf feeling came to a head in the murder of four members of a family allied to the Monaldeschi.[7] The murderers were all members of the leading family of Ghibelline nobles, the Filippeschi, their victims the descendants of a certain Berardino. The crime was immediately followed by a revenge,

[1] C.D., CCCCXIV-CCCCLXXIX, especially CCCCXXX-I, CCCCXLVIII and CCCCLXX (sentences against four Miscinelli, a very prominent Ghibelline family).

[2] For their early history, and that of the leading Ghibelline family, v. App. III.

[3] Illustrated in P. Perali, Orvieto, pp. 70-1; the author states that the plate is of a type that was manufactured in Orvieto, and attributes it to the second half of the thirteenth century on stylistic evidence.

[4] Theiner, doc. CCCCI; C.D., pp. 318 and 326-8. Nicholas IV honoured a Monaldeschi by passing a night at his castle in 1290 (Ephemerides, p. 186).

[5] C.D., CCCCLXXXIII-IV and CCCCLXXXIX, DII, DIV.

[6] Ciarfaglia di Cittadino was Potestà of Modena in 1264 (Salimbene, Cronica, p. 675 of 1942 edn.) and Capitano at Florence in 1286-7 (C.D., p. 337). His brother Ermanno was Potestà of Florence in 1266-7 (Ephemerides, pp. 131 and 157), and of Lucca in 1274 (ibid., p. 349 n.) and Rector of the Romagna in 1288 (Reg. Nich. IV, nos. 6966, etc.).

[7] Chr. Ant., Chr. Pot. 2 and Chr. Pot 4 (Ephemerides, pp. 132, 147, 158) fill in the background to the bare judicial sentence (C.D., DIV).

a Filippeschi being killed by a son of one of those murdered.

As far back as 1240 the Filippeschi had been enemies of the Monaldeschi, and the feud had lasted through the intervening years, though there is no certain evidence that it had previously taken such violent form.[1] Moreover the Berardino family had fallen out with the Filippeschi at least eight years before the murder, for they denounced two members of that family for their failure to pay a fine to which they had been condemned in 1264.[2] Since the Filippeschi were then ordered to pay twenty soldi for each day of the eighteen months that had passed since the sentence, and half this sum was allotted to their denouncers, the hatred between the two families is not difficult to explain!

All the chroniclers of the period emphasize the importance of this murder by describing it in detail. Certainly there had been factional hatred in Orvieto for some time before this (the murder of a Capitano del Popolo in 1267 probably had political motives, and there was fighting among the nobles in the 1240s),[3] but this episode served to crystallize the rival parties and to intensify the tradition of enmity.

The murder was immediately followed by a battle between Guelfs and Ghibellines, after which the Filippeschi principally concerned fled the town. Sixteen of them were found guilty of murder by the Potestà, who outlawed them, condemned them to pay a heavy fine, ordered the destruction of their towers and palaces, and then himself fled to escape the vengeance of their relatives.[4] Twenty-five leading members of each faction were sent into exile, an arrangement which was probably intended to appease the Ghibellines, but in December the case against the Filippeschi was reopened; twenty-one members of the family were fined for refusing to appear at the enquiry into the murder, and another for being an accessory after the fact and making a speech against the Potestà in the Piazza del Comune.

[1] C.D., CCLI (the Monaldeschi-Filippeschi law-suit of 1240). L. Manente often describes fighting between the two families from the year 1226 onwards, but is entirely unreliable on this period.

[2] ACO, Lib. Cond. 1266-7.

[3] The murder of 1257 is described by Chr. Ant., Chr. Pot. 2, 3, and 4, and L. Manente (Ephemerides, pp. 128, 145, 152-4, 304); the fighting of the 1240s in Chr. Pot. 3 (ibid., p. 150). [4] ACO, Lib. Cond. 1272, fo. 3.

Despite the size of these fines (over 7,000 lire in almost every case), a considerable proportion of them was paid in the course of 1273, partly in property.[1] In December of that year the commune decided to come to terms with the Filippeschi over the remainder. The Potestà informed them that 'in view of the excessive heaviness of the fines' (no doubt the real intention was to increase the chance of their being paid), the sentence was commuted to a joint fine of 21,000 lire, of which only two-thirds was to be paid for the present. In addition several of them were to go into temporary exile and to undertake penitential pilgrimages, some to Compostella, others to the Holy Land.[2]

This was still an extremely heavy fine (not long afterwards it took the commune six years to raise 16,000 lire),[3] but the Filippeschi determined to make their peace with the commune and they gave a security of their intention to pay the new joint fine and to keep the peace.[4] This agreement was tolerably well observed in the following years, though there were sporadic troubles; the only serious disturbances, those of 1286, were ended by a formal reconciliation in the Piazza del Comune between representatives of the two parties, in the presence of the bishop, the clergy, and the entire population.[5] In any case the leadership of the anti-Guelf movement had temporarily passed into other hands, as recounted in the next chapter.

---

[1] *C.D.*, DIII, one of four purchases made by the commune from Filippeschi in one day; the price of these properties was then deducted from the fine.

[2] *C.D.*, DIV and notes (summary of Lib. Cond. 1273, 3b, fo.3). Fumi has missed the sentences of 1272 and only gives the alterations to them.

[3] To purchase the revocation of an interdict (see p. 78).

[4] *C.D.*, notes to DIV.

[5] Chr. Pot. 4 (*Ephemerides*, pp. 160-1); there was fighting on the Bolsena road below the town involving Sienese and Perugian detachments. For three weeks the disorders were so serious that no milling could be done (ACO, Rif. 1295, fo. 74).

CHAPTER IX

RANIERI DELLA GRECA'S POPOLO (1280-92)

ONE consequence of the Angevin ascendancy was that the Popolo, whose power had increased in the 1250s, grew steadily weaker. The principal supporters of the Angevin-papal hegemony were noble families such as the Monaldeschi and thanks to this the ill-defined constitutional rights of the Popolo soon began to recede. In 1270 the Council of the Popolo still met, but without its Captain,[1] and indeed this office seems almost to have fallen into desuetude in the next decade. The names of nearly all the Captains of the 1250s and 1260s are recorded, but there is no documentary evidence for the continuance of the office between the captaincy of Guidochiaro dei Galluzzi in 1269[2] and that of Ranieri della Greca in 1280.

After 1280 the presence of the papal Curia and Angevin Court continued to provide the setting against which was enacted the drama of Orvieto's political life, and a rejuvenated Popolo took over from the Ghibelline nobles the direction of the anti-Guelf opposition.

The resurgence of the Popolo in the 1280s was almost entirely the work of one man, Ranieri della Greca, Capitano del Popolo in 1280-1 and 1284. Ranieri, or 'Neri', came of a family that had been prominent in Orvieto for over sixty years.[3] He is first mentioned in a deed of 1274, as an arbiter in the partition of the Aldobrandeschine contado.[4]

The great work of Della Greca was the forging of a new party in which the existing Ghibelline faction was reinforced by fresh elements turned against Guelfism by its identification with a foreign Court, a largely foreign Curia and, worst of all, a foreign garrison.

---

[1] *C.D.*, ccccLXXXIX.   [2] *C.D.*, pp. 298 ff.

[3] Ugolino della Greca, who was probably Neri's father, was a judge in 1215 and represented the commune in negotiations with Todi (1221), Siena (1221) and Florence (1229): (*C.D.*, pp. 69, 90, 93-5, 122-5).   [4] Ciacci, doc. 580.

The Guelfs had long been the 'patriotic' party, but now the rôles were reversed, and many beside the Filippeschi must have been heartened by the omen of the strange and hideous fish 'like a lion' which was caught off the shore of the Orvietan Maremma in 1282, and which—to the chronicler—so manifestly foreshadowed the Sicilian Vespers![1]

Ranieri himself was a patriot rather than a Ghibelline, and only the events of these years link him to that party. What gives cohesion to his long and distinguished career (he was still serving the commune in 1313)[2] is his belief that the interests of Orvieto, especially in the Aldobrandeschine contado, should if necessary override loyalty to the papacy. Thus in 1302, after Countess Margherita had been declared a rebel by Boniface VIII, who was threatening to confiscate her estates, Della Greca helped her by paying rent on her behalf to the Abbot of S. Anastasio, of whom much of her land was held.[3] When the Aldobrandeschine lands were overrun on Boniface's death Neri was chosen to negotiate terms with the towns concerned, and then given the vital post of Potestà of Pitigliano,[4] almost certainly because he alone of Orvieto's politicians had never approved the bargain with the late pope whereby the commune renounced this sphere of influence. Nothing connects him with the contemporary currents of religious unorthodoxy, indeed his relative Ugolino di Aldobrandino was at this very time Archpriest at Orvieto and his son Edoardo a Dominican and Canon of Chiusi.[5]

Though Della Greca was a Ghibelline only through the force of circumstances, it was inevitable that much of his support should come from those who were Ghibelline by tradition. The Filippeschi were sent into exile in 1283, no doubt through Guelf fear of their association with Della Greca; a chronicler names Simone dei Filippeschi as his right-hand man during the troubles of 1284.[6] Though they now found themselves connected with a new movement whose aims (placing Orvieto before Ghibellinism and the

[1] Cont. Orv. Polono, p. 112 ('piscis magnus in effigie leonis captus fuit . . . pellis cuius pilosa erat, pedes breves, cauda leonina et caput leoninum, aures, os, et infra, dentes et linguam habebat quasi leo': this sounds like a seal).
[2] *Ephemerides*, p. 352 n.   [3] Ciacci, doc. 646. (See pp. 72-4.)
[4] ACO, Rif. 1303 (10 December) and *C.D.*, p. 402: *v*. Ch. x.
[5] AVO, Cod. A, fo. 229 v; *Reg. B. VIII*, nos. 2098 and 4030.
[6] L. Manente (*Ephemerides*, p. 318); Chr. Pot. 4 (*ibid.*, p. 160).

PLATE II

THE PALAZZO DEL POPOLO, ORVIETO (mainly thirteenth century)

Popolo before the Ghibelline nobles) had little in common with their own, the Filippeschi were bound to accept such powerful allies in the struggle against the Monaldeschi and Guelfism.

Della Greca's election as Capitano del Popolo in 1280 seems to have arisen out of a popular tumult. 'The Popolo was formed', says a chronicler, 'in Piazza S. Domenico', and Ranieri della Greca was elected by the Consuls of the Arti as first Capitano del Popolo.[1] The description of Neri as 'primus capitaneus populi' indicates how completely the powers of the Popolo had fallen into desuetude in the preceding period. The first act of the new Captain was typical of his policy of raising at the same time the prestige and the efficiency of the popular organization: he ordered the erection of a Palazzo del Popolo and the clearing of a vast *piazza* in front of it.[2]

The Popolo, as resuscitated by Della Greca, began to be included in the formula for the submission of subject territories, for the first time since the 1250s; in 1284 the lords of Viterbo swore an oath of submission to Orvieto's Potestà and to her Capitano del Popolo.[3] At the same time the Council of the Popolo gained the right of electing the Potestà, while the Captain's title swelled to that of 'Captain of the city of Orvieto and of the commune and Popolo'.[4] Not all these alterations were made during Neri's first captaincy (1280–1), but as early as 1281 he had made the authority of the Capitano del Popolo so considerable that the Guelfs considered it better policy to capture the office than to attempt to diminish its powers. Hence the Captains in 1282 and 1283 were two leading Guelf nobles, Bernardino di Marsciano and Ermanno di Cittadino dei Monaldeschi.[5]

Two armed risings mark the zenith of Della Greca's anti-Angevin policy, but the first of these was premature and almost certainly unpremeditated. This occurred in 1281, when a dispute between an Orvietan and a member of the Angevin Court flared up into a serious riot in which many were wounded on each side and one

---

[1] Chr. Ant. and Chr. Pot. 4 (*Ephemerides*, pp. 133 and 159).
[2] *Ibid.*; C.D., DXXIV.
[3] C.D., DXXXI.
[4] *Ibid.*, DXXVIII; *Ephemerides*, p. 185.
[5] *Ephemerides*, p. 159; C.D., p. 328.

Frenchman and several Orvietans killed.[1] When the Angevins called upon Della Greca to hold the fury of his people in check he feigned illness and refused to appear. His resignation, which was doubtless insisted on by the French authorities, followed the pacification.

In 1284 Della Greca was re-elected as Capitano del Popolo, no doubt on the strength of an avowedly anti-Guelf programme, for the pope at once left Orvieto 'unable to bear any longer the malice and wickedness of Ranieri, the Orvietan Captain'.[2] The Ghibelline coup planned by Neri in 1284 was a very different business from the impulsive rising of three years before. The plot turned upon the situation in the Aldobrandeschine contado, so often the key to Orvieto's politics. In May of that year Count Aldobrandino 'Rosso' died, leaving as his heir his son-in-law Guy de Montfort (the murderer of Henry of Almaine and son of the great Earl Simon), who at the time was commanding the papal forces in the Romagna.[3] A neighbouring feudal lord, the Count of Anguillara, took advantage of Guy's absence and at once overran the Aldobrandeschine lands, to which he had no conceivable legal claim. De Montfort soon obtained permission to relinquish his command and returned to his newly-inherited estates to undertake a campaign against his supplanter. The crux of Della Greca's plan was to be the election of the Count of Anguillara as Potestà of Orvieto for the coming year. Almost certainly he struck a bargain with the Count that Orvieto was to assist in the war against Montfort in exchange for the assurance that she would acquire greater rights in the contado if the Count was victorious.

This plot was known as early as August, when the pope wrote to warn Orvieto against carrying it out.[4] It could not come to a head, however, until October, when the election of the Potestà

---

[1] Cont. Orv. Polono, p. 112: the episode is also described in Guillaume de Nangis, 'Vita Philippi III' (*Recueil des Historiens des Gaules et de la France*, xx, p. 516) and in MGH, xxii, pp. 480-1, but these accounts are clearly based on a common source. Ranieri had been in office eight months before this event (ACO, Rif. 1304, fos. 114v-115v), which can be dated approximately to April 1281.

[2] *Lib. Pont.*, ii, 463.

[3] These events are described in the *Lib. Pont.*, loc. cit., and a chronicle in *Historiae Francorum Scriptores* (ed. Duchesne), v, pp. 886-7.

[4] Ciacci, doc. 610 b.

was due to take place. When this time arrived, Ranieri ('grown fat in office', as Polono's Guelf continuator indignantly remarks) held the election at a council-meeting of the Popolo, and the Count of Anguillara was duly chosen.[1] Hearing this, the Guelfs decided to hold a rival election in the nearby Piazza del Comune; they attempted to obtain entrance to the Palazzo del Comune, but this was refused by the Potestà on the grounds—themselves an interesting commentary on the increasing powers of the Popolo—that he lacked the authority of Della Greca. The Guelfs chose no less than three Potestà, in case the first choices were unwilling to accept office; the three were, in order, the Pope, Guy de Montfort (the Count of Anguillara's opponent in the war for the Aldobrandeschine contado), and a certain Guido of Rimini.

On October 17th, two days after these elections, fighting broke out between the rival parties, but it was ended on the 20th by a compromise. It was agreed by both sides that there should be a new Capitano del Popolo, an Orvietan named Monaldo degli Ardiccioni, but the reconciliation was abortive, for the Ghibellines provoked the Guelfs by carrying off the new Captain and inducting him in office while the Guelf bigwigs waited in vain in the Piazza S. Francesco for the procession to begin! Fighting started again, but early in the morning of the 21st the Ghibellines, who had been frightened by rumours of the advent of Montfort, fled from Orvieto and gathered in the Val di Chiana. Perhaps they had guessed what would happen next. The Guelfs proved as unwilling to welcome their new ally as they had been to receive Charles d'Anjou in 1268. To remove the occasion for Montfort's presence they hastily gathered the Consuls of the Arti and the Council of the Popolo in the Palazzo del Comune to elect as Capitano Ermanno di Cittadino dei Monaldeschi, and proclaimed that the Ghibellines might re-enter the town without fear of vengeance. The Ghibellines returned, and the terms offered them were apparently respected.

Della Greca's attempt to crown with a *coup d'état* his work of moulding a new and powerful party from the combined forces of

---

[1] The events that follow are described at length in the chronicle quoted by Monaldeschi (*Ephemerides*, p. 185). The accounts in Chr. Pot. 4 (*ibid.*, p. 160) and Cont. Orv. Polono (p. 116) vary slightly from this, and give the impression of being over-simplified.

Ghibellinism and the Popolo had failed, though it had been saved from disaster by the Guelfs' fear of their uncongenial ally. The regenerated Popolo, however, survived this setback. In 1286 the Council of the Popolo seems still to have exercised considerable authority in Orvieto's affairs,[1] and among its members are numbered the Consuls of the Arti, who are also mentioned in connection with the election of the Potestà in 1284. From their office grew that of the Seven Consuls of the Seven Arti, who after 1292 were to take their place among the rulers of the city. Della Greca's work of behalf of the Popolo had a lasting effect, but it was destined to exert its political power through the Consulate of the Arti, not through the dangerously individual office of the captaincy.

---

[1] C.D., DXLII (the Council of the Popolo orders the construction of a new road).

CHAPTER X

INTERNAL UNITY AND A STRONG
FOREIGN POLICY (1292-1303)

THE pontificate of Nicholas IV (1288-92) marked the close of
Orvieto's domination by the French, for Charles d'Anjou was
dead and his son preoccupied by the struggle with the Spaniards
for Sicily. The power behind the papal throne was now a Roman
family, the Colonna. Nicholas followed what was becoming a
well-established tradition and chose Orvieto as the seat of the Curia
from June 1290 to October 1291.[1] The stay was notable only for
Nicholas' election as Potestà and Capitano del Popolo (it was the
first time a pope had held these offices at Orvieto)[2] and for the
encouragement he gave to the building of the new cathedral, of
which he laid the foundation stone.[3] Nicholas' relations with the
commune seem in general to have been friendly, though he taxed
Val del Lago and appointed local officials there. Orvieto protested,[4]
but took no action, probably bearing in mind that the pope was
old and that, since there was no obvious successor, his pontificate
might be followed, as it had been preceded, by a long vacancy.

As it turned out, the conclave that followed Nicholas' death in
April 1292 was a very lengthy one, more than two years of com-
plicated negotiation intervening before Celestine V, the hermit of
Monte Morrone, was chosen to succeed. The delay was due to the

---

[1] *Reg. Nich. IV*, nos. 2658-6217.

[2] Martin IV was elected Potestà in 1284, but appears to have refused the office. Nicholas
of course held it through a vicar. The practice of electing the pope as Potestà or Capitano
was common throughout the States of the the Church (*v.* G. Ermini, 'La Libertà comunale
nello Stato della Chiesa' in ASRSP, xlix, pp. 27-33) and Orvieto often followed it later.

[3] *Statuti . . dell 'Opera di S. Maria*, p. 7; Chr. Ant., Chr. Pot. 4, Monaldeschi's Chr.
(*Ephemerides*, pp. 134, 162, 186); Cont. Orv. Polono, p. 119. Nicholas also offered
indulgences to those aiding the construction of the cathedral and helped settle the differences arising from the need to demolish some property of the chapter which stood on
the new site (*Reg. Nich. IV*, nos. 5588, 5900, 5923).

[4] Theiner, pp. 317-21; C.D., dlxx (contains a reference to Orvieto's petition to
Nicholas IV concerning the Val del Lago).

evenly-matched strength of two rival factions, the Colonna and Orsini. Orvieto must have watched this struggle with interest. Not only was the personality of the pope of great importance as an indication of the policy he was likely to pursue concerning the Val del Lago, but two of the cardinals were particularly well known to Orvieto through their successive guardianship of the heiress to the Aldobrandeschine contado. The last Count, Aldobrandino 'Rosso', had died in 1284,[1] leaving only a daughter, Margherita, whose adventurous career (she married five times) is closely connected with the history of the commune in the following decade. Margherita's first husband was Guy de Montfort, whose rôle in the events of 1284 has been mentioned above. After Guy was captured off the coast of Sicily by a Spanish naval force in 1287, Margherita lived with, and probably married, a local noble named Nello dei Pannocchieschi.[2] She was evidently considered incapable of assuming responsibility for the vast estates she owned, since Nicholas IV had appointed first Cardinal Benedict Caetani (the future Pope Boniface VIII), and later Cardinal Napoleone Orsini, as her guardian.[3]

Benedict Caetani, as an executor and legatee of the will of Margherita's father, was the obvious choice. He knew that part of Italy well, for he had spent much of his youth at Todi, and had often been with the Curia at Orvieto, where he had been ordained priest in 1291.[4] As Margherita's guardian he was apparently superseded by Napoleone Orsini, who in 1293 married his ward to his brother Orsello, Guy de Montfort having died in a Sicilian prison. Benedict meanwhile was probably more concerned with his hopes that the deadlock in the Curia might lead to his election as pope.

---

[1] Chr. Ant. and Chr. Pot 4 (*Ephemerides*, pp. 133 and 160); *Lib. Pont.*, p. 463; Ciacci, doc. 607 (Count Rosso's will).

[2] For Margherita *v.* especially Ciacci, ch. VI and corresponding docs.; Lisini, *passim*; Caetani, *Domus Caietana*, ch. XVIII (= 'Margherita Aldobrandesca e i Caetani' in ASRSP, XLIV, 1921). For Guy de Montfort, F. M. Powicke, 'Guy de Montfort (1265-71)' in *Trans. Royal Hist. Soc.*, 4th S., XVIII, 1935.

[3] *Reg. Nich. IV*, nn. 5751-2 (Benedict Caetani made Margherita's guardian); Lisini, p. 69.

[4] Boase, pp. 7-10, 25-6, 29, 32, 35-6; Cont. Orv. Polono, p. 120 (an account of the evil portents accompanying Benedict's ordination as priest).

Orsello Orsini showed some reluctance to recognize Orvieto's suzertainty over his newly-acquired lands, though they had been subject to the commune for almost a century; but a short campaign, involving the capture of Saturnia, was sufficient to persuade him to renew the oath of submission.[1]

This attack and a brief expedition against Amelia were the only military enterprises of 1293, but a much more important one had been under consideration. The long papal vacancy made an invasion of the Val del Lago an extraordinarily tempting project. The dispute had dragged on for a century now, and the pontiffs since the defeat of the Hohenstaufen had been even less complaisant than their predecessors. Why not overrun the whole area while the conclave talked and procrastinated and face the new pope, when at last there was one, with a *fait accompli*? It was probably in the spring of 1293 that the commune considered a variant to this scheme, and entered upon negotiations with one who had at least very good hopes of being the next pope. A secret meeting took place at Viterbo between representatives of the commune of Orvieto and Cardinal Benedict Caetani, Margherita's former guardian. It seems certain that at this meeting an agreement was made whereby Benedict, if he became pope, was to recognize Orvieto's rule over the Val del Lago; in return, Orvieto was to support the cardinal's projects for securing to his family the lands of Countess Margherita. There can be little doubt that at this time Boniface planned a Caetani marriage for the Countess, but was forestalled by Napoleone Orsini.

This scandalous proposal to alienate lands held by virtue of a spiritual office and appertaining to that office in return for a favour to the holder's own family has never been remarked upon, except in the bald statement of two reliable chroniclers—one an Orvietan and the other Bolsenese—that Boniface VIII exchanged the Val del Lago for the Aldobrandeschine contado.[2] And even these chroniclers

---

[1] Chr. Pot. 4 (*Ephemerides*, p. 163); *C.D.*, DL-DLII.

[2] Cont. Orv. Polono, p. 120; Bolsenese Chr. cited in *Ephemerides*, p. 163 n. The Bolsenese chronicler was almost certainly a contemporary (his description of the submission to Orvieto in 1294 appears to be that of an eye-witness). Cont. Orv. Polono was not compiled till some fifty years later. Its tone is in general pro-papal, but it is unfriendly to Boniface.

omit, no doubt through ignorance, the essential fact that the deal was made at least eighteen months before Boniface became pope. It is now necessary to recapitulate the evidence for this extraordinary and hitherto neglected transaction, which provides such a vivid and typical example of Boniface's scheming on behalf of his family and has the additional importance of confirming that he expected to succeed Nicholas IV as pope.

The date of the exchange described by the chroniclers is known through the chance survival in the Orvietan Council minutes of a letter written in December 1295 (a year after Boniface became pope) which refers expressly to this bargain. By then Orvieto had overrun the Val del Lago and Boniface had excommunicated her; now Orvieto called upon the pope to implement the 'pacta integre facta olim Viterbii per dominum Benedictum nunc papam', and threatened in dark terms that if he prevaricated Orvieto would not fulfil her share and 'factum non fiat'.[1] The vital importance of this document is that it names Viterbo as the place of the meeting, for Boniface is known to have spent most of the time between the winter of 1292–3 and the autumn of 1293 at this town.[2] The Countess Margherita was married by June 1293 to Orsello Orsini, and since the bargain almost certainly presupposed that she should marry a Caetani, the period to which the agreement should probably be assigned can be narrowed down to the first few months of 1293.[3]

[1] See pp. 65–8. For the negotiations of October to December 1295, ACO, Rif. 1295, fos. 78–133; the letter of 9 December is fos. 113–114 v, and is summarized by Dottarelli, who fails to grasp its implications. It was approved by the Council of twenty-four, by three other Councils 'magnis et diversis', and by a specially appointed Balia of seventeen.

[2] Stefaneschi's verse life of Celestine V in F. X. Seppelt, *Monumenta Coelestiniana*, p. 8. The agreement in any case obviously dates from after the death of Nicholas IV. Stefaneschi says that Boniface went to Anagni in the summer of 1292 and that later he spent most of his time at Viterbo, but he does not make it at all clear when he moved there.

[3] It is not absolutely necessary to the thesis propounded above to suppose that the bargain preceded the Orsini marriage, although this seems highly probable. Boniface knew Margherita's guilty secret, that during her first husband's imprisonment she had lived with Nello dei Pannocchieschi, and he later used this to dissolve her marriage to his nephew Roffredo (see p. 70). He might therefore have proposed to dissolve the Orsini marriage, if he became pope, on the same grounds; this would have had the additional savour of being a snub for his rival Napoleone Orsini. But there is no evidence that he attempted to break up the Orsini marriage and this theory is altogether less probable than the one based on the supposition that the bargain preceded the Countess's marriage to Orsello.

So startling an allegation needs careful defence, especially when there is not absolutely certain proof of it. A number of objections can be raised to the hypothesis just stated, and they require notice. An obvious question is: may not Boniface have been acting at Viterbo on behalf of the cardinals, and reached some agreement in their name with Orvieto? There is no documentary evidence in favour of this, however, and Orvieto's letter implies that they were dealing with him as an individual, while the commune could hardly have thought that an agreement made with the cardinals about papal territory was binding on a pope, whereas it could reasonably be regarded as binding if it was negotiated with the same pope before his election.

Another objection is that Boniface could not know that he would become pope, and that in fact he was not the next pope. The answer is that he was able and ambitious and knew that his chances of advancement were good. Several historians of the period have already suggested that he may have hoped to succeed Nicholas IV,[1] and he replaced the pathetic Celestine V with such alacrity that great scandal resulted.

What seems to clinch the case for the hypothesis stated above is the renewal of negotiations between Orvieto and Boniface as soon as the Countess Margherita again became marriageable. Her husband Orsello died shortly before 21 October 1295 and on the 25th these negotiations were opened[2] (the letter referring to the Viterbo agreement dates from a month later). In the lack of absolutely conclusive evidence the case must remain 'not proven', but this explanation is reconcilable with all the known facts, and I believe that no alternative one is. Above all—and it is by this that it stands or falls—it is entirely in keeping with the character of

---

[1] Boase, pp. 29 and 32; H. Fincke, *Aus den Tagen Bonifaz VIII*, Münster, 1902, pp. 31 and 37; R. Morghen, 'Il Cardinale Matteo Rosso Orsini', ASRSP, XLVI, 1923, p. 319.

[2] Boase (pp. 33 n., 40-1 and 162) puts Orsello's death in the summer of 1294, just before Celestine's election, but he was still alive in June 1295 (*C.D.*, DLXV); G. Tommasi, *Dell' Historie di Siena*, Venice, 1625, pt. 2, p. 138, and L. Manente (*Ephemerides*, p. 328) say Orsello died in October 1295, and this date is confirmed by the visit to the Countess of a Sienese embassy—presumably of condolence—on the 21st of that month (Lisini, p. 73). The brother of Cardinal Napoleone, whose death Stefaneschi mentions as occurring in 1294, was probably the Giovanni whose tomb is in S. Francesco at Assisi (*v.* G. Caetani, *Caietanorum Genealogia*, Table LXIV); this is the opinion of the latest historian of Assisi (A. Fortini, *Assisi nel Medio Evo*, Rome, 1940, p. 234).

Boniface, and with the methods he employed in building up great estates for his family. What is exceptional about the episode is the amount of detailed evidence available, and it is this that justifies so full an account being given of it.

This digression stemmed out of the events of 1293, when Orvieto had contemplated an attack on the Val del Lago but never carried it out. One obstacle had been the hostile attitude of Perugia, but in 1294 the alliance of the two towns was renewed[1], and the cardinals, who were still in conclave at Perugia, drew the conclusion that Orvieto's assault was imminent; on 12 April they renewed their warning that it would entail *ipso facto* an interdict, the excommunication of all municipal officers and councillors, a fine of 20,000 marks, and the loss of any rights Orvieto might possess in the disputed area.[2]

The attack was launched at the end of May, against Bolsena, by an Orvietan force which included large contingents from the contado and was supplied with catapults for siege-warfare. Its commander was the same Orsello Orsini who had been so loth to submit to the commune the previous year. With the aid of some troops sent by the cardinals, Bolsena held out until 11 June, when it surrendered unconditionally. Two days later the other towns of the Val del Lago submitted and a governor was established in each of them. Thence the army moved on to Acquapendente, which was besieged for over a month, but by the third week of July Orvieto abandoned hopes of taking the town and a truce was

---

[1] In June Perugia replied unfavourably to an Orvietan 'feeler' about her attitude in the event of an attack on the Val del Lago, but Orvieto showed Perugia some papal 'litteras gratie' in October (Dottarelli, p. 128). By a deed in ACO (Dipl., Sec. XIII, n. 66) which is partly illegible, Orvieto appointed a proctor to sign this renewal. The date of this document is missing, but it can certainly be assigned to the thirteenth century, on palaeographical grounds, and there is little doubt that it was drawn up during the first half of the year 1294. The evidence for this is the presence of a communal official who was 'Spoletanensis' (his name is illegible); the only recorded Spoletan in office at Orvieto was Celle de' Bustoliti, Potestà in 1294 (C.D., pp. 432-4); since the deed dates from a papal vacancy ('. . . cante pastore' is legible) the period is limited to that before Celestine's election on 5 July. Boase (p. 33) is under the impression that the attack actually took place in 1293.

[2] Theiner, CCCXCII. It is possible that the attack would never have taken place but for the Orsini marriage of the previous year, but it is more likely that, even had the agreement with Boniface held, Orvieto would have had to take the Val del Lago by force. Boniface was hated in the Val del Lago after 1296 (the Bolsenese chronicler calls the exchange of that year 'contra di Dio e contra di rascione . . . e Dio volse che pochu n'ebe bene'); he could hardly have signed the area away without Orvieto even attacking it.

signed. Celestine V had now been elected pope, and the cardinals, whose responsibility in the matter would soon be over, gave their approbation to the truce.[1] Orvieto's next step was to regularize the hasty treaties of June, and in late August the Val del Lago towns accepted full terms of submission whereby they recognized that they were subject to the commune and had been since time immemorial.[2]

Celestine's brief pontificate—from July till December—prolonged Orvieto's breathing-space, for he never achieved a grip on the administration of the Patrimony. Benedict Caetani duly succeeded, and he soon confirmed the sentences already passed on the commune, threatening moreover that Orvieto would be deprived of all rights over her contado unless she promised complete obedience to his commands by March 13th. Orvieto sent an ambassador who took the necessary oath and on April 6th Boniface despatched Cardinal Napoleone Orsini with authority to lift the interdict after receiving from the commune the towns of the Val del Lago and guarantees of future obedience.[3] The Cardinal, however, returned to Rome with his mission unaccomplished, for Orvieto jibbed at these terms. The pope's reply to this was to issue orders that all the clergy were to leave the town in one week if his instructions were not obeyed within that period; furthermore all the inhabitants were threatened with outlawry and the confiscation of their property. The commune persisted in its defiance and, after the clergy had abandoned the town, another bull outlawed Orvieto and withdrew all its papal privileges, depriving its judges and notaries of their powers and all its citizens of the right to hold office anywhere. The Potestà and Captain were to appear personally before Boniface by June 29th, or Orvieto would be deprived of its

---

[1] The campaign is described by Cont. Orv. Polono (p. 119), Chr. Pot. 4 and the Bolsenese Chr. quoted in *Ephemerides*, p. 163, n. 3, Dottarelli (p. 129) enumerates several of the recipients of the cardinals' bull (v. also Potthast, n. 23946, to Viterbo); the copy sent to the Bishop of Todi is in Arch. Vat. A. A. Arm. I, xviii, n. 3590. The cardinals' representative at Acquapendente, a friar, was one signatory to the truce. Orvieto was now under an interdict, and the truce was in no way an acknowledgement of her gains (*C.D.*, dliii and dlxx).

[2] *C.D.*, dliv-dlvi; Dottarelli, docs. xix-xx. The towns also swore to the usual articles of obedience.

[3] *Reg. B. VIII*, n. 741; Chr. Pot. 4 (*Ephemerides*, p. 164), which also mentions the exodus of the clergy in May.

bishopric, and if fifty-four named ringleaders in the attack on the Val del Lago did not appear by the same day, they and their descendants would lose many of their civil and ecclesiastical rights.[1]

Again Orvieto refused to renounce the struggle. Her reply was to strengthen the defence works of Bolsena and the other Val del Lago towns and reorganize their garrisons. She also renewed the assault on Acquapendente, but this attack, begun during May, had not been successful by October, and was presumably abandoned before winter.[2] Meanwhile the pope transferred Bishop Francesco of Orvieto to the diocese of Florence, and appointed no successor.[3]

In October the news of Orsello Orsini's death suddenly brought back the possibility of implementing the bargain of 1293, since Margherita was now available to marry a Caetani. The Capitano del Popolo was at once despatched to the Curia on an embassy; he was accompanied by Bishop Francesco, the commune having asked that old ally to act on behalf of his former diocese. On November 14th the Capitano was back in Orvieto, apparently hopeful for a speedy reconciliation with the pope, for at his sugges-tion the Council appointed a proctor 'ad obediendos mandatos Ecclesiae'. On the 17th he was back in Rome, but negotiations apparently broke down, for on the 20th Boniface confirmed the sentences previously passed on Orvieto.[4] On December 4th, however, messengers from the Capitano reported that the pope, whose intentions appeared to be friendly, had suggested the nomination of Cardinal Matteo 'Rosso' Orsini as mediator.

---

[1] *Reg. B. VIII*, nn. 767-9 and Theiner, CCCCXCIV, which also summarizes the course of events since the previous summer.

[2] Costantini, doc. XVI; ACO, Rif. 1295, fos. 9-75v.

[3] *Reg. B. VIII*, n. 438. Bishop Francesco was a firm ally of the commune, and it is notable that he undertook four episcopal visitations of the Val del Lago, in 1280, 1281, 1286 and 1291 (AVO, Cod. A, fos. 220v, 228, and 231v-2: Cod. C, fo. 98v) and regularly collected tenths there; the area had received only two episcopal visitations in the previous fifty years. At this time the commune was even paying a garrison in the Val del Lago 'de avere episcopatus urbevetanae' (ACO, Rif. 1295, fo. 59v), and it may be significant that the first recorded enactment of the popular office of the Seven Consuls was one in favour of Bishop Francesco (see p. 80).

[4] For all the negotiations of October-December, ACO, Rif. 1295, fos. 78-133. The Bull of 20 November is *Reg. B.VIII*, n. 847; it may represent a temporary breakdown in negotiations, or it may have been a mere bargaining-move by Boniface. For Orsello's death see p. 63, n.

The Council decided to accept this mediation, and despatched on December 10th the important letter that has already been discussed. This message is couched in such vague language that its meaning is obscure, but its general intention was clearly to imply repentance, while giving up nothing.[1] It suggested that the Curia should keep Bolsena and Grotte until a decision was reached, unless this took longer than three months, in which case they were then to be returned to Orvieto; that after settlement the castles of the disputed towns should be destroyed if not retained by the commune as the seats of its governors; that the interdict and excommunications should be withdrawn and Orvieto fined lightly if at all; and that the Curia should aid the commune's taxation of the Val del Lago! The negotiations continued, a new embassy being sent to Rome on December 19th. A week later it was joined by the Captain, and agreement now seemed in sight, for his instructions were 'ad perficiendam, si poterit, compositionem per ipsum factam cum Summo Pontefice et domino Mattheo Rubeo Cardinale'.

Here there is a long gap in the minutes of the Council meetings and there is no indication of the progress of the negotiations till the following March (1296), when at last the Archbishop of Reggio was appointed to receive back the towns occupied by the Orvietans (the commune having promised to obey all the commands of the Church), and to relax the interdict. The town received absolution on March 22nd, and two days later the pope appointed a new bishop.[2] In July Orvieto's reconciliation with the papacy was confirmed by Boniface's election as Capitano del Popolo.[3]

The pope, however, continued to proceed with great caution. The relaxation of the interdict seems to have been arranged to coincide with the bethrothal of his great-nephew Roffredo to the Countess Margherita, and six months later the bargain of 1293 at last came fully into effect, Roffredo Caetani's marriage coinciding

---

[1] See p. 62. The ambassadors who took the letter were specifically informed that they were not authorized to take any oath on behalf of the commune.

[2] Chr. Pot. 4 (*Ephemerides*, p. 168); *Reg. B. VIII*, n. 1574; *C.D.*, DLXVI-DLXIX (DLXIX = *Reg. B. VIII*, n. 1029). The commune had to raise a loan to pay a sum of money demanded by the archbishop.

[3] Chr. Pot. 4 (p. 168 and n.).

with the announcement of the terms involved in Orvieto's absolution.[1] A Bull of September 4th laid it down that while the towns of the Val del Lago were 'Sedi soli subiecti' and Orvieto had no 'imperium' over them, they were to fight on behalf of Orvieto when requested, to pay Orvieto taxes and to perform all the other duties imposed upon towns subject to the commune.[2] The Church did retain the right to appoint Potestà, but on alternate years its choice was to be restricted to a list of four Orvietan nominees for each post; here is a clause in which the bare bones of hard-fought negotiation show clearly through the bland flesh of pontifical pronouncement. Orvieto was given a month in which to decide whether to accept this cession, so inadequately disguised as a deprivation. There was little hesitation, for only six days later the town and its citizens were fully absolved from their excommunication and outlawry.[3]

Margherita's marriage to Roffredo Caetani, who in March had been named Count Palatine and Rector of the Patrimony in Tuscany, took place at Anagni on September 19th. There were great rejoicings and games at Orvieto, both to celebrate papal recognition of the commune's *de facto* rule over the Val del Lago and to welcome Count Roffredo and his bride when they came north; fifty pages and twelve knights, dressed in tunics and fur-lined cloaks, specially made for the occasion, accompanied them from Bolsena to Soana.[4]

The new settlement now received its first check. The Val del Lago towns, who were only informed of the Papal decision in November, refused to accept it. When the commune sent ambassadors to receive their submission and their oath to obey the terms of the Bull of 4 September, each town refused, expressly stating that its Council met only on orders from the Captain of the Patrimony; this action had clearly been agreed on beforehand. They were not sufficiently strong, however, to withstand for long

[1] Roffredo became Count Palatine and Rector of the Patrimony in Tuscany in March (*Reg. B. VIII*, nn. 5452-4), so this was probably when the marriage was arranged.
[2] *C.D.*, DLXX.
[3] *C.D.*, DLXXI-II. One ringleader alone of the fifty-four condemned in 1295 was to remain excommunicated. Acquapendente was granted by a separate Bill, ten days after the towns of the Val del Lago proper.
[4] Caetani, *Caietanorum Genealogia*, p. 52; Chr. Pot. 4 (*Ephemerides*, pp. 169-70).

the powerful combination opposed to them, and they admitted defeat the following spring. At the end of March 1297 the new Potestà of these towns were sworn in and took up office.[1] This was not the end of all resistance, however; the bitterness of our Bolsenese chronicler is probably typical, for in 1298 and again in 1301 there were troubles, the Val del Lago towns refusing to pay taxes to Orvieto, and claiming the right to tax the property of Orvietan citizens within their own boundaries.[2] Yet on the whole the commune seems to have succeeded in securing obedience to its authority.

Boniface's popularity at Orvieto must indeed have been great in 1297, and when he announced his intention of making a prolonged stay in the town elaborate preparations were made for his reception. Jousts were organized, public buildings repaired, and—most spectacular of all—statues of the pope himself erected above the two principal gates of the town. Boniface was re-elected Capitano del Popolo, and Orvieto put a hundred and fifty cavalry at his disposal.[3] From June till November the Curia remained at Orvieto, and two great occasions which made the stay particularly memorable were the canonization of S. Louis in S. Francesco on August 10th and the celebration of the first Pontifical Mass in the new cathedral. The pope was elected Potestà and again re-elected as Capitano for 1298, and before leaving Orvieto he made a characteristic gesture; he excused the commune the payment of the fine imposed two years before, accepting in its stead the new papal palace that the town was building next to the bishop's palace. On his way south he stopped at Bolsena, whence he issued a

[1] Dottarelli, doc. xxv; C.D., DLXXIII-DLXXV; Chr.Pot. 4 (p. 170); ACO, Rif. 1297, fos. 5-10 of loose sheets. On 28 February Boniface issued a bull authorizing Orvieto and the officials of the Patrimony to use force against the towns of the Val del Lago, but it was not needed: Grotte had given in three days before, and the other towns soon followed suit.

[2] C.D., DLXXVII-III; Dottarelli, pp. 161-3; ACO, Rif. 1301, fos. 27v-29v, 40, 162. Orvieto's refusal to allow the Val del Lago towns to tax her citizens' property there was a genuine grievance, for these towns were taxed by both Orvieto and the Patrimony. The amounts paid by them in 1298 as hearth-tax, 'tallia militum', hunting-dues, and 'procurationes' are given by P. Fabre in 'Un Registre Caméral du Cardinal Albornoz en 1364' (in Mélanges d'Archéologie et d'Histoire, Paris, 1887, pp. 185-93). Acquapendente paid the most (276 lire) and Gradoli least (42 lire, 18 soldi): some of them also owed an annual payment of wood (ibid., pp. 193-4).

[3] C.D., p. 397; Chr. Ant. and Chr. Pot. 4 (Ephemerides, pp. 134 and 170). One of these statues of Pope Boniface is still to be seen above the Porta Maggiore.

further indulgence to all helping the construction of the cathedral, to which he also allotted the revenue of a newly-dissolved monastery for the next five years.[1] It was very probably at this period that Boniface successfully urged a reconciliation between the two rival communes with whom he was closely connected, Orvieto and Todi; their long enmity was suspended in 1301 by an alliance and an agreement that the disputed fortifications of Montemarte should be destroyed and their site purchased from Orvieto by Todi for 20,000 lire.[2]

In the meantime Roffredo Caetani's marriage to the Countess Margherita had come to an end after only two years. In October 1298 the Cardinal-Bishop of Sabina was charged by the pope with an enquiry into the legitimacy of this marriage, which had been impugned on the grounds that Margherita had a previous husband who was still alive; if he found the marriage irregular, he was to dissolve it. The cardinal's work was soon done, for Roffredo was betrothed in 1298 to Giovanna dell'Acquila, heiress to the county of Fondi, and their marriage took place the following year.[3]

The previous husband of Margherita referred to is Nello dei Pannocchieschi, with whom she had lived during the captivity of her first husband, Guy de Montfort, and whom she was later compelled to re-marry, on Boniface's orders. It has already been suggested that the pope was aware of a means of dissolving the marriage with Roffredo at the time when that marriage was arranged.[4] It is extremely improbable that Boniface, who knew Margherita and her history well, came to hear of her marriage to Nello only

---

[1] Chr. Ant. and Chr. Pot. 4 (*loc. cit.*); *Reg. B. VIII*, nn. 1851-2179 and 2207-8; *C.D.*, p. 398 and DLXXVI; Theiner, DIX. Boniface had already given the Opera del Duomo 1,000 florins (Cont. Orv. Polono, p. 126). The pope talks of the cancellation of a fine of 40,000 florins, but the bull of 10 September 1296 had seemed to imply that Orvieto was absolved from all her punishments, including the fine.

[2] *C.D.*, DLXXVII-DXCI and DXCVII-III (where the chronology is confused through the date of DLXXVII being read as '1300' instead of '1301'); *Ephemerides*, pp. 172-3 (Chr. Pot. 4) and 215-6 (Chr. of F. Montemarte). Todi had purchased Montemarte once before, in 1291, but its previous owners had constantly harried their Tudertine supplanters. After 1301 there were no serious troubles till 1314, when Perugia claimed that Todi still owed her 6,000 lire over the sale of 1290-1 (ACT, Arm. II, Cas. XI, n. 20).

[3] *Regesta Chartarum*, I, 147; Caetani, *Caietanorum Genealogia*, p. 52. Roffredo and Margherita were probably already living apart in 1297 (Lisini, p. 78: Ciacci, p. 270).

[4] See p. 62 n. and p. 76 and n. If Margherita married Nello she probably did so in 1289; in that year Ranieri da Baschi, the brother of Margherita's stepmother, came with

between 1296 and 1298, yet he should not have allowed her to marry his nephew if he was in possession of the facts before 1296.

It is almost certain that the marriage was arranged in the knowledge that its legality was doubtful, and quite possible that it was intended from the first to be dissolved after a short period. Margherita was no longer young, and if she bore Roffredo no male heir the successor to the Aldobrandeschine estates would be either the son she had had by Nello or one of her sons-in-law (she had two daughters by previous marriages, both of them married in 1296). The marriage could therefore serve a double purpose, for it gave the Caetani a claim to the succession and might at the same time provide the opportunity of depriving Margherita of her lands as a bigamist. The Orvietan chronicler who called Pope Boniface 'homo in rebus mundanis prudens et cordatus'[1] knew his man. But it is quite possible that the divorce was not decided upon till after 1296. Margherita's failure to provide a male heir may have settled the matter, while Roffredo was perhaps not unwilling to lose a wife who was about twice his age. The deciding factor, however, was probably a shift in the direction of Boniface's territorial interests. By 1298 his ambitions were no longer directed towards Southern Tuscany, where he had played all his cards; he was now building up a vast network of possessions south of Rome, hence the Fondi marriage in 1299.[2]

It is probable that soon after this divorce the Aldobrandeschine contado was put by the pope under the custody of Theoderic of Orvieto, a newly-created cardinal.[3] Margherita, however, sought

troops from Todi and carried her away from Orbetello, where she was living with Nello (Chr. Pot. 4, pp. 161-2; Ciacci, pp. 252-6; Lisini, p. 13). It is very unlikely that the marriage was valid, i.e. that it took place after Montfort's death in 1291, for Orsello Orsini would hardly have married her in 1293 in those circumstances.

[1] Cont. Orv. Polono, p. 120. Ciacci (pp. 271 ff.) suggests that Margherita was the 'bella donna' of Inferno, XIX, whom Boniface 'non temesti torre a'nganno . . . e poi di farne strazio', but the reference is certainly to the Church. The legality of the divorce was questioned by Nogaret in 1303, when he drew up a series of accusations against Boniface (Ciacci, p. 276); the surviving documents concerning Boniface's posthumous trial refer to accusations of heresy and immorality and the matter is not mentioned in them.

[2] Boase, ch. VI passim; G. Falco, 'Sulla Formazione e la Costituzione della Signoria dei Caetani, 1283-1303' in Rivista Storica Italiana, N.S., VI, July 1928, pp. 242 ff.

[3] Lisini, p. 89, and Caetani, Domus Caietana, p. 140 suggest this; Cardinal Theoderic was certainly in charge of Saturnia and Marzano in 1300 (Reg. B. VIII, n. 3909). For his career, v. App. IV.

support elsewhere and joined forces with her cousin Guy of S. Fiora, the owner of an Aldobrandeschine county north of Margherita's. The pope's reaction was to incite Orvieto and Siena to war against Margherita and Guy. The pair were at war with Siena in 1299, and in 1300 they inflicted a heavy defeat on the Orvietans, who had been urged on by papal exhortations, expressed through Cardinal Theoderic, to deprive Guy and Margherita of all their lands. Siena, apparently less pliable, had to be promised possession of all conquests made north of the river Ombrone, and in October 1300 Orso Orsini and his nephew Gentile were appointed to the supreme command of the forces opposing the cousins, who were now married.[1] Rumour had it that the pope had promised the Orsini the succession to Margherita's lands, and they cherished hopes at the least, for not only had the Countess married one Orsini but her daughter by Guy de Montfort was married to another, Gentile's son Romano. This in a way made them rivals of the Caetani, but Boniface never minded playing a waiting game, and in September he had secured the Orsini to his cause by awarding them much land confiscated from the Colonna.[2]

The task assigned to the Orsini was the defeat of Guy and Margherita, who were now proclaimed rebels against the Church, and the capture of their lands (the rights of Siena, Orvieto, and Margherita's children remaining inviolate).[3] Orvieto promised assistance, and Gentile Orsini was made Potestà in 1301.[4] Yet the military effort of that year seems to have petered out after a raid on Radicofani, and in August the pope was rebuking Siena for signing a peace with Guy of S. Fiora.[5]

---

[1] Ciacci, pp. 287-90 and doc. 645 (the grant to Siena, later modified to exclude conquests made since 1284); Chr. Pot. 4 (pp. 170- ad 1298- and 172); ACO, Rif. 1300, fos. 21-28v; Reg. B. VIII, nn. 3905-6; Domus Caietana, p. 140.

[2] Reg. B. VIII, nn. 3911-5.

[3] Ibid., n. 3909.

[4] ACO, Rif. 1300, fos. 136v-137 (Orvieto sends ambassadors asking to be excused part of the aid promised) and Rif. 1301, fos. 81v-88. Orsini wrote a tactless letter to the commune, saying that the pope had made him Potestà ('dominus noster summus Pontifex offitium potestarie terre vestre nobis concessit'). His Vicar was unpopular, and there were riots against him (ibid., fos. 151v-152v).

[5] ACO, Rif. 1300, fos. 56v-68 and 1301, fos. 1, 26, 39v-40v, 44, 49,; Chr. Pot. 4 (Ephemerides, pp. 172-3); Reg. B. VIII, nn. 4326 (March, Florence is asked to provide 200 cavalry for the Orsini) and 4387.

Orvieto was provoked to continue the war by subtler means. In April 1302 the commune received a secret communication from Cardinal Theoderic, who stated that he had reason to believe that the pope was thinking of granting the Aldobrandeschine contado to Orvieto and that if they wished to accept it they should dispatch ambassadors to the Curia at once. The same day a Balìa decided that the offer, if made, should be accepted, but somehow the opportunity afforded by Orvieto's possession of a powerful well-wisher in the Curia was missed.[1] There is no reason to doubt the Cardinal's words, for the Orsini are not heard of in connection with the Aldobrandeschine estates after the autumn of 1301, and they were not disposed of until 1303.[2] Orvieto pressed home an attack on Pitigliano so successfully that on 1 May 1302 Guy and Margherita submitted to the commune, but it was not till July that ambassadors were sent to the pope at Anagni 'pro negotiis Marittime', and by then it was apparently too late. Meanwhile the death of Guy had put an end to the intermittent war, the last episodes of which had been fighting at Radicofani and an unsuccessful stand by Guy and Margherita at Acquapendente.[3]

In March 1303 Margherita finally lost her lands, and Boniface's schemes came to fruition ten years after the initiation at Viterbo. The Countess was condemned by the pope to forfeit the tenure of the whole area held of the monastery of S. Anastasio, an investigation by Cardinal Theoderic having proved that she had alienated the monastery's property without its permission and that she had illegally married her cousin, who was, moreover, a rebel against the Church. She was refused the right to appeal. Three days later the Abbot of S. Anastasio granted these lands to Benedict Caetani, a younger brother of Roffredo, and Benedict was invested by his

---

[1] ACO, Rif. 1302, fo. 201 and v. The relevant passage runs: '. . . quod sanctissimus pater dominus noster intendebat commune Urbisveteris praeferre in terris Marittime et comitatu Aldebrandesca ipsum commune extollere et magnificare ac ipsi communi ad censum ipsas terras Marittime concedere et comitatum.'

[2] ACO, Rif. 1301, fo. 90 (October, the last reference to the Orsini).

[3] Chr. Pot. 4 (p. 173); ACO, Rif. 1302, fo. 215 (the July embassy, the first to go to the Curia after April); Theiner DLXI. Acquapendente was probably chosen because it had again been on bad terms with Orvieto. Manno Monaldeschi commanded the Orvietan forces which captured the town.

great-uncle with the contado palatine.[1] In April the new Count
came to the area to receive the submission of his subjects, and paid
a visit to Orvieto, where he bestowed knighthoods on a number
of citizens.[2]

But Benedict's rule in the Aldobrandeschine contado was destined to be short-lived. On September 7th Boniface and his family
(including Benedict) were attacked at Anagni by a large party of
conspirators who had nothing in common but their hatred of the
Caetani.[3] By the 11th news of the outrage of Anagni had reached
Orvieto and the Council of the Popolo met to discuss what action
should be taken 'ad utilitatem et statum et exaltationem communis
et populi Urbisveteris et ad conservationem iurum et iurisdictionum
dicti populi et communis' in view of the 'multe novitates... circa
statum Romane Ecclesie et Summi Pontificis'. On the motion of
one of the Seven it was decided to sign a 'francischia' giving the
inhabitants of the Aldobrandeschine contado the same rights as
citizens of Orvieto and to mobilize a force representing the
commune and Popolo which was to enter the Aldobrandeschine
lands within twenty-four hours and attack any town refusing to
submit to Orvieto.[4] For sheer cold-blooded opportunism this
looting of the property of a prostrate ally ranks with any deed of
the Caetani; the pontifical sower of winds was reaping a municipal
whirlwind.

The town of Saturnia refused to submit to Orvieto's officials,
and it was decided to reinforce the advance-guard of troops with a
'generalis exercitus' consisting of the entire cavalry, a thousand
foot and one soldier from each household of the contado and the
Val del Lago. The next day a letter from Benedict's vicar in the
contado stated his willingness to hand over the towns to Orvieto if

---

[1] *Reg. B. VIII*, nn. 5333-5; also 5337 (Benedict appointed Rector of the Tuscan
Patrimony). The lands concerned were all those held by Margherita; an inventory of
them (dated 1286) is printed by I. Giorgi, 'Il Regesto del Monastero di S. Anastasio' in
ASRSP, I, 1877.

[2] *Regesta Chartarum*, I, 229 (the oath of Montebuono: Caetani dates it 1302, but the
indiction is that for 1303); for the Orvieto visit, L. Manente (*Ephemerides*, pp. 337-9) and
ACO, Rif. 1303, fos. 21 and 31v.

[3] Cardinal Napoleone Orsini, whose rivalry with the Caetani concerning the Aldobrandeschine contado has been mentioned above (pp. 60 and 62) was in touch with the
conspirators (Boase, p. 349) and was a hostile witness at Boniface's posthumous trial
(*ibid.*, p. 368).   [4] ACO, Rif. 1303, fos. 60-63v.

the inhabitants gave their consent, but now the commune became suddenly aware of the dangers of the policy on which they had so irrevocably embarked. On September 16th news was received, in a letter from Cardinal Theoderic, of the pope's liberation, and it must have been a very subdued gathering of the Council of the Popolo which heard a judge's reminder that their recent policy had been 'magni ponderis et magni periculi' and that 'non decet communi Urbisveteris facere contra dominum Papam a quo tanta benefitia recepit'. It was decided to send an embassy to condole with the pope and to congratulate him on his escape; a slip by the notary at this point casts some doubt on the sincerity of the message, for he began to write that the embassy should 'de sinistro casu gaudere', but crossed out 'gaudere' and amended this to 'de sinistro casu dolere et de restitutione gaudere'.[1]

On September 23rd it was known that the pope had returned to Rome, and the Council decided that the 'impresa facta per Populum ulterius non procedat'. The towns already captured were to be garrisoned and a new embassy which visited the pope was to say, if questioned about the Aldobrandeschine contado, that they had no mandate to discuss this matter.[2]

After only three weeks there was once again a dramatic turn in events, for the Pope died on October 12th and the commune at once decided to press home the attack against the remaining Aldobrandeschine towns. Monte Acuto fell in late November after a siege; by then the major towns had all been captured and a small garrison was allotted to each of them for the winter. Throughout this period Orvieto's Capitano del Popolo was a Pistoian deputy for Boniface, who had been elected to the office![3]

The history of Orvieto's dealings with Boniface VIII over the Aldobrandeschine lands and the Val del Lago is incomplete without a brief epilogue recounting their aftermath. In the autumn of 1303 the town was again placed under an interdict, as a punishment for

---

[1] For all these events, ACO, Rif. 1303, fos. 64-6. Difficulty was experienced in raising sufficient troops because the Val del Lago towns had just provided men for the Patrimony and protested at this double imposition. [2] ACO, Rif. 1303, fos. 67-69v.

[3] Ibid., fos. 74-6, 79v-80, 86v-88; C.D., p. 387. Several of the Aldobrandeschine towns submitted formally in January 1304 (C.D., DCIV-DCV).

the onslaught on the Aldobrandeschine contado. The new pope, Benedict XI, though duly elected as Potestà and Capitano, avoided Orvieto when on his way to Perugia in the spring of 1304, and the Bolsenese chronicler says that he revoked Pope Boniface's concession of the Val del Lago, but no such deed is mentioned in the later appeals of Bolsena, so the statement is improbable. There is no doubt, however, of Benedict's unfriendly attitude towards the commune.[1]

Orvieto's war developed into a defence of the contado against Nello dei Pannocchieschi, Margherita's latest husband, but the couple soon parted company, and Nello abandoned his pretensions to the area.[2] For the rest of her life Margherita threw in her lot with the Orsini; her brother-in-law Cardinal Napoleone was her special protector and the heir to her lands was eventually her grandson Guido. The Countess settled in Rome, where she seems at last to have found peace, interrupted only by one curious interlude when an impostor appeared in the Maremma, claiming to be the Countess Margherita.[3]

This settlement, like so many others, was disturbed by the expedition of the Emperor Henry VII. Fearing lest the Countess should place herself under imperial protection and renew her claims to the contado, the commune asked her to come and live at Orvieto and even offered her an allowance. After much hesitation Margherita agreed, but Orvieto's fear that she would take advantage of the new situation was well-founded. In February 1313 she and Gentile Orsini entered the contado and rapidly secured the submission of Soana, Pitigliano and several other towns.[4] Orvieto's

---

[1] The interdict was imposed when one Amato was vicar of the Patrimony (C.D., DCXIV): this dates it to 1303, when Benedict Caetani's vicar was Amato di Giovanni (Reg. B. XI, n. 91); ACO, Rif. 1303, fo. 84 and 1304, fos. 133v and 146v (Benedict XI Potestà and Capitano): the Pope was invited to Orvieto (Rif. 1304, fo. 112) and Ferreto de' Ferreti (Historia, I, 173 in 'Fonti per la Storia d'Italia') says he stayed there four days, but Cont. Orv. Polono, a better authority, gives Acquapendente as the place of his stay (p. 126) and L. Manente agrees (p. 339), adding that he was 'poco amico ad Orvieto'. The Bolsenese Chr. is cited in Ephemerides, p. 174 n.

[2] ACO, Rif. 1304, fos. 109v–153v; Caetani, Domus Caietana, p. 143. Margherita was compelled to marry Nello by Cardinal Theoderic, on papal orders (Ciacci, doc. 651) (see p. 70).   [3] Caetani, Domus Caietana, p. 144; Regesta Chartarum, I, 240.

[4] ACO, Rif. 1312, fos. 220v, 253-5v, 270 and Rif. 1313, fos. 3-16; Chr. Ant., Chr. Pot. 4 and L. Manente (Ephemerides, pp. 136, 178, 350). Orvieto had kept in touch with Margherita, who still owned property there (AVO, Cod. A, fo. 83): in 1308 the commune

reaction to the danger was to send an embassy to Anagni to seek Benedict Caetani and offer him the tenure of all Orvieto's zone of the Aldobrandeschine contado. It is curious that for almost ten years nothing had been heard of Benedict in connection with his former estates, but now he was the obvious choice, for in 1312-13 he played a leading part in the Angevin defence of Rome against Henry VII and the Ghibellines. The negotiations were soon concluded, and on 1 April 1313 Benedict appointed a proctor to swear on his behalf that he would become a citizen of Orvieto and pay 12,000 florins to hold the Aldobrandeschine contado of the commune.[1] Ten years after his death Boniface's schemes continued to bear fruit.

The interdict imposed in 1303 lasted for over ten years, the negotiations for Orvieto's absolution lingering on until December 1313.[2] The death of Benedict XI and the papacy's move beyond the Alps in 1305 delayed the matter and no doubt the pope's remoteness made his threats seem of less importance. Clement V did confirm the interdict, however, and in 1307 the commune at last began a serious attempt to obtain absolution. In 1308 the Abbot of Acquaorte was at the Curia on behalf of Orvieto and was empowered to offer 6,000 florins for absolution, if the papacy would recognize the commune's right over the Aldobrandeschine contado; but in 1309 he reported that 13,000 florins were required. A great effort was made to raise this money, but in 1310 Orvieto rashly fell foul of the authorities of the Patrimony (Montefiascone was sacked after the Captain of the Patrimony had intercepted some grain intended for Orvieto),[3] and the Curia was able to raise

aided her daughter and son-in-law in a war (Ciacci, p. 328; ACO, Rif. 1309, fos. 183v and 217, and 1310, fo. 10) and in 1309 she planned a visit to the town (Rif. 1309, fos. 284v-5). The promised allowance was never paid her.

[1] C.D., DCXI: the deed of submission is no longer extant, but it figures in a 14th-century inventory of the Orvietan archive (Ephemerides, p. 123). For Benedict Caetani's rôle in opposing Henry VII, v. C. W. Previté-Orton, 'The Roman House of Caetani in the Middle Ages' in The Edinburgh Review, vol. 248, October 1928, pp. 303-4. Benedict died in 1322 and was succeeded by Guido Orsini, the son of Margherita's daughter Anastasia de Montfort.

[2] For the whole question of the interdict and the negotiations leading up to Orvieto's absolution, v. C.D., DCXIV and notes. The episode is characteristic of the methods that made Dante call John XXII 'tu che sol per cancellare scrivi' ('you who order only to countermand'), Paradiso, XVIII, 130.

[3] Chr. Ant. and Chr. Pot. 4 (Ephemerides, pp. 135 and 177); ACO, Rif. 1310, fos. 71-2. There was a severe famine in 1310. It is not clear to what extent the interdict was observed

its demands yet again. Another cardinal was put in charge of the matter, and a disillusioned ambassador reported that the number of ecclesiastics concerned with the case was being increased in order that more might receive presents and a share of the fine. In 1312 the commune raised a large loan from its Jewish community and the sorry business at last came to an end in 1313, when Orvieto received absolution on payment of over 16,000 lire. The Curia's rapacious exploitation of Orvieto's treacherous *volte-face* of 1303 makes a fitting end to twenty years of sordid dealings.

These twelve eventful years between the death of Nicholas IV and that of Benedict XI are the great period of the commune's power. Two things especially, one more lasting than the other, bear witness to its strength and its wealth: the magnificent new cathedral, begun in 1290 and mainly paid for by contributions from the town and contado,[1] and the daring policy whereby the papacy was twice defied, and in the interval wooed with an enthusiasm that spoke all too clearly of calculation. Such a policy would have been impossible without a high degree of unanimity within the commune, and throughout the period Orvietan politics are characterized by a unity that is rarely found in all the turbulent history of the city-republics, and contrasts strangely with what had come before and was to follow.

It is significant that the minutes of the Council meetings record only one close vote in these years—and that, symptomatically, is on an unimportant domestic issue concerning weights and measures.[2] When it had been decided that a certain course of action was that

throughout these years, but when Cardinal Fieschi went to Orvieto in 1311 he thought it worth while to obtain papal permission to celebrate Mass there (*Reg. Cl. V*, n. 7545).

[1] For the chronology of the Duomo, *v.* R. Bonelli, *Fasi Costruttive ed Organismo Architettonico del Duomo di Orvieto*, pp. 4-5. For a list of some contributions from the contado, Della Valle, pp. 249-50. The cathedral is as large as that of Siena, which was being built at the same time. Its principal architect, Lorenzo Maitani, was a Sienese. Maitani was also probably responsible for the finest parts of the magnificent bas-reliefs on the facade. Throughout the fourteenth century the Sienese influence on Orvietan art was strong; there was an Orvietan school of painting, following closely the style of Simone Martini, who had worked in the town. Thus artistically Orvieto was almost a colony of Siena, though politically it was usually an enemy.

[2] ACO, Rif. 1300, fos. 62-4. These minutes are extant with few gaps from 1295 onwards.

78

most in the interest of the town it was backed by all, whatever its party connotations. Manente's claim that the new Duomo was built 'to end the discord between Monaldeschi and Filippeschi'[1] is not convincing, but temporarily the same aim was achieved by agreement on a forceful and immensely ambitious foreign policy.

This internal agreement is also to be seen in the careers of several of those most prominent in Orvieto's affairs throughout the period. Whatever the deviations of the commune's policy, the same hands remain at the rudder, oblivious of ideological inconsistency so long as the interests of the town are being served. Domenico di Oradino, a hosier who was perhaps the most frequent speaker in Council meetings of the Popolo between 1295 and 1303 and who played a notable part in many of the events of those years, was so notorious for the rôle he played in Orvieto's invasion of the Val del Lago in 1294 that he was expressly excluded from Boniface's absolution of the ringleaders excommunicated in 1295.[2] Yet only three years later it is he who rises to propose in tones of righteous indignation that Orvieto should obey Boniface's exhortations and attack Guy of S. Fiora for his rebellion against the pope.[3] One Faffaccio di Masseo, who had been Capitano del Popolo in 1285, was singled out for excommunication as a ringleader in 1294, but remained in the front rank of Orvietan statesmen throughout the commune's close alliance with Boniface and in 1303 was sent as an ambassador to the pope himself.[4] Yet another distinguished Vicar of Bray was Neri di Guidetto, also a leader in 1294, who held a series of important posts as ambassador and representative of the commune in 1300-3, was then prominent in the overrunning of the Aldo-brandeschine contado after the outrage of Anagni, and continued to play a big part in Orvieto's politics for the next thirty years.[5]

There are two aspects to Orvieto's new-found unity, one being

---

[1] *Ephemerides*, p. 322.

[2] ACO, Rif. 1297, fos. 19v-20 (see p. 68 n).

[3] ACO, Rif. 1300, fo. 21v.

[4] He was ambassador to Siena in 1300 and in 1301 a director of the 'lira' (direct taxation) and probably Potestà of S. Lorenzo (*C.D.*, p. 355; ACO, Rif. 1300, fo. 28v; 1301, fos. 145 and 148; 1303, fo. 41).

[5] For the leaders of 1294, Theiner, pp. 322-7 (the list is reprinted in *Ephemerides*, pp. 164n.-168n.). For Neri's appointments, ACO, Rif. 1300, fos. 92v and 96v; 1302, fo. 215; 1303, fo. 40, etc.

a truce between Guelfs and Ghibellines, the other the joint participation of nobles and Popolo in the commune's policy. The Popolo was already securing a greater share of political power (its vital conquest, the institution of the Seven, dates from 1292), but its association in the great events of 1293-1303 hastened the process, since it demanded constitutional concessions commensurate with its services.

The Seven (as the office of the Seven Consuls of the Seven Arti was usually abbreviated) came into existence in the spring of 1292, but nothing is known of the circumstances surrounding its origins. Hitherto the Popolo had only had one executive officer, the Captain; its other prominent members were Consuls of the Arti and councillors. Suddenly this institution of the Seven Consuls is found to be issuing executive orders applying to the commune as a whole, the first extant one being a measure forbidding excommunicates from pleading in the Potestà's court.[1] If the minutes of the Council meetings for this year had survived, the origins of this constitutional revolution would be less obscure. In general terms it is explicable by the failure of Della Greca as Captain of the Popolo; if the captaincy was not to be the office through which the Popolo exerted its growing power, another one had to be constructed. This suggestion is confirmed by the situation in 1292, for in that year one Florio of Milan was both Potestà and Capitano del Popolo[2]; in view of his dual position he could hardly be regarded as the ideal leader of the Popolo, and probably this was the immediate occasion of the institution of the new office. In any case neighbouring states had set an example in founding similar executive offices filled by local 'popolani'; the Five had occupied a corresponding position at Perugia since 1270, while the Nine at Siena, who are first heard of in 1277, became permanent with effect from this same year of 1292.[3]

---

[1] AVO, Cod. C, fo. 89 (cited in *Ephemerides*, p. 323.n, with no indication of its provenance). The deed begins 'Placuit 7 consulibus artium de 7 artibus civitatis urbevetanae et ordinaverunt statuerunt et reformaverunt ac provisum est per eos pro utilitate et statu communis urbevetani . . . quod . . . (etc.)'.

[2] *C.D.*, pp. 339 ff.

[3] F. Guardabassi, *Storia di Perugia* (Perugia, 1933-), I, 135; F. Schevill, *Siena* (London, 1909), p. 193. Another influential factor, Florence's régime of the six priors, dates from 1282.

Whether the Seven was at first intended to be a permanent institution it is impossible to say, and indeed the growth of their power and status is as hard to trace as their origin. There is nothing approaching a complete Carta del Popolo extant for this period, but here and there a random clue throws some light on their aggrandisement. By 1293 the Seven were already concerned in the campaign against Orsello Orsini.[1] The importance of their rôle in the Val del Lago attack in the following year is attested by Boniface's singling out for especial commination in his bull of excommunication 'illos qui apud eos Septem . . . dicebantur'.[2] It is not till 1300 that they are found issuing a whole series of orders, regulating the status of condemned criminals.[3] Meanwhile their prestige had certainly been growing. In 1295 they asserted the dignity of the Popolo when the Potestà and his officers insulted their office and the Captain refused to act on their behalf.[4] A similar incident in 1301 led to their obtaining the privilege of immunity from arrest by any officer of the commune, and in the same year the re-submission of a rebellious subject was made to the Captain, Seven, and Potestà, in that order.[5]

The increasing power of the Popolo throughout the period is not only to be seen in the growth of its principal organ. Again the evidence is fragmentary and usually indirect, but by 1298 the principle is implicitly recognized that the ultimate legislative body of the city is the Council of the Popolo.[6] Several times during the decade it is ordered that half the members of a Balia must be popolani, and once that all must be.[7] An example of lesser, but significant, gains is the transfer in 1296 of the corn-market from the Piazza del Comune to that of the Popolo.[8] The total gain was such that by the end of Boniface's pontificate the balance of power seems to have shifted so completely that the Popolo, from a position of subordination to the commune, had reached one of pre-eminence. The evidence of the wording used in deeds must obviously be used with caution, but it seems significant that the Val del Lago campaign of 1294 was the work of the Commune

[1] *C.D.*, DL.
[2] *Ephemerides*, pp. 164-8.
[3] ACO, Rif. 1300, fos. 100v-104.
[4] Chr. Pot. 4 (*Ephemerides*, pp. 165 and 168n.).
[5] *C.D.*, DXCII.
[6] ACO, Rif. 1298, fos. 5-7.
[7] *Ibid.*, fos. 6-8v, etc.; 1302, fo. 201 and v.
[8] Chr. Pot. 4 (*Ephemerides*, p. 170).

and Popolo, while the invasion of the Aldobrandeschine contado in 1303 is called simply the 'impresa facta per Populum'.[1] While the process whereby the Popolo was gaining ground at the commune's expense was an unpremeditated and gradual one, the truce between Ghibelline and Guelf was conceived as an act of policy. The renewed participation of Ghibellines in political offices and councils is marked from at least 1294 onwards. In the course of the next ten years many Filippeschi are found as councillors, members of Balie, Potestà in subject towns, and so on.[2] Most embassies include Filippeschi representatives; often one of two ambassadors, or two of four, is a Ghibelline.[3] Moreover the Filippeschi were sufficiently involved in Orvieto's amity with Boniface for the pope to grant one of them a benefice at Chiusi as a favour to the family.[4] Positions of political importance were also held by members of the other leading Ghibelline families, such as Giovanni 'Bachecha' and Meo dei Miscinelli, who was one of the Seven in 1298 and Potestà of Bolsena in 1298-9.[5] By 1303 the Ghibellines were so influential that the Balia of twelve leading citizens which advised on the military operations of that autumn was 'de utraque parte sex'.[6] Only in 1295 there was a temporary rift; a number of Filippeschi were in exile that summer, but they were apparently readmitted by October.[7]

The Ghibellines' large share of political power by no means entailed the eclipse of the Monaldeschi. When Orvieto's policy was overtly anti-papal they disappeared discreetly from the scene, to re-emerge after the heat of the day, when its gains were at stake. Thus not a single Monaldeschi is to be found among the

---

[1] *Ephemerides*, pp. 164-8 (Boniface's condemnation) and ACO, Rif. 1303, fo. 67. For the Popolo's leadership in the 1303 campaign, see pp. 84-5.

[2] ACO, Lib. Cond. 1295, fos. 78-80; Rif. 1295, fos. 33v, 93, 120; 1300, fos. 26, 68v, 112, 133v, 138, 158; 1301, fos. 145 and 164; *C.D.*, DLXVII; Dottarelli, p. 171 n.; etc.

[3] ACO, Rif. 1300, fos. 133v and 138, etc., etc.

[4] *Reg. B. VIII*, n. 2072. The boy who benefited was a minor and was not in Holy Orders.

[5] ACO, Rif. 1295, fo. 46; Dottarelli, p. 159; *Reg. B. VIII*, n. 2458; etc.

[6] ACO, Rif. 1303, fos. 61-2.

[7] *Ibid.*, 1295, fos. 30, 38, 51v, etc. Città della Pieve was requested in August not to receive 'inbannitos Urbisveteris et specialiter illos de Filippensibus qui apud Fabrum incendium commiserunt'. The Captain's squire was sent to Fabro to destroy the property of these exiles, and in September Chiusi was asked to receive them.

fifty-four Orvietans excommunicated by name for their leading part in the 1294 attack on the Val del Lago, and again in the autumn of 1303 they provided an exception from the general unanimity; to have played a large part in the overrunning of the Aldobrandeschine contado would have been clearly inconsistent with their friendship with its owner, Count Benedict Caetani.[1] Apart from these temporary withdrawals, however, the Monaldeschi maintained their dominating position in Orvietan politics, and in some respects even strengthened it.

Soon after Orvieto had, in 1296, firmly hitched its waggon to the papal star, they began to resume positions of authority, especially in the cavalry and the government of the contado, and as ambassadors, and in the following years they held innumerable political offices.[2] A subsidiary source of strength to the family, and one that fluctuated little with political changes, was the extraordinary number of major ecclesiastical posts occupied by Monaldeschi. At the turn of the century they provided the archpriest and two other canons in the Orvieto chapter, the prior of the local Dominican house (who was later to become Bishop of Orvieto) and the prior of the neighbouring monastery of Samprugnano, while among the many high offices held by Monaldeschi in other parts was the bishopric of the neighbouring diocese of Soana.[3] How great was the influence of the higher clergy in the commune emerges clearly from the career of Bishop Francesco and later those of Bishop Beltramo Monaldeschi and the Archpriest Monaldo.[4] The events of the next chapter will show that ten years of coalition had not seriously sapped the foundations of Monaldeschi supremacy.

---

[1] *Ephemerides*, pp. 164n.-168n.

[2] In 1300, for example, Manno Monaldeschi was Visconte of the piviere of S. Venanzo and Spinuccio Monaldeschi of Fabro, Nericola was a representative of the commune at the Patrimonial parliament, etc. (Rif. *ad an.*, fos. 63, 109v, 133, etc.).

[3] Archpriest Monaldo di Ugolino (ACO, Rif. 1303, fo. 12), and canons Neri di Ugolino (*Reg. B. VIII*, n. 3257, etc.) and Pepo di Pietro (*ibid.*, n. 3858). Simone di Masseo, prior of Samprugnano (ACO, Lib. Don., fo. 11), Monaldo di Ermanno, Bishop of Soana and later Archbishop of Benevento (*Ephemerides*, p. 337n.). Tramo di Corrado, prior of the Dominican house in Orvieto, later Bishop of Bagnorea and of Orvieto (Caccia, pp. 52n. and 123-5). Other Monaldeschi held a bishopric in Dalmatia, a canonry at Arras, and at least two livings in Orvieto.

[4] See p. 66 n. 3, and below pp. 122, 137, etc.

CHAPTER XI

THE DEFEAT OF THE GHIBELLINES (1303-13)

THE years that followed the eventful pontificate of Boniface VIII were quiet ones in Orvieto and their interest lies in domestic affairs. The Ghibellines continued to share in the political life of the commune and there is no evidence of tension between them and the Guelfs.[1] As long as Italy contained neither a pope nor an Emperor the factions lacked the external stimulus and support that had so often set them fighting, and was shortly to do so again. Behind the quarrels of the 1260s and 1270s lay the issue of whether the government of the commune was to be the monopoly of a Guelf party supported by French popes and Angevin garrisons, and the great struggle of 1313 was to be fought over an attempt to introduce a Ghibelline régime backed by an Empire which had again become a power in Italy; between these two periods there was little conflict within the Orvietan nobility.

The unity of the nobles was one cause of the rapid growth in the Popolo's power, for there was clearly greater need to guard against the danger of a noble monopoly of government when Guelf and Ghibelline had ceased to exhaust most of their strength in opposing each other. Not only did the Popolo's power increase continually between 1303 and 1310, but this increase was evidently the outcome of a fixed policy, pursued with patience and determination.

The important part played by the Popolo in the campaign of 1303 has already been mentioned. There was apparently much hesitation among the nobles as to the advisability of overrunning the Aldobrandeschine lands, for the operation was decided upon and organized by the Popolo alone (though they had noble advisers

---

[1] Filippeschi were granted reprisals against a neighbouring town in 1307 (ACO, Rif. *ad an.*, fos. 54-5); they supplied members of important embassies (Chr. Pot. 4, 1309, p. 176), etc.

and nobles were in the army) and measures were passed giving the Popolo special powers to attack and destroy the house of any noble actively opposing the project. At the same time nobles were expressly forbidden to approach the persons of the Captain and Seven, the Popolo elected its own standard-bearers, and diplomatic business in connection with the campaign was conducted by 'popolani' alone.[1] All this demonstrates the great degree of independence that the Popolo was acquiring, an independence that was emphasized and increased on every occasion when its policy diverged from that of the nobles.

The succeeding years saw a continuous stream of pro-Popolo and anti-noble legislation, and all the more important of these measures were added to the written constitution, or Carta, of the Popolo. This constitution had existed at least as early as 1247, but the first occasion on which a series of provisions of the Council of the Popolo is known to have been added to it was in December 1306, when the murder by a noble of a former member of the Seven provoked a spate of orders. These reveal that the Popolo already had a body of a thousand armed men, and typical clauses provided that relatives to the third degree might be held responsible for offences committed against the Seven by nobles, that the list of members of Arti was to be checked and revised, that evidence given in law-courts by nobles should be regarded as suspect, and that popolani should be excused small fines.[2]

In 1307 there was a new series of additions to the Carta del Popolo, and the measures of the previous year were confirmed. If a noble murdered a popolano it was compulsory for the family of the victim to denounce the crime within three days (such orders bring home most vividly how the Popolo needed an artificial legal superiority for its members to guard them against the might of the nobles), and popular officers were forbidden to impede the trials

---

[1] For all this period, notes to *C.D.*, DCII. See below, p. 102, for the significance of the election of popular standard-bearers. By 1309 each Quarter of the town had its own banner (ACO, Rif. 1309, fo. 61). The part played by banners in the formation of popular patriotism is an interesting example of the importance of visual factors in politics.

[2] ACO, Rif. 1306, fos. 10-15v. For the reference to a Carta del Popolo in 1247, see p. 40. Although the 1,000 became the Popolo's army for use against civil enemies, the army of 1303 which invaded the Aldobrandeschine contado also included 1,000 infantry, the lineal ancestor, no doubt, of the 'mille armatos de populo' of 1306 and later.

of nobles. At least half of the personnel of all embassies were to be 'popolani' and the revenue from grazing-rights leased out in the Aldobrandeschine area was to be spent only on buying grain for the Popolo.[1] Another characteristic measure, passed in 1309, restricted the access of nobles to the officers of the Popolo, while these detailed ordinances were always accompanied by more general ones, such as 'quod societas populi et artium . . . fiat', 'quod nulla persona audeat dicere quod populus urbevetanus recipeat diminutionem', and 'quod dominus Capitaneus et Septem et eorum offitium semper sit' (sic).[2] The Popolo was learning, as it grew in strength, to pitch its claims correspondingly high.

The arrival in Italy of the Emperor Henry VII put a sudden end to this period of predominantly domestic interests. Everywhere the snows of indifference melted under the rays of the imperial sun, to reveal the familiar pattern of Guelf and Ghibelline alliances.

Henry entered Lombardy in 1310, and the same year Orvieto joined a Guelf league sponsored by Perugia and including Lucca, Siena, Spoleto and Gubbio.[3] She also strengthened her links with Florence, supplying that town with Captains of the Popolo in the spring and in the winter of 1310, and sending some troops to help in the latest campaign against Arezzo.[4] This close alliance between Florence and Orvieto was the fruit of a very long tradition of collaboration, dating back over eighty years. Together the two communes had stood up to Siena in the great wars of 1229-35 and 1251-4 and together they had upheld the Guelf cause in the dark years between Montaperti and Benevento. Orvieto was much the weaker partner, but her strategic situation was of enormous value, both as the key to the best road to Rome and as a base for a 'second front' against Siena. In additon she frequently provided military aid, even when her own interests were not directly at stake. There was also a continual interchange of communal officials; Florence had on one occasion even entrusted to an Orvietan Potestà, Capitano, and garrison the whole internal security of the

---

[1] ACO, Rif. 1307, fos. 29 and 57v-58v; and Statuti, no. 1a (matr. 26). The Popolo's claim to special rights in this area was based on its organization of the campaign in 1303.
[2] Rif. and Statutes cited above, and Rif. 1309, fos. 55-61 and 70-1.
[3] *Ephemerides*, p. 348n.
[4] Chr. Pot. 4 (*Ephemerides*, p. 177); Degli Azzi, II, docs. 159-61 and 164.

city, while in return Orvieto received as officers members of such celebrated families as the Donati, Cerchi, Frescobaldi, Rossi, Della Tosa, and Tornaquinci.[1] Commercially too the towns were closely interlinked, for several Florentine banking houses maintained branches in Orvieto. These appear to have enjoyed something of a monopoly, and at times the commune was heavily in their debt.[2] There was certainly an element of economic dependence in Orvieto's relationship with Florence, but the distinction between links and chains is rarely a very clear one and the community of interests between the two towns was the vital factor.

The Captains of the Popolo supplied to Florence in 1310 were both Monaldeschi, and this is one of several signs that fear of the Emperor and the consequent Guelf trend of Orvieto's policy were bringing about a pronounced return of that family's supremacy.[3] A letter written in 1312 to the commander of the Florentine garrison at Orvieto bears witness to the special position of the Monaldeschi as the Guelf family *par excellence* and probably the only Orvietan family known by name in Florence.[4] He is instructed to maintain close liaison with them and to rely upon them for news and advice should he find himself cut off from Florence. An understanding between Guelf nobles and Popolo was also springing up in the face of the imperialist menace, to judge from the number of Monaldeschi granted permission to carry arms, while others were temporarily declared popolani.[5]

It was now essential to strengthen the commune and its hold over the contado. Clearly the Aldobrandeschine lands were the

[1] See above, pp. 28, 41-3, etc. For Florentine officials at Orvieto, *v. Ephemerides*, pp. 170, 172, 175; *C.D.*, p. 337; Degli Azzi, II, docs. 160-1, etc. In all, Florence provided Orvieto with eight Potestà between 1228 and 1250 and with four Potestà and five Capitani between then and 1310.

[2] Among these houses which had branches in Orvieto in the thirteenth century were the Spiliati and Spini; the first reference to the former is in 1259 (AVO, Cod. C, fo. 139), the first to the latter in 1283 (L. Gauthier, *Les Lombards dans les Deux Bourgognes*, Paris, 1907, p. 116). By the early fourteenth century the Mozzi (ACO, Rif. 1301, fos. 51-2) and the Bardi (ASRSP, XLVI, p. 376) also had branches there. In 1301 the commune was heavily in debt to the Mozzi and Spini (Rif., *loc. cit.*) and there were loans from Florentines again in 1303 and 1305 (*C.D.*, notes to DCI).

[3] The outstanding figures in the Balie and diplomatic activities of 1310-3 are Ugolino, Buonconte (his son), and Manno Monaldeschi.

[4] See below, p. 89, for this correspondence.

[5] ACO, Rif. 1312, fos. 221, 229, 257v, 266, 271v; 1313, fos. 18v and 25, etc.

most threatened part of Orvieto's territory; the commune's title to them was far from clear and her administrative grip had never been very great, while the Emperor was the obvious source of support for any challenger and the area was of interest to him, since it lay on the route from Pisa to Rome that he would take when he went south for his coronation. The futile attempt to keep the Countess Margherita at Orvieto has been mentioned above.[1] It was also decided to strengthen the defences and administration of the Aldobrandeschine contado. In December 1310 a (non-Orvietan) official was appointed to govern the area and a garrison was despatched there, and a series of tours of inspection was made in the following year, which revealed the complete inadequacy of the defences; each of the towns had a keep, but they were in such a ruinous condition that it was not worth manning them. Meanwhile the inhabitants repeatedly called on Orvieto for more military aid, even informing one committee of enquiry that if the commune could find no remedy for their plight they would bear it no longer, but would submit their town to the Devil![2]

The long-threatened pressure from the Emperor began to materialize in the spring of 1312 when Henry moved to Pisa and set out from there for Rome, taking the coastal route. Supported by such powerful feudal neighbours of Orvieto as the Prefetti di Vico, the Counts of Anguillara, S. Fiora and Marsciano, and the lords of Bisenzio, the imperial forces passed through the Aldobrandeschine contado, but did not delay there. Meanwhile a state of emergency prevailed in Orvieto. A series of regulations passed in May provided that party banners were not be to made, that the Potestà, Captain and Seven were to conduct a search for illicit arms, non-Orvietans were not to possess arms unless they lived in Orvietan households, and among the disorders now punishable was the crying of 'Muoiano i Guelfi!' or 'Muoiano i Ghibellini!'[3]

---

[1] See p. 76.

[2] ACO, Rif. 1310, fos. 81v-83; 1311, fos. 106v, 154, 169-176v; 1312, fos. 206-8v and 212-5 ('nisi subito aliud salutare remedium apponatur per commune urbevetanum, cum amplius sustinere non possunt, darent se diabolo').

[3] Chr. Ant. (*Ephemerides*, pp. 135-6, and n.); Cont. Orv. Polono, p. 129. For various emergency measures, ACO, Rif. 1312, fos. 206 and 210-7.

By August 1312 Orvieto housed a very considerable Florentine garrison, with detachments from Siena, Lucca and Prato. A number of letters containing orders to the commanders of this force has survived and they clearly illustrate Orvieto's strategical importance.[1] The purpose of the garrison was to block the main road from Rome to Tuscany and to provide a base on which the forward army operating near Rome could fall back. If the Emperor appeared to be outflanking Orvieto it would be easy to withdraw the garrison northwards, and this was done at the end of August when Henry's army, which had followed the Tiber valley and thus left Orvieto's possessions untouched, reached Todi. Many a friendship has failed to survive the impact of an allied garrison (Orvieto's troubles with the Angevin troops of the 1280s are an example), but in 1312 the town's relations with its Florentine defenders appear to have been excellent.[2]

Only when he had passed into Tuscany did the Emperor raise with Orvieto the delicate question of the commune's possessions in the Val di Chiana which were held of the Empire. From Arezzo, at the end of August, he sent Cetona a demand for military assistance, at the same time informing Orvieto of this action. The insolence of Orvieto's reply can only be explained by the certainty that Henry was now bound for the north; they hoped, they said, to give an answer within two months concerning the lands they were alleged to hold of the Emperor. Meanwhile Cetona was advised to plead her weakness and the hostility of her neighbours and to say that Orvieto was conducting an enquiry into imperial rights in this area, which she had held 'ab antiquo tempore cuius non est memoria'. In mid-September this enquiry (by twelve judges) had begun and an embassy informed the Emperor that the commune was giving all its attention to the matter and that, should the Divine Grace so permit, their reply would be one pleasing to him.[3] The defiant tone adopted throughout this

[1] Degli Azzi, I, docs. 15-17 and 19-28.
[2] The only sign of trouble is the arrest of two Florentine soldiers, but orders were given for their immediate release (Rif. 1312, fo. 239v). The imperialist forces sacked Marsciano, which lay just within the Perugian contado, but only fifteen miles from Orvieto (Chr. Pot. 4, p. 178), and one detachment may even have lodged at Fabro, the Filippeschi stronghold a dozen miles from the town (Graziani's Chr., ASI, XVI, I, p. 81).
[3] ACO, Rif. 1312, fos. 220v and 250v-253.

transaction is an indication of Orvieto's very firm adherence to the cause of Florence and the Guelfs.

The imperial menace had twice passed close to the town in 1312, but each time it had moved on, leaving the Guelfs in undisturbed command. For 1313 Orvieto's Ghibellines had more precise hopes and with the approval of an imperial dignitary they made plans for a rising to coincide with the departure for Rome and Naples of Henry's army, which throughout the spring and early summer was gathering reinforcements in Tuscany.[1] Meanwhile Orvieto's position had been made yet more difficult by the Orsini invasion of the Aldobrandeschine contado, necessitating the belated recognition of Benedict Caetani and a military campaign which petered out owing to desertions and dissatisfaction among the commune's underpaid troops.[2] Within the town there reigned 'turbatio magna' and a series of emergency measures was passed in June and July; justice was to be administered summarily, without the intervention of executive officials, and the list of those permitted to carry arms was curtailed and closed.[3]

The storm burst soon after the Emperor set out for the south. The Guelfs, who had come to know of the understanding between the Ghibellines and the imperial official, suggested a compromise, the nature of which reveals how weak they felt their situation to be: if the Ghibellines would promise not to admit Henry's troops, they might take over all the principal offices of the commune. The Ghibellines confidently rejected this offer and on August 16th, having news that the Emperor's army had set out from Siena, they rose in revolt.[4]

[1] The fullest account of the events of 1313 is in the chronicle cited by Monaldeschi (*Ephemerides*, pp. 186-9); it has a very strong pro-Guelf bias. There are also long accounts in Chr. Pot. 4 (p. 178) and Cont. Orv. Polono (pp. 131-2). Other sources are Manente (pp. 350-2), Graziani (p. 83), G. Villani (lib. IX, cap. 40) and a Sienese chronicle (RIS, N.S., xv, 6, pp. 245 and 334).

[2] Manente, p. 350, and ACO, Rif. 1313, fos. 7-19. For the events concerning the Aldobrandeschine contado, see pp. 76-7.   [3] Rif. 1313 (July —), fos. 1-6.

[4] The events of 1284, when the Guelfs had profited by the proximity of their ally Montfort but had done everything to discourage him from entering the town, may have suggested the feasibility of the compromise proposed by the Guelfs. It is doubtful whether Henry would have done more than detach a small body of troops to aid the Orvietan Ghibellines, for the town lies some miles from the main Siena-Rome road (which passes through Acquapendente).

The Guelfs regarded the arrival of the Emperor's troops as imminent and saw little hope, yet they decided to send their women and children out of the town and to make a desperate defence. For three days the fortunes of battle fluctuated. Both sides received reinforcements, and the Ghibellines expelled the Capitano from his palace, while the Guelfs captured the palace of the Potestà. On the morning of Sunday the 19th, however, the Guelfs succeeded in driving the Ghibellines back as far as one of the gates of the city. Just at this critical time arrived a large force of Ghibellines drawn from all the pro-imperial towns of the neighbourhood, under the command of the Tudertine Bindo da Baschi. They at once counter-attacked, entering the town by the gate through which their party had been fleeing, and their number struck despair into the hearts of the Guelfs who just before had seemed on the verge of victory.[1]

While the Guelfs prepared to evacuate the town at nightfall, the bishop and clergy, accompanied by the Captain of the Patrimony (who had come on a mission of pacification), implored the Ghibellines to spare their conquered opponents. The reply was that the Guelfs were to drink their cup to the last drop; no terms would be granted them. The Guelfs did not leave that night, and the next day, August 20th, the Ghibellines set about driving them from the town. At once they were thrown back, and many of them fled, 'plorantes et clamantes', by the Porta S. Maria and the Porta Pertusa.

Yet once again the pendulum swung back just when all seemed lost. As the Guelfs abandoned the town, crying in vain for aid, they heard a voice from the heavens (says the chronicler), bidding them to return, for aid was arrived from Perugia. This piece of celestial intelligence proving to be well-founded, the Ghibellines were at once counter-attacked with the aid of some two hundred Perugian cavalrymen.[2] After driving the Ghibellines back as far as the fountain of S. Stefano, the Guelfs achieved an important success, for the Tudertine leader Bindo was unhorsed and killed

---

[1] One chronicler says they had 500 cavalry, another 800 cavalry and 2,200 foot.
[2] Graziani says 200, Cont. Orv. Polono puts them at only 150, Monaldeschi's chronicle at 1,200 horse and as many foot.

by infantrymen; the Guelfs cut off his hands and then, 'benignitate motos', removed him to S. Francesco for burial. A Florentine Ghibelline, Bernardo degli Acerbi, succeeded Bindo in command, but before long he too was killed, in the Piazza San Domenico. The day was becoming a rout and the Ghibellines 'fled like eaglets and on St. Bernard's Day in August lost both their Bernard and their nests'.[1] A new leader, a Tudertine, was also killed, and at dusk the Ghibellines began to retreat from the town. The five days' battle was over.

The higher issue was about to be settled in an even more decisive fashion. Had the Ghibellines won, it would have been a hollow victory, for some forty miles to the north the Emperor fell sick, and on August 24th he died, and with him Ghibelline hopes throughout Italy. But Orvieto's Guelfs had not fought in vain. Their enemies had been shattered irreparably and, as a chronicler says, 'this battle was the ruin of the Filippeschi, for from henceforth they were defeated and dispersed; they never had any strength afterwards'.[2] The victory had been so complete and so spectacular that it stood out in an epoch accustomed to such events; Giovanni Villani gives it a whole chapter and it was in Dante's mind when he used Monaldeschi and Filippeschi as the great example of factional hatred.[3]

---

[1] Cont. Orv. Polono, pp. 131-2. Among those killed in this stage of the fighting was the imperial functionary who had undertaken the negotiations between the Orvietan Ghibellines and the Emperor. The eagle was of course the emblem of the Empire.

[2] L. Manente (*Ephemerides*, p. 352: '. . . questa battaglia fu la rovina de Philipensi, che andaro sottomessi et spersi, che non hebbero mai più forza alcuna'). One chronicler puts the total killed on both sides at 4,000, but this is almost certainly an exaggeration. Several hundred houses were burnt.

[3] *Purgatorio*, VI, 106-8. The *Purgatorio* was probably written between 1314 and 1319.

CHAPTER XII

THE RULE OF THE FIVE (1313-15)

THE victorious Guelfs proceeded to consolidate their position through a radical alteration of the constitution. By August 30th, just over a week after the defeat of the Ghibellines, two emergency offices, of 'Rettore e Difensore della Terra', and 'Capitano della Città', had been specially created, and two lords of the contado appointed to them; these posts were intended as a temporary expedient and by January of the following year had been abolished.[1] A more fundamental change was the substitution of the Seven by Five 'sapientibus ad defensionem communis praepositis'. The new institution of the Five is the most important phenomenon of the period that follows the Guelf victory of 1313, and it must be considered at some length.

The Five was in origin a committee dedicated to the consolidation and exploitation of the Guelf victory, as its composition clearly shows. The original Five were all nobles of leading Guelf families; two, or perhaps three, of them were Monaldeschi, one a Montemarte, one a Medici.[2] The personnel of the Five altered each month, and its composition is known for 14 of the 28 months of its existence. In twelve of these months there was at least one Monaldeschi among its members, and twice there were two. Moreover an investigation of the personnel of Balie during the same period reveals that four Monaldeschi were each members of more Balie and embassies than any other citizen. All the other leading Guelf families were represented on the Five, the Montemarte twice, and the Ardiccioni twice. Its composition was not, however, entirely noble, in fact popolani slightly predominated after the

---

[1] Chr. Pot. 4 (*Ephemerides*, p. 179). Unfortunately almost all the Council minutes for the latter part of 1313 have been lost, but those of 29 and 30 August have survived by the chance of their transcription in a chronicle cited by Monaldo Monaldeschi in his *Commentari* (p. 75: reprinted in Pardi, *Signori* 5, p. 13).

[2] Monaldeschi's *Commentari*, *loc. cit.*

first period; the popular members of the Five consisted in the main of those who played a prominent part in the Popolo both before and after this interlude.[1] Each Five nominated a Balia of eight, who in turn elected the next Five, so there could be little fear of any very fundamental alteration in the interests represented by the Five.[2]

The *raison-d'être* of the Five was in the repression of the defeated Ghibellines, and this remained the fundamental part of its policy. Its first recorded action is the election of a Balia of 16 to advise on the treatment of Ghibellines and their property; when the Five met with this addition on the following day it was decided unanimously, on the motion of Manno Monaldeschi (one of the 16), that all Filippeschi should be declared rebels and outlaws; their homes were to be destroyed, and their property confiscated to the commune.[3] In the next three months a list of Ghibelline outlaws was drawn up and several times revised, while a census was compiled of their property. Only a fragment of the census has survived, but this provides a vivid illustration of the absorption by the great Guelf families of the land of their conquered adversaries. It concerns the area of Salci and Fabro, where the Filippeschi and Miscinelli (another leading Ghibelline family) had held large properties adjoining those of Buonconte di Ugolino Monaldeschi and Count Pietro di Montemarte; by the time of the census these two had bought up most of this Ghibelline land. A scandalous scramble over the property of their victims seems to have ensued after the Guelfs' victory, and it is not till March 1314 that there are signs of a concern for legality and the economic well-being

---

[1] Pietro Fallastate, one of the Five in April 1315, had been one of the Seven in 1308 (ACO, Rif. 1308, fo. 218 and Pardi, *Signori* 5, p. 24), while other leading popolani who played an important part in the politics of this period were Ciuccio di Zacharia (Cardinal Theoderic's nephew), Nallo della Terza—both these held office as members of the Five— Lippo degli Alberici, and the inevitable Neri di Guidetto. Pardi's otherwise useful study of the five gives the misleading impression that there was little continuity in the personnel of the government before and after August 1313.

[2] ACO, Rif. 1315, fo. 54. The formula employed when the five entered office in September 1314 (Rif. 1314, fo. 5) and November 1315 (Pardi, *Signori* 5, p. 24) seems to imply they they were chosen by lot ('Infrascripti sunt illi 5 qui debent esse pro presenti mense septembris ad offitium dominorum 5 communis civitatis Urbisveteris quorum nomina scripta reperta sunt in una cartuccia reperta in una ex palluttis in pisside existentibus que stat apud ecclesiam sancti Iohannis . . . ', etc.): but this is probably a case of a constitutional form surviving the abolition of its substance. [3] Monaldeschi, *loc. cit.*

94

of the commune; then Manno Monaldeschi successfully proposed that all concessions of Ghibelline property should be subject to reconsideration, and that the 'rebels' dwellings in the contado should be destroyed. But the re-allotment of the property by the commune does not appear to have been entirely satisfactory, for in the following years there are frequent references to the impossibility of securing the cultivation of all the confiscated Ghibelline land.[1]

In the spring of 1315 the Guelfs tempered the severity of their anti-Ghibelline measures by introducing a division of Ghibellines into three different categories, according to their danger as potential opponents. Some were now re-admitted, but at times of crisis one, two, or all of the categories could be sent into temporary exile, according to the seriousness of the situation; or all could be sent into simultaneous exile of varying degrees of severity.[2] Meanwhile legislation of a sort characteristic of the Italian communes regulated the status of the returned Ghibellines; they were admitted to a kind of restricted citizenship, subject to peculiar penalties and disabilities. Thus they were liable to double the normal punishment if they injured or killed Guelfs (and in the latter event a special measure secured to the relatives of the victim half of the property of the murderer); they had to provide horses for the commune's campaigns, but were not to take part in the fighting themselves, or if they did, they were not paid; and Guelfs were to have preference even in medical treatment.[3] The office of the four Captains of the Parte Guelfa, which was created in May 1315,[4] both symbolized and maintained the tyranny of Guelf over Ghibelline.

[1] For example in October 1314 and February 1315 (Rif. cited in Pardi, *Signori* 5, pp. 16-7). For Manno's proposal, ACO, Rif. XIII (Rosso), fos. 10-11 (also for references to legislation of the previous October and November). The census is ACO, 'Bono Communis Urbisveteris olim Rebellium'. Count Pietro di Montemarte was himself the father-in-law of one of the wealthiest rebels, Petruccio di Simone di Ranieri (Rif. 1321, fos. 141v-142).

[2] Pardi, *Signori* 5, p. 19. The first category was exiled in July 1315 (*Ephemerides*, p. 355n.), the other two joining them in August: in October all three were re-admitted (Pardi, pp. 19-20). Another time the three categories were ordered to withdraw to a distance of over eight, four, and two miles, respectively, from the town (*C.D.*, p. 800n.). Ghibellines banished in this manner were compelled to 'check out' at the gates as they left.

[3] Ciacci, I, 352n. ; Pardi, p. 20; *Ephemerides*, p. 355n.   [4] ACO, Rif. 1315, fos. 6-7.

The foreign policy of the Five was naturally one of friendship with those who had brought about victory in August 1313, and with Florence and the Angevins, the two great sources of Guelf power in Central Italy. In October 1313 a solemn perpetual alliance was signed with Perugia.[1] In November 1314 Orvieto was represented at the general Guelf Parliament held at Florence, and between then and the following July she several times sent military assistance to the Florentine and Angevin forces engaged in a war with Pisa. Once Siena warned her of a proposed Pisan campaign against Orvieto, but this never eventuated. Orvieto was also prominent in the Umbrian Guelf League, formed by Perugia in the autumn of 1315 to take on three hundred mercenaries in the interests of mutual defence; this alliance was linked with the Guelfs of Tuscany, for King Robert financed it and gave it his blessing.[2]

The policy of the Five during the first two years of their rule was so successful that there seemed no reason why what had begun as a quasi-revolutionary committee should not continue as a permanent organ of government. Yet the train of events which was to bring about their fall can be traced back to 1314. It is curious, though very far from unique in the annals of Guelf history, that the 'little rift within the lute' took the form of a dispute with ecclesiastical authority. A quarrel between Bisenzio and Grotte caused Orvieto to fall foul of the authorities of the Patrimony.[3] After a campaign in 1314 Bisenzio claimed from Grotte compensation for some damage done to her crops and to the indignation of Orvieto the claim against her subject was backed by the Vicar of the Patrimony. To a letter from the Vicar (which is no longer extant) Orvieto retorted that the commune had advisers of its own and needed no instructions from him, with more in the same vein.[4] The following May Orvieto refused to

---

[1] *C.D.*, DCXII.   [2] *C.D.*, DCXIX and DCXXI; Pardi, pp. 21-2.

[3] In 1313 relations had been friendly, for Orvieto contributed to the Patrimonial army troops to fight the rebellion of Viterbo and Corneto (Antonelli, 'Dominazione Pontificia', XXV, p. 361).

[4] 'Quod domini 5 habeant illos sapientes iuris quos habere voluerint qui sapientes deliberent quomodo et qualiter et qua forma creari debeat syndicus . . . et utrum fieri debeat nec ne . . . ' (ACO, Rif. 1314, fos. 19v-27v). For payment of the troops who fought in the campaign against Bisenzio, Rif. cited in *Ephemerides*, p. 355n.

pay the Vicar taxes, in June Acquapendente appealed for protection against his 'molestia et questiones' concerning criminal jurisdiction and the election of the Potestà, and in July Grotte and S. Lorenzo again sought support against Bisenzio and the Vicar. The crux of the dispute, as is clear from a document of 1317, was the still undecided problem of the Patrimony's rights in the Val del Lago, and particularly of its powers of taxation.[1]

Many towns and nobles had fallen out with the Vicar and when the rebellion came, in November, it was on a formidable scale. This Vicar, Bernard de Coucy, was a great intriguer and, it would seem, something of a Ghibelline by force of circumstances if not by sympathies. In October he demanded troops of Grotte, Acquapendente and Proceno for a Ghibelline campaign against the lords of Farnese, and this finally decided Orvieto to join a number of towns and nobles of the Patrimony in open rebellion.[2]

The signal for the revolt was given when the Guelfs of Montefiascone rose against Bernard's Ghibelline supporters; Orvieto had news of this on 25 November 1315 and decided at once to send support to the Guelfs. With the aid of the troops from Orvieto and the Vicar's many other enemies, the whole town was carried, Bernard remaining surrounded in the citadel. On the 29th, however, strong Ghibelline forces arrived headed by the Prefetto di Vico and the Viterbese; the Orvietans, under the rash leadership of Manno Monaldeschi, at first sallied forth against the newcomers, but finding themselves outnumbered in cavalry by five hundred to fifty, they fled back into the town. Here they were caught up in a general flight of the Guelfs, who lost over a hundred killed and two hundred prisoners in a disorderly and disastrous withdrawal.

The fiasco of this rebellion was the immediate cause of the fall of the Five, for the grave crisis in the commune's affairs suggested the need for a new and broader government, while not only had the Five forfeited the confidence of the commune, but their

---

[1] ACO, Rif. 1315, fos. 13v-14v, 17-8, 32 and (July) 9-10v; C.D., DCXX.

[2] Rif. 1315, fos. 37-44v. The best sources for the rebellion are the text of the condemnation of the rebels by the Vicar in December 1315 (given in full in Antonelli, 'Una Ribellione'), Cont. Orv. Polono *ad* 1315, pp. 132-3, and Chr. Pot. 4 (*ad* 1316, in error) in *Ephemerides*, p. 180. Toscanella, Montalto, and Poncello Orsini were other ringleaders in the revolt.

removal would presumably help to placate the wrath of Bernard de Coucy. On December 3rd a Balìa was appointed to advise such emergency measures as it might consider necessary, and on the 14th a special meeting of the Council of the Five, the Twenty-four, the Forty 'sapientes', and the Consuls of the Arti discussed the situation and in particular the proposition 'quod populus guelfus fiat et sit' in Orvieto, and the form that such a Popolo should take.[1] This virtual suicide is probably explained by the chronicler's remark that on the previous day cries of 'Viva il Popolo!' were heard in the streets, and there was an atmosphere of discontent, at which the Monaldeschi (here used to personify the supporters of the Five) 'ceperunt timere'. In the Council meeting it was decided, on the motion of a Monaldeschi, that the Guelf Popolo, with the Seven as its administrative organ, was to supersede the Five; Ranieri di Zacharia was to be Capitano del Popolo till the following April and Poncello Orsini Capitano di Guerra for nine months. Further decisions provided that the Five then in office were to share power with the Seven until the end of the month (this was probably a face-saving measure), while the external alliance and the anti-Ghibelline legislation of the Five were to be treated as sacrosanct. The same day the Consuls of the Arti elected the new Seven.

---

[1] For this Council meeting, Pardi, pp. 25 and 30-1; it is also mentioned in Chr. Pot. 4 (*Ephemerides*, pp. 179-80), which misleadingly describes it partly under 1315 and partly (but clearly in error) under 1316.

CHAPTER XIII

THE POPOLO OF PONCELLO ORSINI (1315-22)

NAPOLEONE, or 'Poncello', Orsini is the most important figure during the next six or seven years of the commune's history. He was a member of the famous Roman family which produced Pope Nicholas III and many cardinals, among them the Cardinal Napoleone Orsini whose acquaintance we have already made. He is first heard of in connection with Orvieto in 1313, when he aided the Countess Margherita and others of her Orsini relatives-in-law in their invasion of the Aldobrandeschine contado.[1] In 1315 he played a double part in the rebellion against the Patrimony, as the commander of the forces sent by Montalto and as a rebel in his own right. The Vicar's deed of condemnation and Polono's Orvietan continuator agree that Poncello was one of the leaders of the revolt, and his selection as Capitano di Guerra was clearly due to the assumption that he shared to the full Orvieto's appetite for revenge against Viterbo, the principal author of the Guelfs' defeat.

Orsini's tenure of this office was eventually prolonged so that he held it for fifteen months, until March 1317, and in the meantime changes in nomenclature gave recognition to the widening scope of his powers; in April 1316 he was 'Capitano di Guerra del Comune e del Popolo', while in October of the same year he is referred to simply as 'Capitano del Comune e del Popolo'.[2] He did not, however, remain continually at Orvieto to exercise these powers in person, for his son Pietro acted as his vicar during some of the latter part of 1316.[3]

This period of Orsini's captaincy roughly coincides with the duration of the crisis that followed the revolt of November 1315. During it the commune's most important activities were the

---

[1] See p. 76.   [2] ACO, Rif. 1316, fo. 25; C.D., p. 439.
[3] ACO, Rif. 1316, fo. 71. etc.

prosecution of a war of revenge against Viterbo and negotiations aimed at securing a pardon for Orvieto's share in the rebellion. The Vicar's condemnation of the rebels is dated 14 December 1315, and they were not pardoned until 21 June 1317.[1] An appeal against the heavy fine imposed was made to the Curia in May 1316[2] (two ambassadors of the commune were despatched to Avignon), but it had no success; the vacancy of the papal throne no doubt made such business more difficult than usual to conclude. This reduced Orvieto to treating with the much-hated Vicar, and the negotiations which terminated in the general absolution of June 1317 had been in progress since February of that year. Orsini was nominated as one of the commune's representatives and helped to bring about the agreement whereby Orvieto obtained a complete pardon on payment of 4,000 florins.[3]

The war against Viterbo was Orsini's main business, however, and in this he played a much more important part, commanding the Orvietan army in the orgy of mutual destruction and plundering that lasted through the spring and summer of 1316.[4] The year began with an attack by all the Ghibellines of the Patrimony, including the Prefetto di Vico, Guittuccio Signore of Bisenzio, Orvieto's exiles, the troops of the Vicar himself, and many others on the contado of Orvieto. Acquapendente was captured and looted, and the army returned through Sugano, leaving behind it a trail of destruction; a small party even raided Petroio, an outlying suburb below the rock of Orvieto, but the town itself was not attacked. Next Orvieto's army sallied forth, under Poncello, and after a short siege achieved the capture of Bisenzio; Guittuccio's wife and child yielded the castle and fled, leaving behind his two children by a former marriage, who were taken to Orvieto as captives. The same army then embarked on a highly successful raid into Viterbese territory which resulted in the capture of ten thousand head of cattle. Viterbo availed itself of the

---

[1] C.D., DCXX (where the year is given wrongly as '1315'). [2] C.D., DCXXII.
[3] ACO, Rif. 1317, fos. 37, 43v-45v; fos. 19-20v (March-April), 91; fos. 10, 40, 53v-54v (May-June).
[4] For this campaign, Chr. Pot. 4 (Ephemerides, pp. 180-1: the events of 1316 are related under 1317, as those of 1315 were under 1316); Cont. Orv. Polono, p. 133; ACO, Rif. 1316, fo. 72 (April) and fos. 6, 18, 20, 36, 40 (May-June); C.D., DCXXIII (the truce) and DCXXVI (the treaty).

absence of Orvieto's army to conduct reprisals in the Tiber valley, where several Orvietan outposts were looted and destroyed; Orvieto's reply to this was to intensify her operations against the undefended villages of Viterbo's contado; Sipicciano was burnt, and three other villages the next day, 'et multa alia loca destruxerunt et ceperunt predam maximam'. Such campaigns can have had few dangers for those who were fortunate enough to be combatants, and early in June Orsini was writing indignantly to Orvieto about a rumour that negotiations were being conducted with a view to concluding a truce. He wrote frequently to demand fuller powers, and the suggestion that Orvieto might make peace without his consent was one that incensed him greatly. But the rumour was denied, and in June he was able to attack Celleno, ravaging all the surrounding area; a raid to the very walls of Viterbo did lead to one Orvietan casualty (the chronicler evidently notes this as a rarity), but the horse-races held nearby in defiance failed to achieve their object of drawing out Viterbo's army. So the Orvietans returned disconsolately, stopping only to destroy one more town on the way, and in September a truce was at last arranged, presumably with Orsini's consent. Till then it must have seemed that this absurd and ghastly game might continue indefinitely. Soon afterwards peace was concluded, Viterbo agreeing to urge the Vicar of the Patrimony to reach an agreement with the erstwhile rebels. The independence of Orsini's position is indicated by his inclusion in the peace-terms as a separate party.

Meanwhile yet another bloodthirsty episode had marked this merciless war. The men of Bolsena had built and launched a ship to protect their fishermen on the Lake from the assaults of Guittuccio of Bisenzio and the inhabitants of the islands subject to him. When the news reached Orvieto that the islanders had captured this vessel, a furious mob attacked the Palazzo del Comune, where Guittuccio's two small sons were held in captivity, and the children were dragged outside and torn to pieces.

By the end of this campaign Orsini's influence was not restricted to the external affairs of the commune, and the legislation of 1316 designed to strengthen the position of the Popolo bears witness to his influence, and shows how he acquired the reputation which led to his recall in 1321.[1] The first of these measures date from April 1316,[2] and emanated from two successive meetings of the Council of the Popolo presided over by Orsini himself. They are described as 'stantiamenta et decreta facta ad corraborationem et fortificationem Populi et officii dominorum Capitanei et Septem', made necessary because 'Populus et Artes sint reformate . . . sed Carta Populi . . . sit . . . defectiva'. The provisions were the conventional ones designed to improve the Popolo's constitutional position and to raise its prestige. Clauses with the former aim included ones threatening punishment for any conspiracies against the Popolo and the Capitano, and trebling the normal punishment for offences against the Seven, while some anti-Ghibelline legislation was renewed. The organization of the Popolo was strengthened in a number of ways. A new list of its members was to be made, and all of them had to be Guelfs; the Gonfaloniere della Giustizia was to have a banner bearing the arms of the Popolo together with a lily, a trellis, and a crowned lion carrying the keys and a sword; each Arte and each of the four Quartieri (districts of the town) was also to have its own banner and standard-bearer; at the sound of the bell of the Palazzo del Popolo all popolani were to assemble in arms; and they were to be reinforced by a thousand armed popolani from the country districts (the 'pivieri') of the contado. Such was Orsini's first reform of the Popolo, a thorough and business-like effort with a typical emphasis on pageantry. In November 1316 it was supplemented by a measure increasing the punishment for all nobles committing offences against popolani (other than Ghibellines).[3]

Orsini's work on behalf of the Popolo outlasted his departure, yet there are some signs of a weakening in its position between 1318 and his second captaincy in 1321. In April and May 1317, soon after he had left office, legislation was passed to quadruple the punishment of all nobles offending popolani, to forbid the judicial torture of popolani, and to provide that each of the twenty-one 'rioni' into which Orvieto was divided was to have

[1] For his title of 'Capitano del Comune e del Popolo' in the autumn of 1316, see p. 99.
[2] ACO, Rif. 1316, fos. 55v-61v. [3] ACO, Rif. 1316, fos. 18-20.

its own banner.[1] In 1318 the offices of the Gonfalonieri were confirmed, and the right of the Popolo asserted to govern the parts of the Aldobrandeschine contado that were reconquered from the rebellious lords of Baschi.[2]

The following year a more radical measure was passed, but while transforming the Popolo it also to some extent weakened it. The amalgamation of several Arti was ordered so that they now numbered sixteen instead of twenty-five, while the Seven were no longer to be chosen entirely from the Consuls of the Arti but four were to be taken thus and three from the seventy councillors of the Popolo.[3] Finally the powers of the Captains of the Parte Guelfa were greatly increased. This office was in being at least as early as 1315;[4] of its four members two were nobles, and two 'Capitanei populares partis Guelfe' (these also were chosen from the seventy councillors, by a vote of the whole Council of the Popolo). The Guelf Capitani were now given the power to veto any acts of the Seven for the remainder of the year (the measures date from September 22nd); they were to assist the Seven in correcting the Carta del Popolo and at the end of the same period they and a special Balia of forty chosen by the Seven were to reconsider all anti-noble legislation. Finally a new Council was to be formed, consisting of thirty-two 'populares', sixteen 'magnates', and the Capitani di Parte Guelfa of the past and the present year.[5] Both the increased powers of the Capitani and the introduction of sixteen 'magnates' into what had previously been an exclusively popular assembly suggest infiltration into the Popolo's institutions by noble elements, and this tendency fits in with the temporary suspension of anti-noble measures. There can be little doubt that this legislation represents a victory, if a veiled one, for the nobility. Orsini was already being missed.

[1] Rif. 1317, fos. 88 and v (April), 6v and 14 (May).

[2] Rif. 1318, fos. 125-126v ('quod omnes terre Marittime que venirent ad manus communis quoadcumque custodiantur per populares urbevetanos'). The Popolo's claim was presumably based on its campaign of 1303 (see p. 86 and note).

[3] Rif. 1319, fos. 102v-108. The reform was short-lived in so far as it affected the composition of the Seven, for in 1321 (Rif. *ad an.*, fo. 1v) six of them were chosen from the Consuls and the other from the forty 'popolani'. The seventy (till then sixty) were elected members of the Council of the Popolo, the Consuls of the Arti being *ex-officio* members.

[4] See p. 95.   [5] For the composition of this and other Councils, *v*. App. I.

Despite the peace with Viterbo, the Vicar's absolution and the settlement of Bisenzio on Vanne di Galasso, Guittuccio's relative and enemy,[1] there was no period of repose for Orvieto. As early as 1317 there was a new outbreak of fighting with Viterbo, who had re-occupied S. Savino.[2] The year 1317, in fact, was a particularly stormy one, for Orvieto had to fight two other campaigns, both in the Marittima, where Siena and Orvieto were faced with the complete defiance of their powerful subjects. The most prominent of these were the Count of S. Fiora and the lords of Baschi (rulers of Montemarano and Vitozzo). Already in 1316 Orvieto had suffered from the depredations of the latter of these nobles, and had sent Siena some aid against the former; that autumn the two communes signed a treaty of mutual assistance against the rebels, and there was fighting throughout 1317 until Orvieto recaptured its principal objective, the town of S. Salvatore.[3] In 1318 both nobles swore oaths of submission to the commune, but they were without effect, for there was fighting against Ugolino of Baschi in 1318 and 1319, while in 1320 there was again trouble at S. Salvatore.[4] This year and the next there was a full-scale campaign against the Ghibellines of the Patrimony, who were now headed by Corneto, Toscanella and Orvieto's old enemy Guittuccio of Bisenzio.[5]

The commune's connection with the Guelf-Angevin system of alliances in Central Italy was continued. In 1317 King Robert was twice chosen as Potestà.[6] The letter informing him of his first election, after commending Orvieto to its 'domino et benefactori ...et...refugio', asks for aid against her Ghibelline neighbours, and in particular pleads with the King to use his influence at the Curia to secure the removal of that 'guerrarum et scandalorum seminator', Bernard de Coucy, Vicar of the Patrimony. How much Orvieto was felt to be part of this great Guelf network is demonstrated by a Bolognese request for help against Cane della Scala in 1318 (it

---

[1] C.D., DCXXVII. [2] Ephemerides, p. 362n.
[3] C.D., DCXXV and notes; ACO, Rif. 1316, fos. 27-9, 34v-37, 40-1 (Sept.-Oct.) and 15-16v, 59v (Nov.-Dec.); Rif. 1317, fos. 16v, 41v, 49-55 (May-June), 7-9, 14, 53v, 65v (July-Aug.), 11 (Sept.); Ephemerides, pp. 359n.-361n.
[4] Ephemerides, pp. 101 and 109, 182 (Chr. Pot. 4), 363n.-367n.; ACO. Lib. Cond. 1320, fos. 11-17.
[5] Cerlini, 'Carte Orvietane' in BRDSPU, XLI, pp. 11-33; Ephemerides, pp. 369-70n.; C.D., DCXXIX. [6] C.D., DCXXIV; Ephemerides, p. 359n.

could not be granted, but Orvieto wrote a lengthy letter of apology) and by the celebrations held in 1319 in honour of the Genoese victory of King Robert.[1] Meanwhile the town did its duty as a pillar of the Umbrian 'Parte Guelfa Ecclesiastica', sending aid to Perugia against Assisi and Spoleto in 1319 and the two following years.[2] In 1319 Bernard de Coucy was transferred and Guitto Farnese, Bishop of Orvieto, became Rector of the Patrimony, so the tension with the Montefiascone Curia was considerably relaxed, and requests from the papacy for aid against Ghibelline rebels became frequent and confident.[3]

The circumstances accompanying the re-election of Poncello Orsini to the captaincy of the Popolo in 1321 are unfortunately wrapped in mystery. The Council minutes are extant for this period, but they preserve a tantalising reticence which the chronicles do nothing to remedy. The known facts are as follows. On January 11th the Council of the Popolo discussed a list of four towns from which they were to select the Captain due to enter office on February 1st: San Gimignano headed the list, but it had already declined to offer a candidate.[4] The matter is not mentioned again until February 2nd, when the new Captain should already have been in office. Then the Seven summoned a 'generali Parlamento et arenga hominum et personarum civitatis Urbisveteris' in the Palazzo del Popolo and in it Poncello Orsini was proposed as 'Capitano Generale del Popolo e di Guerra'.[5] Now the Parliament of all the citizens, while still retaining a theoretical place in the constitution of the commune,[6] was an unwieldy and anachronistic assembly, of which this is the first recorded meeting since 1251. Moreover the Seven had just executed a rapid *volte-face*, for, shortly

---

[1] *C.D.*, DCXXVIII and notes; Fumi, *I Rapporti fra Genova e Orvieto nel sec. XIV*, Orvieto, 1892, cols. 6-9. This Cane della Scala was the famous Can Grande, the patron of Dante.

[2] *Ephemerides*, pp. 368n.-369n.; ACO, Rif. 1319, fos. 23v-32, etc.; 1320, fo. 73v (March), 19-20 and 44-5, 53v-54, 61v-63, 105v-111, 117v (May-Sept.); 1321, fos. 53v, 105v, 147v.   [3] *C.D.*, DCXXXI-III and DCXXXV.

[4] ACO, Rif. 1321, fo. 199v.   [5] *Ibid.*, fos. 212-3.

[6] Its authority, for example, was required for the re-election of the Capitano del Popolo for two consecutive periods (Rif. 1316, fos. 54-6). For its existence in 1251, *v. C.D.*, CCLXXXV. It is noteworthy that in Florence the Parlamento of all the citizens was the conventional vehicle of the *coup d'état*; this easily handled and apparently democratic organ played the rôle in the fourteenth century that the plebiscite was to play in the nineteenth and (in many countries) the general election in the twentieth.

before, they and the Potestà had issued a special order forbidding
the holding of any meetings that day. If confirmation is needed
for the suggestion that part of the Popolo was employing exceptional methods to bring about what they knew to be a highly
controversial election, it is provided by the motion proposed in
the same meeting that the Arti should be 'libere prout erant
antequam discordia esset in civitate urbevetana' (this presumably
refers to the great 'discordia' of 1313) and that Poncello Orsini
and one representative of each Arte should correct the Carta del
Popolo; the order forbidding meetings that day was also to be
quashed. Both this motion and Orsini's election were approved,
'quasi omnibus sedentibus'. Clearly the choice of Poncello Orsini
as Captain was part of a policy designed to strengthen the position
of the Popolo, his previous spell of office having procured him a
reputation as the ideal leader of a strong Popolo against the nobility.
This fact of his re-election by a party with a definite programme
makes it particularly regrettable that none of the details are known
of the scheming which must have intervened between the discussion of January 11th and the election, for they would certainly
cast much light on the methods and personnel of the popular party
at this period. A useful scrap of information is the action of the
Seven (together with the Potestà) in prohibiting meetings on
February 2nd; they must have had wind of the projected Parliament
and its purpose, and at first sight it is curious to find the officers
of the Popolo as enemies of Orsini. But a strong Captain meant
less power for the Seven, and in any case membership of the Popolo
did not necessarily imply agreement with an anti-noble policy;
the history of the following years was largely to be conditioned
by divisions within the Popolo.

Orsini's popular reforms of 1316, together with his further
reforms of 1321-2 and his ejection by the nobles in 1322 attest
sufficiently the justice of his reputation. Three entries in the
chronicles make it clear that he had particularly strong enemies
among the Monaldeschi, those arch-nobles who 'non estimavano
nisciuna altra casa di nobiltà de Orvieto'.[1] Since he was contem-
poraneously occupying the position of Capitano di Guerra at

[1] L. Manente (*Ephemerides*, p. 375).

Perugia,[1] he had for several periods to be represented by a vicar;[2] the first of these was at the end of March 1321 and the chronicler remarks significantly that those who recalled him after it were the popolani and 'pars Monaldensium'. Luca Manente states that Poncello's special enemies among the Monaldeschi were Manno di Corrado and Napoleone and the other sons of Pietro Novello.[3] Nevertheless the letter from the commune to King Robert which has already been quoted[4] commends Poncello and Bertoldo Orsini for their great services to Orvieto and the 'Parti Guelfe ecclesiastice', which suggests that Poncello's championship of the Popolo was not incompatible with orthodox Guelf sentiments.

The influence of Orsini was soon evident in a new reform of the Popolo. In April and May measures provided for the internal discipline of the Arti and their defence against the nobility, while all nobles and the representatives of each 'piviere' of the contado were to swear to obey the orders of the Capitano and to preserve the Arti.[5] In November there came a spate of legislation on behalf of the Popolo. On the 8th Poncello was confirmed in office and it was decided 'quod fiat . . . reformatio et federatio coniuratio et sotietas firma et perpetua inter homines parvos mediocres et magnos populares civitatis'.[6] New orders on the 13th dealt with the organization of the armed Guelf popolani in regions, again doubled the punishment for nobles committing offences against popolani, prohibited the latter from associating with the former, and ordered the formation of a new Council of thirty-two popolani, whose consent—together with that of the full Council of the Popolo—was now needed before a noble could be a member of any Council: finally, Orsini was given full powers to dismiss any office-holder of whom he disapproved, substituting whomever he might prefer.[1] This last clause is a vivid illustration of the personal nature of Poncello Orsini's reforms; he seems to impart strength to an organism which tends to wither whenever deprived of his control. A week later new measures provided 'quod nobiles et barones comitatus hobediant domino Poncello' and 'quod non possit fieri aliqua inquisitio contra aliquem popularem' (only the headings are reported, hence their generality); also a mission was to go to Siena to enquire into the legislation on behalf of the Popolo of that city.[2] On the 23rd a Balia was chosen to correct the Carta del Popolo, but its authority specifically excluded any detraction from the powers of Poncello Orsini and the Seven.[3]

The end of January 1322 saw a new series of reforms.[4] There was to be a Gonfaloniere della Giustizia (this was a popular office, based on a Florentine model, which only came into being in time of emergency, its holder being a sort of native assistant to the Capitano, who had to be an outsider); all the Arti, quartieri, and rioni were to swear an oath of obedience to the Gonfaloniere, and he was to have the power to convene meetings of the Council of the Popolo. The powers of the Seven were also increased, to those they held before 1313; they were to have twenty-five armed servants; and all of them were now to be chosen as representatives of an Arte.[5] A list of noble families was drawn up, and new restrictions were placed on all members of these families; the Seven were empowered to add names to the list, but not to subtract them from it.[6] A number of miscellaneous measures on behalf of the Popolo included one which allotted to the Arti one of the three keys to each of the city gates. At the same time Poncello Orsini was sworn in as Captain for a further year.

In February a measure was passed, bold in intention though

---

[1] ACO, Rif. 1321, fos. 13-15.　　　　　　　　　　　[2] Ibid., fos. 23-4.
[3] Ibid., fos. 25v-27v.　　　　　　　　　　　　　　　[4] Rif. 1322, fos. 63-69.
[5] Ibid., fo. 1 (March). For previous changes in the method of choice of the Seven, see p. 103 and note. Evidently it was held to strengthen the popular nature of the office if each of its members was the direct representative of an Arte. It at least ensured that the poorer trades were represented frequently; when three of the Seven represented the Popolo generally they probably tended to be chosen from the wealthier Arti.
[6] The list was issued on February 8th and is extant in the Rif., fos. 76v-79v.

there is no evidence that it was effective, aiming at securing control
of the contado by the Popolo.[1] Four popolani, one of each
quartiere, were to be appointed Captains or Vicars 'totius comitatus
et districtus et baronium et districtualium civitatis Urbisveteris':
approximately a quarter of the contado was assigned to each, but
the division was a piecemeal one, for it was no doubt felt that
rule over a compact territory would be too great a temptation to
individual ambition. At the same time the Popolo put forward
a claim to appoint Potestà to all the towns of the contado, from
its own members.

Confronted with this rapid advance in the Popolo's pretensions
the Monaldeschi began to plot Orsini's downfall. The crisis came
in the second half of April, at a time when Orsini was absent.
On the 20th the Council of the Popolo met to consider the
emergency, and in particular the rumour that the Monaldeschi
(tactfully referred to as 'certi cives urbevetani') were planning to
bring about a *coup d'état* by the use of 'foreign' cavalry and infantry.[2]
It was decided that a pact and alliance should be made between
the Popolo and all the nobles except the Monaldeschi to preserve
the Popolo, the commune, and the Parte Guelfa.[3] The same day
some emergency measures were passed to discourage disturbances; one provided that 'Nulla persona debeat gridare vel
clamando dicere "Vivat" vel "Moriatur" aliqua spetialis persona'.
By the 23rd news of the troubles had reached Perugia, which
decided to send an embassy to reconcile the two parties.[4] Some
fighting between popolani was discussed in the Council meeting
of the 26th,[5] and on the 28th it was decided that the Seven due to

[1] *Ibid.*, fos. 79v-81.
[2] Rif. 1322, fos. 39-41 (April). They met 'cum nuper in civitate urbevetana sint multi
suspectus et varietates discordie et ipsa civitas propter defectum et culpam hominum
ipsius sit parata ad scandalum et turbationem' and 'cum dicatur quod certi cives urbevetani
requirant forenses equites et pedites ut veniant ad dictam civitatem pro turbatione boni
et pacifici status civitatis'.
[3] They were to swear 'unionem, sotietatem, coniurationem et confederationem
perpetuam ad statum et salutem populi urbevetani et communis et partis Guelfe civitatis
ipsius et dominorum 7': each rione was to take the oath through its representatives, and
the members of this alliance were to promise each other mutual military assistance. The
pact was to be renewed annually.
[4] *C.D.*, DCXXXVII. This embassy arrived and on May 4th was given powers similar to
those of an existing Balia of nine to bring about a peaceful settlement.
[5] For the events of the next three weeks, *v.* ACO, Rif. 1322, fos. 46v-59.

retire at the end of the month should remain in office for two further weeks in view of the gravity of the situation.

It is not possible to reconstruct exactly the events of the next few days, but it is almost certain that Monaldeschi threats persuaded the Popolo to perform the manoeuvre of dropping the pilot, in exchange for guarantees that there were to be no recriminations. The Council of the Popolo, which met on May 2nd by order of Poncello Orsini, in accordance with the usual formula, assembled on the 4th, 'de mandato dominorum 7'. It is the events of the 4th which suggest that the Popolo's unity had proved inadequate to the force of Monaldeschi pressure. On that day Orsini left Orvieto,[1] and the other known events of the 4th are a popular assault on the Seven,[2] and the passing of a law that any Monaldeschi committing an offence against a popolano was to suffer a quadruple penalty. This new law suggests that the Popolo was allowed to retain its authority and even to ensure the Monaldeschi did not abuse their victory—all no doubt as a *quid pro quo* for the abandonment of Orsini. Meanwhile popular resentment against this desertion was expressed in the attack on the Seven, the obvious scapegoats when traitors to the Popolo were being sought. The mild treatment of most of those concerned in the disturbances of the 4th (the assailants of the wounded member of the Seven were excepted, however) confirms that the Monaldeschi blended their threats with cajolery.

One chronicler records that Poncello Orsini left Orvieto 'dovi restò la ciptà in potestà de' Monaldensi'.[3] Their triumph may have entailed finesse but it was none the less clear-cut for that. On May 7th a Monaldeschi and a member of the Montemarte family (who have already been met with as close allies of the Monaldeschi)[4] were appointed joint Captains of the Popolo, while the former was also to be 'Difensore del Popolo' and Gonfaloniere della Giustizia. On the same day all who had fled during the crisis

---

[1] Chr. Pot. 4 (*Ephemerides*, p. 182) says he was 'expulsus . . . de palatio populi', and when he was at last paid his salary for his unfinished term of office it was admitted that 'per eum non steterit quod non perfeceret et serviret in dictis officiis' (ACO, Rif. 1324, fo. 129v). But there is no evidence that his expulsion was achieved by physical force.

[2] They were attacked with stones, and one was gravely injured. Their banner was also taken.

[3] L. Manente (*Ephemerides*, p. 376).   [4] See p. 93.

were ordered to return. Orsini at first went only to Civitella d'Agliano, eight miles from Orvieto, and for the next few weeks precautions were taken lest he should attempt an armed return,[1] but he had probably lost interest in the ungrateful institution to whose power he had contributed so much. Orvieto's Popolo never found a leader to replace him, and the hesitant but characteristic policy which led to the bargain of 1322 and Orsini's abandonment must often have been regretted.

---

[1] *Ephemerides*, p. 378n. and ACO, Rif. 1322, fos. 60v ff.

CHAPTER XIV

THE NOBLES IN CONTROL (1322-32)

THE nine years that had passed since the defeat of the Ghibellines had seen a succession of important changes in the government of the commune. The régime of the Guelf nobility had fallen through a failure in foreign policy and a period had followed in which the Popolo played as large a part as the nobles in the management of the commune's affairs. During Poncello Orsini's two terms of office as Capitano the Popolo had even presumed to restrict the powers of the nobility very considerably, and this had eventually driven the most powerful of the noble families into open opposition to him. Before investigating the underlying causes of the Popolo's weakness and the reasons for the Monaldeschi's success in April 1322, it is relevant to enquire to what extent the apparent political changes of the period 1313-22 correspond with changes in the personnel of those who were wielding political power. Avowed alterations in the direction of public affairs may purposely or accidently conceal what is only a 'ministerial re-shuffle'. They cannot be taken at their face value, and must be compared with an analysis of the personnel of the office-holders during the same period.

A consideration of those holding political offices during these years (which is here taken to include membership of important Balìe and embassies) leads to some interesting and surprising conclusions.[1] When a list of the twenty-six persons who held the greatest number of offices during the rule of the Five is confronted with a similar list for the years between the fall of the Five and that of Poncello Orsini it is found that no fewer than twenty names appear in both. This striking similarity between the two lists reveals clearly that the break in continuity in December 1315 is only apparent. Of the six names that find a place in the first list but

---

[1] These lists are compiled from references in the Rif. of the relevant years.

not in the latter, five are those of Monaldeschi, which does suggest a decline in their influence, and the basis of their grievance against Orsini; but, although they have been passed by others in the frequency of their election to offices during the later period, all six continue to play an important part in Orvietan politics, so that the list for 1316-22 would only need to be extended to include the thirty-two most frequent office-holders for the names of four of them (all Monaldeschi) to be found in it. Of the twenty names that appear in both lists, eight are those of Monaldeschi, six of other nobles, and six of popolani. It has already been observed that a small nucleus of popolani, comprising a few names that are ubiquitous in the political documents of the period, had held a number of offices during the régime of the Five and, for that time at least, can be regarded as allies of the Monaldeschi and the Guelf nobility; this is a class of which much more will be heard later. The figures given above make it clear that those who apparently fell from power in 1315 continued to play a big part in the commune's politics. Many of these personalities, both noble and popolani, had indeed been very prominent even before 1313. A mere handful of men, some of them Guelf nobles and others popolani, remained at the helm despite apparent upheavals such as that of 1315, and this is very relevant to the problem which has now to be considered, that of the causes of the Popolo's defeat in 1322.

It has already been suggested that lack of unity was the principal cause of the Popolo's weakness. The clue to this deficiency is to be found in the participation of almost all the prominent popolani in the Guelf régime of 1313-5, which may have mitigated what began as a noble tyranny, but at the same time committed the natural leaders of the Popolo to an alliance with the nobility. Such an alliance provokes the question: how far did the formal distinction between nobles and popolani correspond to a real difference in political interests and traditions? To answer it, it is necessary to investigate the social and financial position of the popolani most prominent in Orvietan politics, as well as their careers.

The predominance within the Popolo of members of the more prosperous trades is very marked. While this must often have

113

seemed a grievance to the humbler Arti it naturally tended to develop in the absence of a strong policy opposing it, not only in view of the superior influence, experience of affairs, and education of the wealthier tradesmen, but because they had more leisure to devote to politics. Indeed it is arguable that it was in the interests of the Popolo to resign itself to their leadership, whatever doubts were entertained about their devotion to its cause. The alternative, a demagogic type of direction, entailed strong leadership from a member of the lesser Arti or from an outsider: the former was never forthcoming, the latter only in 1316-7 and 1321-2. Thus the guilds of Merchants and Mercers provided a high proportion of the popular office-holders, together with the lawyers. The importance of the part played by the latter from the twelfth century onwards in the development of the Italian city-states, and indeed in colouring the whole nature of that 'Italian World in which the level of the Western Civilization had been raised precociously to such a high degree that the difference of degree became tantamount to a difference in kind',[1] is now a common place to the mediaeval historian. Nowhere is it more vividly illustrated than in the minutes of the communes' Council meetings. There the judges stand out as by far the most loquacious of the councillors; often special Balie composed only of judges are appointed to advise on some question entailing judicial knowledge, but their representation and influence in Councils, embassies, and Balie is out of all proportion to the number of their members. The majority of the popolani most prominent in the early fourteenth century, men such as Neri di Guidetto, Giovanni di Federico, and Pietro di Andrea 'Fallastate', were lawyers. The politics of the Italian communes call for investigation as a study in 'dikastarchy'.

The census of 1292 reveals the existence of a number of wealthy popolani at that period,[2] and the fragmentary evidence available in the form of documents relating to taxation and loans and to the liability to provide and maintain horses for the commune's cavalry shows that in the next decades the group of popolani playing the

[1] A. J. Toynbee, *A Study of History*, London, 1934-, vol. III, 300.
[2] Unfortunately the published extracts only relate to property within the town. The vast volumes concerning possessions in the contado would certainly repay study, but probably only someone living *in situ* could undertake this lengthy task.

PLATE III

THE PIAZZA DEL DUOMO IN THE FOURTEENTH CENTURY

From the frescoes by Ugolino di Prete Ilario in the Duomo

biggest part in politics contains several wealthy men. In 1316 at least ten popolani were among the wealthy class responsible for the maintenance of a horse, and a list for 1326 contains the names of six popolani, every one of them a name occurring constantly in the Council minutes of the time.[1] One of these, Cardinal Theoderic's nephew Neri di Zacharia, was particularly wealthy and his loans to the commune between 1317 and 1328 total almost a thousand florins.[2] A census of about the year 1330[3] reveals Neri di Guidetto (mentioned several times above) as the owner of forty-two agricultural holdings in one area of the contado alone. The nephews of Cardinal Theoderic call for special mention as members of a small but influential class, the descendents of noble families who had been granted the privileges of membership of the Popolo. This class of pseudo-popolani also included Filippo degli Alberici and his son Facietto. All these four had distinguished careers and leading popular offices.[4]

Sufficient evidence has been mustered to suggest that there were men among the popolani whose social and financial standing was such that their interests and sympathies might be expected to lie with the nobles rather than with the exponents of minor trades, and that it was mainly from this same class that the Popolo's political leaders were recruited.[5] The alliance of 1313-15 was a sign of this state of affairs. An even clearer illustration of its consequences was the number of popolani formerly prominent in the affairs of the Popolo who continued to hold political office after 1334 under the tyranny of the most powerful of the Guelf nobles, Ermanno Monaldeschi.[6]

[1] They include all the three lawyers mentioned above (p. 114), members of the Della Terza, Toste, Vaschesi and other leading popular families, and Neri and Benedetto di Zacharia, the nephews of Cardinal Theoderic (ACO, Rif. 1316, fos. 23-27v, and 1326, fos. 38v-40v).

[2] Rif. 1317, fo. 84; 1321, fo. 25; 1328, fos. 89-94: for a loan in 1320 BRDSPU, XLI, p. 27.

[3] ACO, 'Catasto 5, sec. XIV'.

[4] For the sons of Zacharia v. Genealogical Table III. Neri was once Capitano del Popolo (C.D., p. 431, etc.), Facietto twice a member of the Seven (ACO, Rif. 1330, fo. 1 (May) and 1334, fo. 49).

[5] There is a recognition of this in the direction of some popular legislation against not the nobles alone, but 'nobiles et magnates' (e.g. ACO, Rif. 1332, fo. 57). By the middle of the century a chronicler is writing of 'grossi populari . . . homini artefici et ricchi', and 'populari grassi' (Ephemerides, pp. 9 and 67). [6] See p. 138.

The only possible remedy for the lack of homogeneity in the Popolo's composition was strong leadership, but here it faced the appalling disadvantage that the captaincy had to be held by an outsider.[1] This provision, which was common to all the Italian communes, was designed to prevent the office becoming the vehicle for the tyranny of a local inhabitant. Fear of the acquisition of too much power by one individual was most characteristic of the Popolo, and it paid a heavy penalty for it. While the natural head of the Popolo was its Captain—it will be seen that when in 1332 the Popolo realized at last how its powers were being sapped, its first action was to increase his jurisdiction[2]—the Gonfaloniere della Giustizia, who was chosen from citizens of Orvieto, might have acquired the leadership had he been granted greater authority and a term of office longer than three months. The Capitano del Popolo himself was normally elected for six months, a period so short that it was unlikely that any real sentiment could grow up binding him to the institution he served and moving him to something more than a conscientious prosecution of his duties.[3] Not only did he lack knowledge of local politics, but even Poncello Orsini, the apparent exception to these generalizations, in the last analysis valued his personal security more than the well-being of the Popolo of a town that was not his own. A mercenary General is better than none at all, but when that General has to be changed at frequent intervals there is no hope of securing continuity in strategy, and little hope that the General will desert his peaceful headquarters to direct a battle in the outcome of which he has no interest. This handicap was at least as disastrous to the Popolo as the unreliability of its leading members.

These weaknesses are illustrated by a phenomenon that at the same time helped to increase their effect, the infiltration of the nobility into power in despite of forms of government designed to safeguard the political supremacy of the Popolo. The class of pseudo-popolani has already been mentioned, but even recognized

---

[1] It is possible that had Orvieto produced an outstanding personality within its Popolo he might have secured the abrogation of this constitutional clause, as Della Greca had done in the 1280s.

[2] See pp. 126-7.

[3] The practice of electing municipal officers twice yearly was almost universal.

members of the nobility exerted much influence through their membership of Balie and embassies. The Balia is one of the most characteristic institutions of the government of the Italian city-states; it was customary to pass on all important business for consideration by one of these *ad hoc* committees, the Councils, whose time was thus saved, limiting themselves to the consideration (and, usually, adoption) of the advice of the Balie. The first reaction to important news was invariably the appointment of a Balia, so much so that at times one has the impression of an almost superstitious belief in their efficacy. It was customary for Balie to include a proportion of noblemen which varied according to the matter under consideration. The advice of nobles was particularly desirable on military and diplomatic questions: when the contado was invaded in 1328 by the forces of Louis of Bavaria a Balia of eight that was given special powers during the emergency included seven nobles.[1] Usually the proportion was lower, but the same advantages secured them representation on all important embassies; the commune could not afford to send emissaries liable to feel and look out of their element in high places. Finally the Captains of the Parte Guelfa, who had considerable influence, were recruited half from the nobility and half from the Popolo; the division between Guelf and Ghibelline intersected that between noble and popolano and made it less clear-cut.

This account of the Popolo's delicate constitution has to be complemented by a consideration of some of the other sources of instability in the commune to account for that attitude of political agnosticism to which the advent of Ermanno's tyranny must largely be attributed.

One most important factor was the continued maintenance of the Guelfs in a position of legal superiority to the Ghibellines, and their nourishment on the property of their defeated opponents. The evils of one-party rule are too familiar to the fifth decade of the twentieth century to need describing here. Particularly baneful is the corrupting influence of a situation in which party membership automatically secures preferential treatment. To hold office in Orvieto after 1313 it was necessary to be a Guelf, at least in name.

[1] ACO, Rif. 1328, fo. 87v (March).

Inscription as a member of that party carried with it privileges that even included fiscal preference; when a forced loan was raised in 1320 Ghibellines were to pay forty soldi, twenty, or ten according to their wealth, while the liability of the Guelfs was half that of the equivalent category of Ghibelline.[1]

Furthermore the Ghibellines, although they were so shattered in 1313 that, as a chronicler says, 'non hebbero mai più forza alcuna',[2] were constantly employed as a bogey to excuse the continuance of the Guelfs' political monopoly. But Ghibellinism was more than a convenient red herring. It was one of the mainstays of the commune's finances, for the Ghibellines whose property was confiscated in 1313 included some of Orvieto's richest citizens.[3] Again and again in the years betweeen 1313 and 1330 when the commune was pressed for money to pay for a war or some other enterprise the solution adopted was to use the revenue from the confiscated property of the 'rebels'. The sale or lease of these lands ensured the growth of a class interested in the preservation of the current régime, though many of them were acquired by nobles whose Guelfism needed no such incentives.[4] Finally the Ghibellines' possessions were used as a bribe to the Popolo; not only did the Arti purchase some of them as investments, but the grain grown on the confiscated lands was on at least one occasion earmarked to be sold retail to popolani only.[5] The corrupting influence of a similar situation in classical Greece has been noted by Burckhardt:[6] 'in the Greek cities', he writes, 'the grip on the property of the parties exterminated by exile or massacre, which had been seized in the name of some principle or other—demos or aristocracy— was apt to turn into a tyranny to which both democracy and

[1] ACO, Rif. 1320, fos. 61v-63 (August).

[2] L. Manente (Ephemerides, p. 352).

[3] See p. 94. Simone di Ranieri di Guido, one of those condemned in 1313, had been the richest but one of all Orvietans in 1292 (Pardi, Catasto, p. 242). The Filippeschi at the same period were Orvieto's third family in point of wealth.

[4] 'La (casa) Philipense era quasi declinata; et cosi epsi Monaldensi possedivano loro beni' (L. Manente, Ephemerides, p. 375). For purchases by members of the Monaldeschi and Montemarte families, see p. 94.

[5] ACO, Rif. 1326, fos. 30v-31v (April), where it is decided 'quod pensiones bonorum rebellium vendantur artibus civitatis urbevetane'. Rif. 1319, fos. 6v-15v (December): the exiles' grain 'vendi debeat minuatim popularibus urbisveteris.'

[6] Reflections on History (English trans.), London, 1943, p. 154.

aristocracy succumbed.' It is striking that this parallel contains also a correct prophecy of Ermanno's Signoria.

It was the very awareness that a tyranny was a possibility that had always to be guarded against that lay behind the tendency to restrict the power of all individual political offices, a tendency that has already been remarked in connection with the captaincy of the Popolo.[1] The same suspiciousness led to a lack of continuity in the affairs for which Balie were primarily responsible, for their composition was also changed frequently; in May 1317, for example, the entire personnel of the Balia of twelve in charge of the prosecution of the war against Viterbo is changed, simply because it has been in office long enough.[2] This handicap has of course its corresponding advantage, which is succinctly expressed in an uncharacteristic statement of principle when the shortening of a term of office is recommended 'ut maior communitas (sit) inter cives urbevetanos et ut unusquisque de honoribus communis sentiat';[3] the rarity of such justifications of political action makes this one particularly interesting.

Ultimately it was the existence of the Popolo as a State within the State that upset the delicate balance of the commune's machinery, for the nobility, with a superiority in cohesion and at least equality in military and financial resources, had to attempt the destruction of a monopoly based on the constitutional privileges of a weaker rival. Safety-valves such as the noble participation in Balie and the captaincy of the Parte Guelfa were inadequate, and the years from 1322 see the nobles in possession of a growing control over the affairs of the commune. A belated stand by a weak but now alert Popolo held up this growth from 1332-4, but in the latter year it collapsed before the *coup d'état* of Ermanno Monaldeschi.

After 1322 the leaderless Popolo drifted and grew weaker. In the next ten years it rarely gave signs of the vigour it had possessed under Orsini. An exception to this was the period during 1324 when the danger of a civil war among the Monaldeschi after the

---

[1] Note Aristotle's remark that 'formerly tyrannies were more common than now, on account of the very extensive powers with which some magistrates were entrusted' (*Politics*, Bk. v).

[2] ACO, Rif. 1317, f. 7v.　　　　　　　　　　　　[3] Rif. 1320, fo. 182 (December).

murder of Giovanni Gatti[1] provoked a series of emergency measures reminiscent of the reforms of 1316 and 1321. Not only were the Monaldeschi compelled to reach agreement, but the 'unio et sotietas' between the Arti was renewed, the body of a thousand armed popolani re-formed and set to guard the town, and Gonfalonieri chosen to assist the Capitano and Seven.[2] There was another revival a year later when a similar situation arose among the Monaldeschi, but it did not outlive the emergency, for in December 1325 the Council of the Popolo voluntarily abnegated much of the Popolo's powers.[3] What had formerly been the Council of forty popolani was now to be composed of twenty-four popolani, twelve nobles, and the four Captains of the Parte Guelfa. At the same time it was decided that the Seven should no longer be chosen from the Arti in rotation, but by lot from a list of 210 (later increased to 336) popolani: it has been suggested above[4] that such a system tended to sap the *esprit de corps* of the artisans. The following spring the Council of the Popolo even voted away to the Forty the power of electing its Captain,[5] an extraordinary act of abdication.

The decadence of the Popolo was both reflected in and actuated by an ever-increasing tendency for its offices to be held by a small *coterie*. Three families in particular, the De la Terza, the Toste and the Avveduti are outstanding in this clique, but a number of other names recur with monotonous frequency.[6]

In view of this tendency it is not surprising to find non-noble families involved in the feuds of the nobles. When there was a

---

[1] See p. 122.

[2] ACO, Rif. 1324, fos. 111v-140v; chronicle cited by M. Monaldeschi, p. 85v, reprinted in *Ephemerides*, p. 189 (this describes the episode *ad* 1323, in error).

[3] Rif. 1325, fos. 78-83 and 96-7.   [4] See p. 103.

[5] ACO, Rif. 1326, fos. 19v-21 (April).

[6] Among these are Nicola di Meo, Nicola di Berardino 'Nasi' (both of these were lawyers), Nucciolo dei Vaschesi, Lemmo 'Insegne', Cecco di Puccio 'Grani', Vanne di Andrea 'Vele' and Bernardo di Pietro di Leonardo. In eight years (from 1326 onwards) members of the Della Terza family provided one of the Seven eight times and filled forty-nine other offices ('offices' is here used to include membership of important Balie and embassies). The corresponding figures for the Avveduti are nine and thirty-two, and for the Toste four and twenty. During the same period Nicola di Meo and his relatives provided members of the Seven twice and filled twenty-seven offices, Nicola di Berardino 'Nasi' and his four members of the Seven and seven other offices, while each of the others named above was represented at least once on the Seven and none of them less than eighteen times in minor offices. (These statistics are founded on the Rif. for the years 1326-34.)

great pacification in 1330 the Della Terza (no less than twenty-four of them are named), the Avveduti, and the Vaschesi were all officially reconciled with their enemies.[1] The Della Terza were certainly allies of Manno Monaldeschi: it was a member of this family who proposed the formation of the Balia of twelve which gave Manno full powers for life, and among the twelve was another Della Terza, as well as a Toste, an Avveduti, the brother of Nicola di Meo, and two other representatives of the small *coterie* into whose hands control of the Popolo had passed.[2]

The decline of the Popolo was also accentuated by the increasing indebtedness of the commune to the nobility. Between 1324 and 1333 the Monaldeschi alone lent over four thousand florins; Ermanno's share of this, which was about three-quarters, will be discussed later in connection with the origins of his Signoria.,

As soon as the Guelf nobles had achieved control of the commune in 1322 they were torn by internal dissensions. A sort of law seems to have prevailed in communal politics that no party could crush its opponents without itself splitting, the antagonisms latent within the party only becoming evident after a mutual enemy had been overcome. The most famous example of this is the scission of the Florentine Guelfs into the Blacks and Whites, but the history of any commune illustrates this protozoa-like tendency in the parties.

The first signs of a split within the Guelf nobility (or, more precisely, within the Monaldeschi, its leading family) are to be found during Poncello Orsini's second spell of office, in the years 1321-2, and they have already been mentioned.[3] Luca Manente says that owing to the Monaldeschi's great wealth and power they split up 'in dui divisioni (chi) a parte guelpha et chi a parte gibellina', the former, including the sons of Corrado, of Pietro Novello, and of Ugolino di Buonconte, opposing Orsini, while those who supported him were Sceo di Vanne and the sons of Ciarfaglia, of Nericola, and of Catalano.[4] The terms 'Guelf' and 'Ghibelline' were certainly not used of these two parties, but for

---

[1] Loose fos. (unnumbered) in Rif. Vol. xxx (See p. 123.)
[2] See pp. 135-6.   [3] See p. 107.
[4] *Ephemerides*, pp. 375-8.

the rest the documentary evidence suggests that the chronicler's statement is accurate, and his account of the wounding of Neri di Sceo by a son of Pietro 'Novello' should probably also be accepted.

Two years later another feud became entangled with the internecine quarrels of the Monaldeschi, bringing to them a new contribution of hatred and bitterness. The Montemarte, Orvieto's second greatest Guelf family, had been deadly enemies of the Gatti of Viterbo since 1315, when Count Cecco Montemarte had been killed in the saddle by Silvestro Gatti in the Montefiascone fighting.[1] Silvestro's son Giovanni married a daughter of Buonconte di Ugolino Monaldeschi, and one day in April 1324 two members of the Montemarte family waylaid him as he was walking in the streets of Orvieto with his brother-in-law Ugolino. Giovanni Gatti was killed in the ensuing scuffle, and Ugolino Monaldeschi and Ceccarello Montemarte were wounded. It was the imminent danger of civil war breaking out after this episode that led to the special measures of the Popolo described above,[2] and henceforward the Montemarte and this branch of the Monaldeschi were sworn enemies.

By the following year the sons of Pietro 'Novello' Monaldeschi had become allies of the Montemarte and had fallen out with Ugolino di Buonconte; in March they and their followers were involved in a street-fight, several on each side being wounded. The Popolo at once passed a series of emergency measures. The Captain was given special powers as Gonfaloniere della Giustizia and the thousand 'armati de populo' mobilized, a Balia of nineteen was appointed to arrange a truce and those who had been concerned in the brawl were confined to their *palazzi*. These included Buonconte and his son Ugolino, the Archpriest Monaldo and his children, three sons of Pietro 'Novello', and many members of the Montemarte family.[3] The crisis lasted several months. In June four Monaldeschi (Ugolino and the three sons of Pietro 'Novello') were found guilty of causing the fight in March, and each fined 500 lire.[4] Late in July the pope wrote to the Rector of the

---

[1] See p. 97; also Chr. of F. Montemarte, *Ephemerides*, pp. 216-7.
[2] See p. 120.
[3] ACO, Rif. 1325, fos. 65v-75.   [4] ACO, Lib. Cond. 1325, fos. 105-6.

Patrimony and to the parties concerned to urge a reconciliation, and it was probably soon after this that a truce was agreed on, to last five years.[1]

The period 1325-30 saw no further developments in the split within the Monaldeschi, and the family's political ascendancy grew yet more pronounced. A Balia of eight which was given special powers in military affairs during the expedition of Louis of Bavaria (1327-8) included no less than seven Monaldeschi.[2] During this brief phase of internal tranquillity the decision was taken to readmit the Ghibellines; after seventeen years of exile they were now suffered to return, albeit as pariahs. This decision was reached at Whitsun 1330, and at the same time it was agreed 'quod omnis pax inter omnes odiosos civitatis et districtus fiat'. On June 5th the Buonconte branch of the Monaldeschi was reconciled with the Montemarte in the Piazza del Popolo, in the presence of the bishop (who preached a sermon) and many hundreds of spectators. Their amity was sealed by the marriage of Giovanni di Montemarte to a grand-daughter of Ugolino Monaldeschi. Other reconciliations, involving popular as well as noble families, took place on the following days, the last one on July 5th. A sort of Festival of Love marked Orvieto's new-found unity, for on June 14th the Captain, who had helped to secure these agreements, was knighted by a grateful commune, and there were jousts and great public celebrations.[3] But the joy of the participants was the feverish joy of those who see violence not banished but postponed, for a new feud, between Manno di Corrado Monaldeschi and Napoleone di Pietro 'Novello' and his brothers, had long been smouldering, and was soon to burst into flame.

Altogether there is something hectic about these years in Orvieto, though the feeling becomes stronger yet in the years 1332-4. One aspect of the crisis was the commune's weakening control over its contado. There disturbances broke out continually; Orvieto's territory seemed too large for her, for if revolt was put down in one place it broke out instantly in another. In 1325 there was a

---

[1] Arch. Vat., Reg. Vat. n. 113, fos. 85-6; L. Manente (*Ephemerides*, pp. 417-8).

[2] ACO, Rif. 1328, fo. 87v.

[3] ACO, Rif. 1330, fos. 12v-22v and unnumbered loose sheets in the same volume; chronicle cited by M. Monaldeschi (*Ephemerides*, pp. 190-1.)

serious rising at Rochette, while the war between the Counts of
Parrano and the Viscounts of Campiglia convulsed the northern
part of the contado.[1] In 1327-8 there was the yet more serious
episode of the temporary loss of Chiusi to Perugia.[2] The town of
S. Salvatore was in revolt in 1327 and again in 1329,[3] and it was
these border-areas of Orvieto's Aldobrandeschine possessions which
were both most liable to revolt and most vulnerable to assault.
In 1331 a peace was patched up with the Counts of Santa Fiora
and the turbulent lords of Montemarano,[4] but it was impossible
to check the depredations of flocks and other property which seem
to have represented the source of livelihood of so many barons; in
one typical raid on the Aldobrandeschine contado Count Romano
Orsini and his followers stole five thousand sheep and several oxen,
as well as killing three men and carrying off another.[5] Noteworthy
as a symptom of this loss of control is the treaty with Siena signed
in 1316.[6] The two neighbours, who had been enemies almost
continually since 1229, renewed their twelfth-century alliance in
answer to conditions which had become analogous to those of the
twelfth century; now that they no longer had a firm grip over
their respective territories, and were no longer neighbours *de facto*,
it was again in their interest to combine against the unruly subjects
of both.

The chaos of the Orvietan contado had a parallel in the condition
of the Patrimony in Tuscany. Here the existence of a strong
nucleus of Ghibelline barons with sympathetic towns, and a series
of inadequate Rectors whose master was far away at Avignon, led
to the loss of all control over the Patrimony's nominal subjects.
An illuminating report from a Vicar to the Pope in 1319 or 1320[7]
has an added interest because the Vicar was Bishop of Orvieto.
Bagnorea, he reports, is obedient to him in everything, because it
is impoverished and feeble, and situated close to his Court.[8] Hardly
any other town is described as obedient; Orvieto, typically, is

---

[1] C.D., DCXL; *Ephemerides*, pp. 383-4n.; Ughelli, p. 121.   [2] See p. 129.
[3] ACO, Rif. 1327, fos. 17v-19 (April) and 1329, fos. 52-4 (July).   [4] C.D., DCXLVI-II.
[5] ACO, uncatalogued letter, dated 7 December (probably 1323).   [6] See p. 104.
[7] M. Antonelli, 'Una Relazione del Vicario del Patrimonio a Giovanni XXII in
Avignone' in ASRSP, XVIII, 1895, pp. 447-67.
[8] '. . . propinqua est curie . . . pauperrima et vilissima est, et ideo in omnibus est
obediens.'

PLATE IV

ORVIETO IN THE FOURTEENTH CENTURY

From the frescoes by Ugolino di Prete Ilario in the Duomo

insubordinate and pays no taxes 'on account of its strength',[1] while another noteworthy entry remarks that the inhabitants of Nepi 'do not fear the spiritual arm, for their officials and councillors have long been excommunicated, and the town under an interdict; this does not worry them'.

The collapse of the Patrimony in Tuscany meant that Orvieto suffered from constant disorders on her southern boundary, while she was frequently at war with the Ghibellines who sought to win Orvieto for the Filippeschi and her other exiles. The war of 1320-1 with Corneto and Bisenzio has already been mentioned.[2] There was another war against Ghibelline forces in 1322, and one against those led by Viterbo in 1325-6.[3] Louis of Bavaria's expedition found a host of supporters, who threatened Orvieto from every side; they included Todi, Viterbo, Toscanella, Corneto, the lords of Montemarano, and the Count of S. Fiora. In these circumstances Orvieto was fortunate to escape so lightly; she suffered only one attack by the Count of S. Fiora in 1327 (in the Val di Chiana), and the pillaging and destruction of the imperial troops in 1328, when they surprisingly failed to capture Bolsena but wrought havoc against the other towns of the Val del Lago.[4] The episodes mentioned above are only some of the more violent disturbances of these years, for the symptoms of the commune's loss of its hold over the contado were general and they became each year more evident, as will be seen in the following chapter.

[1] Orvieto had two quarrels with the Patrimony at this period: she was found guilty of an unstated offence in October 1323 (Ephemerides, p. 380n.), and after December 1326 there was a violent dispute concerning the commune's right to make a census of property in the Val del Lago.   [2] See p. 104.

[3] Ephemerides, pp. 375n. and 385n.; L. Fumi, Balneoregensia, Orvieto, 1895, docs. XII-XVI; C.D., DCXLI.

[4] C.D., DCXLV (Todi); Ephemerides, pp. 420-4n. and Antonelli, 'Dominazione Pontificia', p. 257 (the 1327 campaign); Ciacci, II, 311 (the lords of Montemarano); ACO, Rif. 1328, fos. 49-98 (February-March) and 103-127v (May-June); Antonelli, art. cit., pp. 258-60 and Theiner, docs. DCCXLIII and DCCLIX (devastation of Val del Lago); L. Manente (Ephemerides, pp. 422-5), Perugian Chr. in ASI, XVI, i, p. 100, Sienese Chr. in RIS, N.S., XV, 6, pp. 469-79), and Bolsenese Chr. in Ephemerides, pp. 189-90 (a participant's account of the siege of Bolsena).

CHAPTER XV

THE CRISIS AND MANNO MONALDESCHI'S
COUP D'ÉTAT (1332-4)

THE ever-increasing rigidity of the Monaldeschi monopoly and
the crisis of the contado naturally called forth a popular reaction,
but the last fight of the Popolo never came near to succeeding, and
indeed there is a curious air of unreality about it, which should
probably be attributed to pessimism about its outcome occasioned
by the lack of a leader and the equivocal allegiance of most of the
prominent popolani.

The first sign of the revival of the Popolo is to be found in 1331
when a Gonfaloniere della Giustizia was elected and the corps of
a thousand armed popolani reorganized.[1] It was not till the
following year that the powers of the Captain were increased and
the movement assumed its characteristic form. The reform of
March 1332 altered the name of the office to 'Capitano Difensore
del Popolo', and the defence of the Popolo was further stressed
by the allotment of fifty cavalry and fifty infantry to the direct
command of the Captain, who was also specifically entrusted with
the formulation and execution of anti-noble legislation. At the
same time nobles were threatened with greatly increased punishment (in most cases, tenfold that previously given) for any offences
they committed, and the thousand were empowered to take the
law into their own hands in dealing with offenders against the
Popolo. The prestige and discipline of the Popolo were also
strengthened in the way now always associated with such revivals;
each Arte and the whole Popolo elected standard-bearers, the
Seven were allotted more servants and buildings, and so on.[2] All
these measures were approved by the Council of Forty Popolani

[1] ACO, Rif. 1331, fos. 2-3v (September).
[2] ACO, Rif. 1332, fos. 57-75. A foretaste of this reform had been the measure of
21 February (ibid., fo. 41) exempting popolani from the payment of forced loans.

and Nobles after their passage through the Council of the Popolo, and it is interesting that as late as this strongly pro-popular legislation could muster a majority there. Perhaps it grew recalcitrant after this concession, for the next move of the Popolo, the following spring, was to abolish this Council, replacing it by the Council of Forty Popolani which it had itself superseded in 1325.[1]

The policy of unifying the Popolo by increasing the powers of its Captain was carried a stage further in December 1333 when, by a special proposal that entailed the abrogation of nineteen clauses of the Carta del Popolo, the Council of the Popolo invested the Captain with all the powers hitherto possessed by itself.[2] At the same time the Council annulled the clause in the Carta stating that the Aldobrandeschine contado should never cease to be the property of Orvieto; the Popolo was opposing the foreign policy of Manno Monaldeschi (who wished to yield Chiusi but hold the Aldobrandeschine lands)[3] as well as trying to combat the Monaldeschi tyranny. The events of 1334 were thus to find a Popolo which had in theory been reformed and strengthened in the last few months, but the feebleness of its opposition to Manno's *coup d'état* shows the inutility of institutional reinforcement in the absence of a will to resist in the human component.

These changes in the Popolo took place against a background of deepening crisis. Between 1332 and 1334 the situation in the contado had gone from bad to worse. The extremities, and in particular the Val di Chiana and the Aldobrandeschine lands, were the parts affected. In 1332 Lugnano was attacked by the restless lords of Montemarano and, although they submitted, in January of the next year four other feudal families of the contado (the Count of Parrano, the lords of Morrano, Trevinano, and one Guido di Simone) and the town of Cetona were outlaws.[4] That

---

[1] The last recorded meeting of the old Council of XL was on March 22nd (Rif. 1333, fo. 98v); on April 11th, forty Popolani were elected, presumably to replace it. (*ibid.*, fos. 119v-120v). Its abolition was doubtless decided between August and December 1332, months for which the Rif. are not extant; the measure is mentioned at a Council meeting in 1334 (Rif., fos. 137-43). For the origins of the old Council, see p. 120.

[2] ACO, Rif. 1333, fos. 79-85v; only the Council's powers of punishing popolani were denied the Captain.

[3] See p. 130.

[4] C.D., DCXLVIII-DCI; ACO, Rif. 1333, fo. 7v.

year saw a rapid succession of troubles in the contado. Pian Castagnaio, which had been in revolt, submitted in February, but both it and Manciano had to be garrisoned. In March Sarteano was attacked by some Sienese, while S. Salvatore refused to pay its taxes. So far the unrest had been centred in the north-western extremity of the contado, but in May it spread south when Count Guido Orsini conducted a raid against Acquapendente. In the summer the disturbances centred around the Val del Lago and the most easterly part of the Aldobrandeschine country. Proceno attacked Montorio in May, and there was a war of retaliation in July. Meanwhile Iugliano, a little further south, had risen in revolt against Orvieto.[1]

These events in the contado were bringing into operation a vicious circle of fiscal embarrassment. While less and less money was forthcoming in taxes from the contado, more and more revenue was needed in order to attempt the reconquest of the commune's rebellious subjects. The consequence was a financial crisis which curtailed the freedom of action of the commune (it will be seen later that the virtual exoneration of the authors of a political murder was to be justified on fiscal as well as other grounds) and contributed to the general unrest. Between April 1333 and May 1334 the frenzied fiscal activities necessitated by this crisis included the levying no less than seven times of a 'lira', or tax on property, two attempts to demand the 'tallia militum' (a payment in lieu of military service) in the contado, the raising of three forced loans, the extensive sale of pardons to outlaws and condemned criminals, and the sale of monopolies in salt, the importation of grain, fishing-rights, and the municipal brothel and gambling-den.[2] When a serious shortage of grain was added to these grievances, it can be understood that the people of Orvieto were in the state where radical remedies recommend themselves by their very radicalism. The situation was ripe for a tyranny.

[1] C.D., DCLII (P. Castagnaio); ACO, Rif. 1333, fo. 93 (Sarteano); ibid., fos. 96v-97 (S. Salvatore); ACO, letter (catalogued in error as '1334', though of May 9th, 1333) (Acquapendente); Rif. 1333, fos. 30v, 55v, 72 and M. Antonelli, 'Nuove Ricerche per la Storia del Patrimonio dal 1321 al 1341' in ASRSP, N.S., I, 1935, p. 122 (Montorio and Proceno); Rif. 1333, fos. 34-44 and 60v-62v (Iugliano).

[2] Information from Rif. 1333-4. For the shortage of grain early in 1334, Rif. ad an., fos. 29v and 46.

It is necessary to turn back to the most serious of the crises in the contado, since it became closely connected with the origins of Ermanno Monaldeschi's tyranny. This was the Perugian threat to Chiusi, once a great Etruscan city and the capital of Lars Porsena, and still a strategically important strong-point in the Val di Chiana. At least as far back as 1313 Perugia had cast envious eyes on this distant outpost of Orvieto, for the treaty of that year[1] prohibited her citizens from entering Chiusi, as Orvietans were excluded from nearby Città della Pieve, Perugia's outpost across the valley. Between 1315 and 1318 there was continual internal discord at Chiusi, and in June 1317 it was decided that there was no hope of Orvieto's mediation being effective unless Perugia also agreed to recognize it and to make a statement that she did not intend to acquire any rights over the city of Chiusi.[2] In 1318 Chiusi used Perugia's well-known ambitions as a bargaining-point, threatening to submit the town to Perugia if it was not granted the degree of independence it demanded.[3] An Orvietan punitive expedition put an end to Chiusi's pretensions and for nine years nothing is heard of Perugian claims to Chiusi. Then Perugia's leading part in the Guelf opposition to Louis IV provided her with a ready-made excuse for the capture of the town. Early in the summer of 1327 Perugia had complained of a nucleus of Ghibellines (including Orvietan exiles) which had settled just inside her frontiers, at Città della Pieve. In October they had moved on to Chiusi, and this provided Perugia's opportunity. She lost no time in attacking and capturing Chiusi.[4]

Despite her own preoccupation with the imperialist threat (on which Perugia had no doubt reckoned), Orvieto spared the troops for the vital undertaking of the recapture of Chiusi, and had achieved this by the beginning of 1328.[5] But the failure of one scheme did not mean that Perugia had abandoned hopes of gaining

[1] See p. 96.
[2] ACO, Rif. 1317, fos. 60v-62v.
[3] Rif. 1318, fos. 76v-78v, 87v, 100v-101, 105, 126, 135-137v, 140v (September-December).
[4] Rif. 1327, fos. 11v-12v and 69 (June-August), 61v-62, 80v-84v (October-November), and other Rif. cited in *Ephemerides*, pp. 419-20n.; L. Manente, ad 1326 (*Ephemerides*, p. 420).
[5] ACO, Rif. 1328, fos. 1-22; *C.D.*, DCXLIV (Chiusi resubmission, mis-dated '1329').

Chiusi. Orvieto's internal dissensions and evident decline, combined with the tantalizing closeness of the prize to her boundaries, tempted Perugia to renew her attempts, and in the spring of 1330 she laid a formal claim to the possession of Chiusi.[1] By 1332 Orvieto regarded a Perugian *coup* at Chiusi as imminent, and in January 1333 she appealed to the pope for the protection of her rights; the matter was referred to a papal legate at Foligno, and two years later the lawyers of Bologna were being consulted.[2] But while the case dragged on, some Orvietans had taken the law into their own hands, and the dispute had become inextricably bound up with the internal politics of the commune. At the very end of 1332, just before the appeal to the pope was made, Napoleone di Pietro 'Novello' Monaldeschi decided to organize a private defence of Chiusi against Perugia; the expedition had no official backing, and was presumably motivated by patriotism together with a desire to raise his own prestige. Undismayed by the possible consequences of their action, Napoleone's rivals Manno and Buonconte at once attempted, though in vain, to drive him out.[3]

The question of Chiusi had thus become the crux of the feud within the Monaldeschi family. Napoleone had chosen the retention of Chiusi as the main plank of his platform and the source of his prestige, while Manno found himself thrust into opposition to this policy, although just before he and Buonconte had made a large loan for this very purpose.[4] He was doubtless able to justify his view by claiming that it was in keeping with Orvieto's traditional foreign policy of keeping at peace with her eastern neighbours in order to exert her domination to the full in the west. It had now come to mean appeasement, but if the first act of Manno's

---

[1] ACO, Rif. 1330, fos. 5v-7v (April) and other Rif. cited in *Ephemerides*, pp. 425-6n.

[2] ACO, Rif. 1332, fos. 220-1; *C.D.*, DCLI; Rif. 1333, fo. 33 etc. and other Rif. cited in *Ephemerides*, p. 431 n. A deed of 1333, now lost, is described in a 14th-century inventory of the Archive (*ibid.*, p. 112) as the legate's award ('lodo')—but the case was still *sub iudice* in 1334 (Rif. *ad an.*, fos. 97-8).

[3] L. Manente *ad* 1332 (*Ephemerides*, pp. 430-1) and Chr. 1333-1354 = Cod. Urb. 1738, *ad* 1333 (*ibid.*, p. 192: this mistakenly calls Napoleone 'Pietro'). The only evidence for this episode comes from chronicles: it therefore dates from one of two parts of 1332—between March 12th and May 13th, or between August 1st and December 31st—as these are the only gaps in the Rif. for those two years. I am inclined to put it late in 1332, since this fits in with the doubt about the year, the appeal to the pope, and Manno's loan; but Manente says it took place in March.　　　[4] ACO, Rif. 1333, fo. 6 (January).

tyranny was the cession of Chiusi to Perugia the second was a declaration of war against the turbulent lord of the Aldobrande-schine contado, Guido Orsini.

Before describing the rapid series of events that made Manno Signore of Orvieto, it may be well to glance back at Napoleone's career and at Manno's thus far. Napoleuccio, as he was usually known, was more of a soldier than a statesman. He commanded Orvietan forces in 1314 (against Pisa), 1315 (at Bolsena), 1317 (at Perugia), 1318 (against Montemarano), 1322 (at Bagnorea), 1325 (in support of Florence), 1327-8 (when he recaptured Chiusi from Perugia) and 1330 (against S. Fiora).[1] The Chiusi victory was his greatest achievement, and was followed by a spell as Potestà there; it is noteworthy that this is the only known case of his holding such an office, while he is only twice heard of as an ambassador. Evidently he was associated in the popular mind with Chiusi and its retention, and this led to his defiant gesture in 1332 when he tried to hold the town on his own, and defended it even against his rivals and relatives, Manno and Buonconte. It is not easy to know how this episode affected his prestige, but Francesco Montemarte calls him the 'maggior cittadino e signore d'Orvieto' and Villani its 'signore',[2] while Manno's desperate tactics in 1334 also suggest that at this time Napoleone's party was gaining the ascendancy.

Manno's career calls for a fuller account. He had held important posts since his youth. When his father was killed in 1300 he was almost certainly aged under thirty, but he took on his father's office as Visconte of the 'piviere' of S. Venanzo at once, and he held office at Acquapendente in 1302 and at Gubbio (an important post, this) and Bagnorea in 1304.[3] From this time onwards he filled numerous communal offices. He played a leading part in the Guelf victory of 1313 and was joint Captain after it, when he proposed the most rigid anti-Ghibelline measures. During the period 1313-15 he held office more frequently than any other Orvietan, while he was surpassed only by two in 1316-22. Very

---

[1] L. Manente (*Ephemerides*, p. 353); Dottarelli, p. 178; ACO, Rif. 1317, fo. 62; 1318, fo. 47; *Ephemerides*, pp. 378 n., 382 n., 420 and n., 428 n.

[2] *Ephemerides*, p. 216; G. Villani, lib. 11, cap. X.

[3] ACO, Rif. 1300, fo. 118v; 1302, fo. 220v; 1304, fo. 130v; Chr. Pot. 4 (*Ephemerides*, p. 175).

frequently he acted as Potestà in towns of the contado;[1] this seems to have been the sort of post for which he was best fitted. He ruled Cetona at a time when the town was tormented by party hatred, but he did so with such success that the inhabitants pleaded that he might be compelled to accept a new term of office.

As a soldier Manno was less conspicuous, and one chronicler blames him for the débâcle of 1315 at Montefiascone.[2] He was more than a mere administrator, though; everything about him suggests an aristocratic capacity for style. His mother came of the family of the Visconti di Campiglia (whose fief lay on the boundary of the Sienese and Orvietan contadi), while his own first wife was a daughter of one of the lords of Baschi, and his second was no less than a Caetani and daughter of the Count Benedict who acquired the Aldobrandeschine estates in 1303.[3] The accounts of a typical embassy reveal him as being accompanied by seven servants, while no other member of the embassy— including several of his own family—had more than three.[4] He must moreover have been a man of very considerable wealth. His father had been one of the richest citizens in 1292, and the confiscation of 1313 had enabled him to add considerably to his estates. The fragmentary census of circa 1330 contains references to very large holdings of his at Paterno and Botto, and he had other property at Bolsena.[5] His loans to the commune are the surest proof of his wealth. Between 1318 and 1333 he loaned to Orvieto well over five thousand florins; the town's next greatest creditor, Manno's rival Napoleone, had lent 650 in the same period.[6]

As the Napoleone-Manno feud crystallized around the question of foreign policy its severity increased. In 1333 a leading supporter

[1] For example at Grotte and Montacuto in 1313, at S. Lorenzo and Grotte again in 1317, at Grotte and Acquapendente in 1319, Cetona in 1322 and Bolsena in 1328 (*Ephemerides*, p. 179; Pardi, *Comune & Signoria*, pp. 60 and 64; Rif. 1319, fo. 84 and 1322, fo. 95; Dottarelli, p. 203).

[2] Cont. Orv. Polono, pp. 132-3.

[3] Pardi, *Comune & Signoria*, p. 58; *Reg. B. VIII*, n. 1917.   [4] ACO, Rif. 1331, fo. 25v.

[5] Pardi, *Catasto*, p. 243 (see above, p. 94); ACO, Catasto 5, sec. XIV; Dottarelli, docs. XLII and XLIV.

[6] ACO, Rif. 1318, fos. 40v, 43v, 97v; BRDSPU, XXXVII, pp. 64 and 71; *ibid.*, XLI, p. 71; Rif. 1319, fo. 141; BRDSPU, XLI, p. 27; Rif. 1321, fo. 81; 1322, fo. 72; 1324, fo. 134; *Ephemerides*, p. 385n.; Rif. 1328, fos. 65, 89, 170v; 1329, fo. 26v; *Ephemerides*, p. 428n. and 430 n.; Rif. 1332, fo. 38v (February); 1333, fo. 6 (January).

of Manno, Ugolino della Greca, was murdered by Napoleone's supporter Vanne de' Mazzocchi.[1] The same year Manno was condemned with two close relatives and thirteen servants for being involved in a brawl, and he and two servants, together with Napoleone and one of his, were found guilty of carrying arms illegally; but the needy and frightened commune allowed them to purchase pardons.[2] At the same time there was a serious crisis in the Popolo, the Captain sentencing the entire personnel of the Seven to death for 'conspiracy against the Popolo'.[3] The sentence was not carried out, and the whole episode is wrapped in obscurity, but it seems safe to assume that the crime committed by the Seven was that of favouring one of the noble parties.

The year 1334 promised to be no less stormy than its predecessor. In January a Ghibelline was condemned for an armed attack on one of the Seven, and in April the authors of two more attacks— one of them on a Della Terza—purchased pardons.[4] The next day, the 20th, Napoleone was set upon in the street and murdered by Manno's son Corrado, Ugolino di Buonconte, and many of their supporters and servants.[5]

The murder of Napoleone set off a train of events that concludes with Manno's election as Gonfaloniere for life on May 14th, and there is sufficient evidence for the occurrences of these three weeks to make it possible to study the technique of a Signore's *coup d'état*. What is impossible is to decide whether the revolution was already planned when the murder took place, but it seems rather probable that Manno intended to exploit the situation arising out of the murder if it evolved in a manner favourable to him. The fact that the murder was apparently committed in cold blood (it is nowhere described as a revenge for an episode immediately preceding it), the degree of premeditation implied by the schemings of the next three weeks, and the proximity of the change of Captains of the Popolo (the obvious period for a *coup*) all suggests this. In any case Manno did not commit himself fully at this stage,

[1] Chr. 1333-54 (*Ephemerides*, p. 192); ACO, Rif. 1334, fo. 27.
[2] ACO, Rif. 1333, fos. 59-60 (July).
[3] *Ibid.*, fo. 6 (January); C.D., DCLIII.
[4] ACO, Lib. Cond. 1334, fos. 12v-13 and Rif. 1334, fos. 103v-105.
[5] Chr. cit. in *Ephemerides*, p. 192; C.D., DCLV.

for the murder was actually carried out by two members of a younger generation, Ugolino di Buonconte and Manno's son Corrado. Such was the effect of the murder and the standing of those involved that the commune allowed eight days to pass before a decision was reached about the punishment of the murderers. When it was announced the decision seemed almost ludicrously favourable to the guilty party, who perhaps began to regard their revolution as already achieved: the murderers were to pay a fine of 1,500 florins![1] This virtual acquittal was probably due to a decision by the Captain (with whom the matter principally rested) that in a prudent compromise lay the best hope of averting a *putsch* by Manno, though the influence of the commune's fiscal crisis is again to be noted. There is a flavour of defeatism about this policy, but events were to show that the Popolo had not yet abandoned an attitude of vigilance and suspiciousness.

The first phase of the revolution, the removal of Manno's principal rival, was now over. The next event was the arrival of the new Captain, the Florentine Giacomo dei Bardi, who took office on May 6th; thus the responsibility for the survival of the Popolo was thrust on to new shoulders in the middle of a crisis.[2] The first Council of the Popolo to be convened by the new Captain was held on the 9th, and firmer measures were decided upon; all those responsible for the murder of Napoleone were to go into exile, together with their leading sympathizers (including all Della Grecas) and Napoleone's two brothers and their chief supporters. The Captain was given command of a special force of twenty-five cavalry and seventy-five infantry, and he was to have extraordinary powers to punish all offences. Also a Gonfaloniere della Giustizia was to be chosen.[3] The nomination of exiles from both parties reveals that the policy of compromise with Manno was still being followed, but at least the Popolo had issued a distinct challenge and put itself in a state of armed emergency.

[1] *C.D.*, DCLV (Rif. of 28 April); the Rif. are the chief authority for the *coup d'état*, but it is referred to in Chr. 1333-54 (*Ephemerides*, p. 192), L. Manente (*ibid.*, pp. 432-3 *ad* 1333), F. Montemarte (*ibid.*, p. 216), G. Villani, lib. 11, cap. x and the Sienese Chrs. in RIS, N.S., xv, 6, p. 513.　　　　[2] ACO, Rif. 1334, fo. 133v.
[3] *Ibid.*, fos. 134-6v (extracts in Pardi, *Comune & Signoria*, app. 1). All the measures were approved by very large majorities. For the nature of the Gonfaloneria della Giustizia, see above, p. 108.

134

The next move clearly lay with Manno and it was probably now that he formulated a plan for the completion of his revolution in two phases. May 11th was the critical day on which the first stage was successfully carried out. At a meeting of the Council of the Popolo one of the Seven proposed, with the consent of his colleagues, that a debate should be held on the state of the contado and the need for constitutional reform (made evident by the 'brigas, dissensiones et scandala' of the past few days). Cecco di Guidetto della Terza then rose and proposed the suspension of no less than thirty-four clauses in the constitution, all of them safeguards against the radical measure he now put forward. This was the formation of a Balìa of twelve, to be chosen by the Captain and Seven and to receive, jointly with them, full powers in all matters concerning the welfare of the city, commune, and Popolo;[1] they were to be the sole legislative body of the commune (assuming the constitutional authority of the full Council of the Popolo), to appoint all officers, and to have the power to make war and peace. Should the Captain be unable to attend their meetings, or refuse to, their power was to be unaffected. This motion was passed by 102 votes to 4.

Although the Council of the Popolo had been carrying measures unfavourable to Manno only two days before, it had now approved by a large majority the move that led directly to his Signoria. Moreover the final clause of Della Terza's motion makes it clear that opposition from the Captain was expected; it was not simply a case of the Council being outwitted by Manno and not realizing that the new rulers of the commune would be favourable to him, on the contrary it was a conscious act of abdication. What had happened since the 9th to decide the Popolo to accept the tyranny of Manno will never be known; Pardi talks of intervention by hired troops,[2] but I can find no documentary support for this attractive hypothesis.

[1] ACO, Rif. 1334, fos. 137-43 (extracts in Pardi, Comune & Signoria, app. II). The Captain, Seven and twelve were to have 'bayliam . . . liberam et absolutam generaliter et particulariter totum et quicquid et omnia et singula que ad bonum statum, defensionem, custodiam et salutem dicte civitatis . . . et utilitatem communis et populi . . . noverint pertinere'.

[2] Comune & Signoria, p. 69.

The twelve were chosen on May 12th[1] and, as mentioned above, over half of them came from that small clique of ruling popular families who provided almost all the officers of the Popolo. Probably the Seven, like those of the previous year, were uninterested in the cause of the Popolo, but supported that of Manno. The election of twelve popolani favourable to his Signoria had almost certainly been organized by him as the next stage in the revolution. When the Seven and 12 met for the first time, on May 14th, the Captain, as anticipated, refused to attend. If he could not prevent the emasculation of the popular régime he could at least refuse to countenance the process by his presence. At the short, businesslike meeting on the 14th Manno and Ugolino di Buonconte were rewarded with the full powers so recently conferred on those who now passed them on and Manno was appointed Gonfaloniere del Popolo and Gonfaloniere della Giustizia for life, with plenary powers to be defined later; finally, he, his son Corrado, his nephew Monaldo di Berardo, and Ugolino were empowered to sit in all Councils, and to vote as ordinary members of them. The first clause was passed with one contrary vote, the rest unanimously.[2]

This was the final day of Manno's *coup d'état*, the third phase of which was now over. The absolution of the murderers and the haughty brushing aside of the Patrimony's tardy intervention[3] represent the beginning of the consolidation. If the Captain and those who had the cause of the Popolo at heart began now to ponder on the 'lessons of the campaign', they were clear enough.

[1] ACO, Rif. 1334, fo. 143 and v. The seven of the 12 coming from important popular families were Nallo di Cecco Della Terza, Cecco di Giannuccio Avveduti, Nuciarello di Ranieri Toste, Pietro di Meo di Nicola, Vannuccio di Pietro di Ranieri di Lodigerio, Giacomo di Angelo di Giacomo di Gerardo, and Cecco di Giacomo di Ranieri di Guglielmo.

[2] ACO, Rif. 1334, fos. 145-7v (extracts in Pardi, *op. cit.*, app. III). The clause relating to Manno alone runs: 'Quod supradictus Mannus domini Corradi sit et esse debeat ex nunc Vexillifer populi et Vexillifer iustitie civitatis Urbisveteris toto tempore vite sue et habeat et habere debeat toto dicto tempore illud et tantum offitium, arbitrium, potestatem, auctoritatem et bayliam que quot et quantas per presentes convenientes et ipsorum Consilium fuerint declarate et ordinate.'

[3] Rif. 1334, fos. 8-9 (4 June: the sentences are quashed). For the intervention of the Patrimony, Arch. Vat., Reg. Vat. Joh. XXII n. 117, fo. 278 and v; M. Antonelli, 'Notizie Umbre tratte dai Registri del Patrimonio', BRDSPU, IX, 1903, p. 482; Rif. of 16 May and 19 June cited in *Ephemerides*, p. 432-3n.

The Captain had been compelled to fight almost a lone battle against an astute opponent whose schemes were laid before ever the unfortunate Florentine set eyes on Orvieto. In any case his task was the hopeless one of saving an institution in spite of itself. The Popolo had always lacked coherence, and the real rulers of Orvieto were now clearly the Monaldeschi. With the family divided against itself, one branch seemed bound ultimately to prevail; the fiscal crisis and the situation in the contado called for determined measures, and when Manno offered himself as a strong man with a definite programme it is not surprising that the Popolo accepted him rather than face a continuation and perhaps intensification of the crisis.

There are two other factors, one of which certainly operated in favour of Manno, while the other probably did. The first is the support of his brother Beltramo, who had become Bishop of Orvieto in 1328, and was not only one of the principal adherents of the Signoria, but the heir-presumptive. He used the enormous influence of his position in favour of his brother.[1] The second is the conjectural support of Perugia. Manno's open advocacy of the cession of Chiusi to Perugia provides a *prima facie* case for this hypothesis, and one small piece of evidence supports it. On 15 April 1334 (five days before the murder of Napoleone) Orvieto received a letter from Perugia warning her that a Ghibelline attempt to capture the town was likely to take place in the near future.[2] Now nothing more is ever heard of these Ghibellines, which leads to the question whether they ever existed. Was Perugia assisting Manno's *coup d'état* by raising a false alarm, calculated to make the atmosphere of Orvieto yet more nervous, and to draw off the glances of suspicious eyes in the search for external threats instead of internal ones?

It remains to suggest which were the social elements whence Manno drew his support. In 1330, a year of famine, Manno had

---

[1] Pardi, *Comune & Signoria*, p. 77; for his unsuccessful attempt to succeed Manno in 1337, Chr. of F. Montemarte (*Ephemerides*, pp. 217-8). Bishop Beltramo is the earliest Orvietan personality of whom we have a definitely identified portrait. He appears (as donor) in the Magdalen panel of a polyptych painted by Simone Martini in 1320 which now hangs in the museum of the Opera del Duomo at Orvieto.

[2] ACO, Rif. 1334, fos. 91v-92.

made a loan of 1,000 florins expressly for the purchase of grain. This may imply a wooing of the populace, and the most important of all the popular families, the Della Terza, have already been described as his allies.[1] It was the Popolo that gave him extraordinary powers as Gonfaloniere for life, and most of the leading popolani continued to hold office under him. But Manno was not the conventional demagogic tyrant familiar to students of the Greek city-states. If the popolani served him, this was at least partly because they could not afford the honour and salt bread of exile, as Ghibelline nobles could; their financial situation compelled their consciences to compromise. Moreover the most prominent popular families, who provided so many of Manno's supporters, were essentially a middle-class, conservative, element. Their common interests and common outlook with the nobility were the most important cause of the Popolo's weakness, and though Manno may have had negative approval from the plebeian class, his active support came mainly from the popular bourgeoisie.

The chief enemies of the future Signore were of course his noble competitors. Napoleone, the hero of Chiusi, was the most eminent of these, but another power to be reckoned with was Ugolino di Buonconte, the head of the branch of Monaldeschi that had quarrelled with the Montemarte. Pardi suggests that until this quarrel broke out Ugolino and his father had been enemies of Manno, but that he then won them over;[2] they were certainly allies by 1333, when they made a joint loan to the commune and fought side by side against Napoleone at Chiusi, but their friendship did not long survive Manno's *coup d'état*, despite Ugolino's special powers under the Signoria.

The tyranny of Ermanno Monaldeschi marks the close of the history of the free commune, though a short and stormy interval elapsed between his death and Orvieto's integration into Cardinal Albornoz' strongly centralized States of the Church. The city at least had produced its own Signore, for Monaldeschi had lived in Orvieto for two hundred years or more, and in a way there

[1] See p. 121.
[2] *Comune & Signoria*, pp. 65-6. I have not been able to trace Pardi's authority for this statement, but Ugolino was an enemy of Napoleone in 1325 (see above, p. 122) and therefore at least a potential ally of Manno.

138

was little loss of continuity, since most of the popolani prominent in the politics of the previous periods maintained their position.[1] But the Signoria, the form adopted by the city-state in the attempt to survive in a new world of larger political entities, lies outside the scope of this investigation.

---

[1] ACO, Rif. 1334-7. An exception is Antonio di Lotto, a leading popolano who was exiled in 1335 (Rif. *ad an.*, fo. 51, July), but I have found no others.

ORVIETO IN THE AGE OF THE TYRANTS

AFTER 1334 Orvieto was no longer a democratic city-state, but the process of its absorption into the Patrimony was a gradual and painful one: not until the second half of the fifteenth century did the town's history lose its political flavour and lapse entirely into municipal mediocrity. For twenty years, until 1354, faction raged within Orvieto more fiercely than ever before. The city fell under a succession of tyrants, none of whom was able to resist for more than a few years the combined onslaught of his adversaries. The turning-point in Orvieto's loss of liberty was Cardinal Albornoz' reconquest of the Papal States. Economically exhausted and already deprived of most of its subject-territory, the town now ceased to count as an independent factor in Italian politics, though it was destined, through its strategic position, to play an occasional part in the disturbed history of Central Italy during the period of the condottieri.

In the years between 1334 and 1354 the crisis of the preceding period grew yet more acute, as the intensification and subdivision of factional hatred, together with plague and economic distress, worked upon a community already weakened by continuous warfare and the gradual loss of its contado. The lengthy absence of the papacy and the consequent chaos within the Patrimony took their toll and Orvieto found itself forced to relinquish much of its thirteenth-century empire. We have already seen Manno, its first tyrant, sign away Chiusi to the Perugians. The process whereby control was lost over the northern and western territory is obscure, since Orvieto seems usually to have lost the substance of power long before its former possessions were recognized as independent or ceded or sold to other towns. For much of the time exiled factions occupied and ruled parts of the contado, and sometimes they sought allies by recognizing the usurped suzerainty of Siena or Perugia in these areas. Certainly Cetona and Sarteano in Val di Chiana had been lost to Perugia by the second half of the fourteenth century, and Chianciano (in the same district) with S. Salvatore, Pian Castagnaio and Marsigliana in the Aldobrandeschine country to Siena. Later Sienese rule was recognized in Val d'Orcia and Val di Paglia, and probably the best that Orvieto could do was to gain some small financial consolation for these losses, as it did in 1374 when Monteleone and Montegabbione, already virtually lost, were sold to a Count Montemarte. The loss of the vast Aldobrandeschine contado is undocumented, but there is no mention of resistance by Orvieto to Count Guido Orsini later than Manno Monaldeschi's partially successful war of 1334-5.

Orvieto's economic decline, of which there is evidence as early as 1313 (many of the houses then destroyed were never rebuilt) coincides with the general recession of the period. The pestilence of 1348 struck the town with great force, and if we need not believe, with one chronicler, that nine-tenths of its population died, there is no need to doubt the statement of another that in that year no mill was working, while abandoned houses were destroyed and pillaged for firewood, so that Orvieto lay like a heap of ruins, dominated by its cathedral.

The succession of revolutions that occupied the twenty years after Manno's usurpation do not warrant detailed treatment. On Manno's death (in 1337) the Monaldeschi split into four parties who took their names respectively from the hind, the viper, the dog, and the eagle. Of these branches, the first descended from Manno and his brother Berardo, the second from Manno's erstwhile ally Buonconte, and the third from the murdered Napoleuccio. The sound and fury of the following years conceal a monotonously simple pattern: no single party was sufficiently strong to retain power in Orvieto, so that each in turn was overthrown by an alliance of enemies, internal and external. Thus in 1338 we find as 'Cavallieri del Popolo' and virtual tyrants of Orvieto Ugolino Monaldeschi (head of the Vipera faction) and his ally Count Pietro Montemarte. They are succeeded by Ugolino's brother Benedetto and Matteo Orsini, but a coalition of the other factions, known as the Beffati (or, later, Muffati) wages continual war on the Vipera

or Malcorini (later Mercorini). Attempts to exile all the parties
were made, but the issue of one of these attempts (in 1338) is
probably typical: after all the leaders had left the town one faction
broke its word and returned, thus becoming—according to legend
—the Malcorini (or 'faithless') while the 'deceived' parties outside
the town became the Beffati. In 1343 Benedetto di Buonconte
and Matteo Orsini were supplanted by a would-be neutral papal
governor, Bernardo del Lago, and in 1345, after Orsini's murder,
peace was at last made, under Sienese auspices, and the Beffati
readmitted. Siena's effort to keep the peace was a failure, for the year
1346 saw in control, in rapid succession, Benedetto di Buonconte
Monaldeschi, Corrado di Manno (della Cervara), and finally Count
Guido Orsini. The Beffati were in power for four years from 1347
(their authority being somewhat mitigated, at the instigation of
Perugia, by the re-introduction of some popular institutions after
1348), but there was a Malcorini coup in 1351 which restored
Benedetto di Buonconte, to whom his nephew Buonconte succeeded in the following year. 1352 was the last year in which a native
of the town ruled in Orvieto; Buonconte was superseded by his
kinsman Pietro (del Cane), and thereafter Orvieto fell under the
control first of the Visconti and (later in the same year) of the
lords of Vico. The resistance of the Prefetto di Vico to Cardinal
Albornoz involved Orvieto in war against the papal reconquest,
but in 1354 the Prefetto abandoned the struggle and the town
readily submitted to papal rule. The Council's decision to appoint
the cardinal as ruler of Orvieto for life (as the pope's vicar) was
approved, 'nemine surgente sed omnibus et singulis indifferenter
sedentibus'.

The frenzied years 1334-54 were followed by twenty-four years
of comparative peacefulness. The independence that had been
voluntarily abnegated in 1354 can hardly have been regretted.
Although the tradition of faction continued, it now ruled the
town's destinies less completely, and the quiet of this period must
have been some consolation for a further loss of power in the
contado.

The beginning of the Great Schism, in 1378, ushered in a new
period of strife in the Patrimony, though Orvieto, once a piece

on the Italian chess-board, was now merely one of the squares. In these years the town changed hands several times: originally Urbanist, it fell to Clementist troops in 1380, passed back to the Roman obedience in 1390 for one year, was recaptured by the Clementists and held by them (with the Perugian Michelotti as Signore) until 1398, when it finally reverted to Boniface IX. Within the cathedral chapter itself 'some prayed for Pope Boniface of Rome and some for Pope Clement of Avignon', but the townsmen themselves are more likely to have prayed for peace. The greatest scourge of these years was the band of Breton mercenaries which oppressed Orvieto and its area from 1380 to 1398. In 1380 they sacked the town, killing more than three thousand of its inhabitants and burning hundreds of houses. Much of Orvieto lay derelict in the ensuing years and many of the churches were abandoned; the number of hearths, which had been over three thousand in 1380, had fallen by 1397 to one thousand. During the siege of 1389, says a chronicler, the population fell to less than five hundred, and they were reduced to eating mice.

In the disturbed conditions of this period Orvieto, like most of the other towns of the Patrimony, lost to nobles of the countryside the last remnant of her contado,[1] but in the fifteenth century she still makes an occasional appearance on the historical stage. In 1413-4 Orvieto fought for John XXIII against King Ladislas of Naples, and fell to Ladislas in 1414. By 1415 the town was again in papal hands and was placed under the lordship of the celebrated condottiere Braccio da Montone in the years 1416-9. In the 1430s and 1440s Orvieto was twice lost to Eugenius IV, first when the Patrimony was invaded by Francesco Sforza, and on another occasion when rule was temporarily usurped by Antonio and Gentile Monaldeschi. Thereafter Orvieto showed no flicker of political independence.

Before we leave Orvieto, let us again glance at its condition in the fifteenth century, to point the contrast with the flourishing city of two hundred years before. The echo of departed glories

---

[1] The process whereby these towns yielded up their territory to feudal lords in the fourteenth and fifteenth centuries has been described in detail by Jean Guiraud in his *L'État Pontifical après le Grand Schisme.*

and of ancient hatreds even today lends to the town an atmosphere of tragedy which must then have been felt yet more strongly. A fifteenth-century chronicler described the Orvieto of his day; after giving a long list of houses destroyed in the many revolutions within the city, and of whole villages destroyed in what had once been its contado, he concludes with these words: 'Fuerunt etiam destructa multa alia castra, ville, turres fortilia ubique per comitatum . . . quasi pro maiori parte omnia sunt destructa, que vix possent numerari: et illa que erant comunis Urbisveteris devenerunt ad alios possessores. Et sic finitus.'

THE COUNCILS

O wing to the informal, improvisatory nature of all the institutions of the Italian city-states, it is an extremely hard task to trace the composition and evolution of the municipal Councils. The relevant evidence is indirect and, until the late thirteenth century, very fragmentary. Moreover some of the Councils were in origin Balie but came to acquire permanency; it is thus impossible to differentiate clearly between temporary committees and permanent Councils. In any case only the broad outlines of their development can be described, for it would require a whole volume to recount every tortuosity in the city's pliable constitution.

The characteristic organ of the nascent commune is the parliament, or 'arenga', of all the citizens, such as is known to have existed in Orvieto in 1170(*C.D.*,xl). The first reference to councillors occurs in a document of 1203 (*C.D.* lxxiv), when the Potestà of Orvieto signified the town's consent to a Sienese treaty 'de consilio et auctoritate omnium consiliarorum infrascriptorum eiusdem civitatis qui credentiam juraverunt et jurejurando tenebantur consulere'. The formula suggests that the council involved was a purely temporary body.

Not until the 1220s is there evidence of the existence of fixed Councils. In 1224 the Council of 100 met by order of the Potestà to give its advice concerning a monastic boundary dispute (*C.D.*, clxix). Its next recorded meeting, in 1225, was again in connection with a judicial matter (*ibid.*, clxxi), and in 1226 both this Council of 100 and a Council of 400 were consulted by the commune's judge (*ibid.*, clxxv). There is no clue as to the composition of these Councils.

A most important stage in the development of the permanent Councils is their acquisition of competence in diplomatic affairs. Both the Greater Council (whose numbers had now decreased to 200) and the Lesser Council took part in the peace negotiations with Siena in 1232, by which time they were officially recognized as the representatives of the city. When a papal emissary came with a message for the 'Popolus' of Orvieto and demanded to speak to the whole population he was assured by the Potestà that this would be unnecessary 'quia Consilium hic adunatum gerit vicem totius populi . . . et per ipsos (sc. consiliarios) regitur civitas, et quicquid per eos fit firmum habetur et ratum, et quid nobis hic congregatis dicitis toti populo dicitis, et quid nos respondemus vobis pro toto populo respondemus' (*C.D.*, CII).

The Potestà's statement, which gives the first clear definition of the Councils' status, is also the first clue to their composition, for it mentions that they included officials of the Arti and 'anteregiones'(representatives of each 'rione' of the city). Thenceforth the two Councils always included delegates of both these elements, though their nomenclature alters in bewildering fashion; the Arti were usually represented by Rettori or Capitudini of the Arti and Società, the 'quartieri' or 'rioni' not only by Anterioni but at times by Gonfalonieri (standard-bearers) and Conestabili. By 1247 the Councils of 200 and 100, though still convened by the head of the commune, the Potestà, and apparently presided over by him, had become known as the Councils of the Popolo (*C.D.*, CCLXIV, CCLXVI, CCLXXIII, CCLXXVII). At the same time an inner Council of twenty-four representatives of the Arti came into being; it often met in conjunction with the two larger Councils. The last stage in the development of the Council of the Popolo is the addition to it of the Capitano del Popolo. In 1264 the Capitano sat in the General Council, together with his Anziani (there is no evidence as to the nature of his office), but the meeting was still convoked and presided over by the Potestà (*C.D.*, CCCLXXXVII).

Although known as the Councils of the Popolo, these Councils appear to have been regarded as organs both of the Commune and of the Popolo—or perhaps of each on different occasions—for even in the fourteenth century they sometimes met under the Potestà. By that period, however, it was normally the Capitano who summoned the Councils and put forward proposals in them, though these always required the approval of the Seven. Clearly the Seven were by then the dominant power in the Council meetings; the Potestà was rarely present and the Capitano, though his attendance was required by the constitution (*v.p.* 135), had ceased to exert much influence except during the two captaincies of Poncello Orsini and the attempted reform of 1332-4.

The structure of the conciliar machine may be compared to that of an onion. It consisted of a central core, whose members (the Capitano and Seven) had to be present at every Council meeting, while around this there existed a succession of layers, and the numbers of these that would be called to a given meeting varied in accordance with the nature of the business to be transacted. Very frequently the Capitano and Seven met with the Inner Council (or Consiglio di Credenza), which normally numbered twenty-four (occasionally sixteen). This Council was at times reinforced by the presence of the consular representatives of all the Arti; it then numbered about sixty, and was known as the Council of the Consuls of the Arti. Other components of the greater Councils were the councillors (or non-consular delegates) of the Arti, and the 'anterioni'; the latter usually numbered either forty or sixty, a quarter of them from each 'quartiere' of the city. Neither the number nor the exact composition of either of the two largest standing Councils, the Consiglio Generale and the Consiglio Speciale, is ever defined, but probably the normal strength of the former was 300 and of the latter 200.

Almost all the councillors mentioned in the last paragraph were 'popolani', the only exception being the nobles admitted to membership of the Council of forty between 1319 and 1333 (pp. 103, 120 and 127). Yet the noble representation in Council meetings was often quite high, since it was extremely common for Balie to be present at Council meetings. A 'Council of forty nobles and popolani' (which is not the same as that of the forty popolani referred to above, for the two are mentioned separately in the same document) frequently formed part of the Greater Councils; its constitutional origin and status is obscure, but not improbably it started as a Balia dedicated to the consideration of some special matter and somehow acquired permanence. This is supported by the frequency of Council meetings of the Capitano, the Seven, and a Balia (whose membership was often thirty-two, or forty); only the Consiglio di Credenza (the twenty-four) seems to have met more often.

Information concerning the election of councillors is available only for the period after 1295, and this subject too has to be treated in outline owing to the commune's incurable experimentalism.

The Seven, who were officers of the Popolo and commune rather than councillors, were normally selected from the Consuls of each Arte in turn, from a roster of the twenty-five Arti; the term of office was two months, so that each Arte supplied a member of the Seven approximately every six months. At certain periods only some of the Seven were selected this way, and others (at first one, later three) co-opted from the members of the Council of forty popolani; after 1326 they were all chosen by lot from a list of 336 prominent popolani (p. 103). The Seven themselves nominated their innermost circle of advisers, the twenty-four 'di credenza', while the various Guild representatives were of course elected within the Arti. The forty or sixty delegates of the 'quartieri' were chosen by a system of indirect election. The ten or fifteen members for each 'quartiere' were usually named by the four 'mediani' for that 'quartiere', who had themselves been chosen either by the Seven or by the Consiglio Generale, according to fluctuations in the constitution. This system is typical of the commune's widespread use of indirect election.

Both this tendency and the intricacy of the constitution are well illustrated by a characteristic decision of 1317 (Rif., Sept., fos. 38v-40) concerning the election of the sixty regional councillors. The Consuls of the Arti and the fifteen representatives of each 'quartiere' (in the sixty for the present half-year) were together to choose sixteen mediani, four per 'quartiere': the mediani for each 'quartiere' were then, in conjunction with the four Captains of the Parte Guelfa, to elect the fifteen representatives of that 'quartiere' for the next half-yearly period.

APPENDIX II

THE GOVERNMENT OF THE CONTADO

THE commune's relations with its subject-territory would require a volume of their own if the question were to be treated adequately. Again the evidence is fragmentary, but it is sufficient for the purpose of this Appendix, which is to give a brief outline of the organization of Orvieto's possessions, of the commune's legal rights in them and its actual powers, and of their value as a source of revenue and military aid.

The contado consisted partly of 'terrae' or 'castra' submitted by their feudal lord or their commune, partly of 'pleberia' (parishes), which were the country districts and villages possessing no governmental organs of their own and thus directly subject to Orvieto. These un-attached rural districts were divided topographically into 'pleberia', each of which was ruled by a 'Viscomes', appointed by Orvieto every six months. It is not known when the system of 'pleberia' came into use, but they are first mentioned in 1278, when a Potestà ordered a 'reinventio confinium omnium et singulorum pleberiorum comitatus urbevetani' (two copies of this are extant in ACO, in 'Istrumentario Sottop. I' and in Cod. De Bustolis, fos. 191-9). In 1278 there were thirty-one 'pleberia', but soon after this they were reorganized, for in 1292 the area was divided into only twenty 'pleberia' (ACO, census of contado *ad annum*). The office of the Viscounty was farmed out, normally to an Orvietan, though on occasions the 'pleberium' itself purchased the right to appoint its own Viscount.

Apart from the institution of the Viscounts there was little difference between the status of the territory directly subject to the commune and that of the 'terrae' submitted by their lord or municipality. Each was compelled to submit its statutes annually to Orvieto for approbation and to obtain the commune's consent to any important legislative measures. The degree of independence granted to the judicature of subject bodies varied considerably. It is curious that few submissions included among their terms any definition of the powers of Orvieto's law-court over its new subjects, but that of Soana in 1216 (*C.D.*, cv) was an exception: it laid down that all cases involving fines of over sixty soldi and all appeals were to be heard at Orvieto. In 1276 it was enacted that all contado lawsuits were to be tried at Orvieto, except that the courts of Acquapendente, Chianciano, Sarteano and Cetona were granted competence in cases involving fines of over ten lire (Chr.

Pot. 2, *Ephemerides*, p. 148); this decision does not seem to have remained effective, for in 1300 we find the Viscounts of the 'pleberia' being deprived of their right to try all cases involving less than twenty-five lire (Rif. 1300, fo. 116).

Obviously the independence of the components of Orvieto's empire varied very widely in accordance with their nature. A fair-sized town like Chiusi, Acquapendente, or Bolsena with an intricate municipal organization of its own and its own political tradition required different treatment from a small village or country district. These towns themselves possessed much the same institutions as Orvieto; Chiusi had its own Parte Guelfa, Bolsena its Popolo and guilds (Rif. 1295, fo. 17, August), and so on. Every town of the contado remained a legal corporation and retained its own property ('communalia') and the right to hold Council meetings, and the larger ones even had commercial reprisals granted against them.[1] Since Orvieto appointed the Potestà of all towns in the contado, the power given to the subject-communes was not really subtracted from its own.[2]

Each town was in principle responsible for its own defence (Rif. 1298, fo. 32, May, etc.), but the exigencies of war often compelled Orvieto to strengthen local garrisons. Indeed the realities of political power are far more relevant to an assessment of Orvieto's control over its subject-territory than are the precise definitions of inoperative legal documents. A certain degree of disorder was endemic in the contado, but the situation did not become critical until the fourteenth century. The Aldobrandeschine lands were always the most vulnerable part of Orvieto's territory, owing to their distance from the city, but until 1284 they were ruled by a Count and the commune's weakness did not result in chaos. Not many records of the Orvietan law-court are extant for the period before 1334, but from those that have survived it would seem that it was not uncommon for 'contadini' to appear when cited before the commune's court, though a great many failed to do so. In the same way dependent communes and 'pleberia' submitted their statutes and legislation for approval on many occasions, but certainly not regularly. That Orvieto so rarely complained of this lack of punctiliousness suggests that it was little disposed to pick a quarrel so long as relations continued to be smooth.

In the thirteenth century the only challenger to the contado, Siena, was beaten off in a series of wars. Orvieto's rule was no less efficient in the following century, but the pressure upon it had increased enor-

---

[1] A system was current whereby the default of merchants could be compensated by the legal seizure of an equivalent amount of money or goods from other merchants of the same town. For the application of this to Bolsena, *v.* Theiner, DLXXV.

[2] In the fourteenth century some of the contado Potestà-ships were allotted to the Arti in rotation, on the same principle as membership of the Seven (*v.* App. I, p. 147).

mously. The crisis in the contado which came to a head in 1332-4 is described in Chapter xv; its principal causes were the pretensions of Perugia to Orvieto's possessions in the Val di Chiana and the chronic anarchy of the Tuscan Patrimony after the migration of the papal Curia.

The commune's wealth was derived to a very large extent from the contado. Each subject agreed on submission to pay an annual 'census', but the sum involved was often small. More important sources of revenue were the hearth-tax (which was paid annually by Acquapendente as early as 1207—C.D., LXXIX—and throughout the Aldobrandeschine contado after 1216—ibid., CVI) and the 'lira' (the normal form of direct taxation) which was frequently applied to the whole contado.

The amount of land owned directly by the commune was very considerable. Orvieto began to acquire 'communalia' in the twelfth century, for the occasion (but not the main cause) of the early wars with Acquapendente was disagreement over the ownership of the Monte Rofeno 'communalia' which were situated half-way between the two towns (Ephemerides, p. 279). The most important purchases made later were those of Bisenzio in 1215 (C.D., XCIX) and of two large towns in the Val di Chiana, Cetona in 1256-60 (ibid., CCCXXXIII and CCCLXXII) and Sarteano in 1280 (Fumi, Chianciano, notes to doc. XVI). After 1303 the commune regularly leased out the grazing-rights of the Aldobrandeschine lands, which seem to have been a very notable source of revenue.

It was the duty of the contado to feed its overlord, and every grain-producing area within it was obliged to bring grain to Orvieto. The amount required was laid down in accordance with the normal yield of the zone in question, and in no case was the export of food outside the Orvietan contado permitted. The Val di Chiana was rich in grain, but the produce of the contado was not always sufficient, and in years of shortage the possession of the port of Orbetello was an invaluable aid in the importation of grain (Rif. 1303, fos. 20, 26-7, March, etc.).

Finally the contado furnished military aid, in men and provisions. Whenever a major campaign was planned, troops were demanded of Orvieto's subject-towns and nobles. This was probably the greatest service performed by the commune's baronial dependants, who often provided large contingents of cavalry. Of the towns, those in the Val di Chiana were the most frequently called upon, though the Val del Lago was also a valuable source of troops. Aid in provisions was requested from any part of the contado where there was an Orvietan military force (an example during the 1293 campaign against Orsello Orsini is C.D., DL).

THE ORIGINS OF THE MONALDESCHI
AND FILIPPESCHI
(See also Genealogical Tables I and II)

LUCA MANENTE, the fifteenth-century chronicler, introduces Orvieto's great Guelf and great Ghibelline family into his history under the year 1200, and at the same time finds an origin for their contention. Two sisters of the Prefetti di Vico, he relates, inherited the property of their family after a brother had been outlawed and put to death; one of them married Monaldo Monaldeschi, the other Ranuccio Filippeschi, and the descendents of these two leading Orvietan nobles shared the inheritance, which was for ever a cause of enmity between them (*Ephemerides*, p. 280).

There is no direct documentary confirmation of this tale, but several pieces of evidence suggest that it contains an element of truth. Two members of the family of the Prefetti appear to have been involved in the murder of Pietro Parenzo in 1199; many of the guilty are known to have fled to Rispampani, a fief of the Prefetti (*Parenzo*, § 12) and in 1201 Tebaldo and Goffredo de' Prefetti were deprived of the tenure of Rocca Sberna, a fortress near Orvieto (*C.D.*, LXII). It is also confirmed that the Monaldeschi had acquired possession of Rocca Sberna at least as early as 1211 (*Ephemerides*, p. 212). The support given by this documentary evidence to Manente's version (which was no doubt the accepted tradition at a period when the struggle between Monaldeschi and Filippeschi was within living memory) suggests that two facts can be accepted: both families came into prominence at the beginning of the thirteenth century, and the rise of the Monaldeschi was connected with the confiscations following the martyrdom of Pietro Parenzo.

The first certain reference to a member of either family in a deed still extant is one to Pietro di Cittadino, the ancestor of the Monaldeschi; in 1157 he held some land by the river Paglia (*C.D.*, XXXVII). This Pietro di Cittadino is mentioned in several other documents, the last occasion being in 1195 (AVO, Cod. B, fo. 114).

There is no evidence concerning the wealth of Pietro di Cittadino, except that he also held land at Pantano, near Orvieto (*C.D.*, XLVI). Much more is known of his three sons and especially of the one, Monaldo, who was to give his name to the family. This Monaldo and one of his peasants were among those miraculously cured through the intervention of S. Pietro Parenzo in the first months after his martyrdom (May 1199) and the terms in which Monaldo is described by the contemporary author of the Legenda (a canon of Orvieto) are of great interest. He is 'dominus Monaldus, nobilis civis urbevetanus, sapiens, humilis, potens et divitiis perhabundans' and his family are 'nobiles viri' (§ 22-3). The status of the Monaldeschi at this period is also indicated by the signature of diplomatic agreements 'in palatio Monaldescorum' in 1200 and 1203 (C.D., LXX and LXXIV). Evidently the family was established by the turn of the century as one of the wealthiest and most respected in Orvieto.

The fact that it was Monaldo and not his father who gave his name to the family suggests that it only acquired this position with his generation. He was the first Monaldeschi to play a prominent part in the affairs of the commune, which he represented in 1210 and 1215 in important diplomatic negotiations (C.D., LXXXII and c).

Beltramo and Simone, the brothers of Monaldo, seem to have played little part in public life, but his mantle was worthily assumed by his son Pietro. The distinguished career of Pietro included tenure of the consulate in 1211-2 and 1219-20 (C.D., pp. 59, 85, etc.), of the Potestà-ship of Acquapendente in 1223 (ibid., p. 108), and in 1226 the Potestà-ship of Siena, a highly responsible post (RIS, N.S., XV, 6, p. 47). He was wounded and captured in the fighting against Siena in 1229, and died a prisoner (Ephemerides, p. 143, etc.).

The most prominent of Pietro's cousins was Cittadino di Beltramo, whose public life stretches over the period 1223-68. The offices he held included the consulate (Ephemerides, p. 150) and the priorate of the Popolo (C.D., pp. 191 et seq.), and he was Potestà of Rieti in 1263 (Potthast, n. 18515, etc.). Cittadino's brothers Monaldo (who was Treasurer to the commune in 1238: C.D., p. 158) and Trasmondo donated the site on which was built S. Domenico, the first church in Italy to be dedicated to that saint (Ephemerides, p. 291n.).

Other Monaldeschi to attain distinction before the middle of the thirteenth century included two grandsons of Pietro di Monaldo, Giordano and another Monaldo, and Buonconte, a son of Monaldo di Beltramo. This Buonconte was a Consul in 1241 (C.D., p. 170), Rettore del Popolo in 1251 (ibid., p. 186), Rettore dei Malefici in 1266 (ibid., p. 252) and joint Rettore della Città in 1269 (ibid., p. 295, etc.); in 1260 he was elected Capitano del Popolo at Florence, but owing to the defeat of Montaperti he never assumed office (Degli Azzi, I, 255).

The purpose of these rather monotonous biographies of early Monaldeschi has been to suggest that by the second half of the thirteenth century the family had attained a commanding position in the politics of Orvieto. Their quarrel with the Filippeschi can be traced back as far as 1240, when there was a lawsuit between the two families (C.D.,

CCLI), but it did not continue uninterrupted, for in 1248 some Filippeschi acted as guarantors for the Monaldeschi's peaceful tenure of Rocca Sberna (*C.D.*, CCLXXVI). By the 1260s the tradition of hatred between the families was already a strong one. Its development in the next half-century is described in Chapters VIII–XI.

The Filippeschi take the stage with less of a flourish. The first identifiable member of the family, Bartolomeo di Filippo, was a contemporary of the first Monaldo Monaldeschi (di Pietro di Cittadino), but his father Filippo, who gave the family its name, was presumably a person of some importance. This Bartolomeo, who is mentioned in a number of documents between 1202 (*Calef. Vecch.*, I, 74) and 1222 (*C.D.*, p. 99, etc.), had four sons, of whom only one, Enrico, played a really large part in the affairs of the commune.

Enrico was a Consul in 1213–4 and 1241 (*C.D.*, pp. 66–9 and 170), conducted the defence of Carnaiola on behalf of the commune in about 1239, and acted as its representative in an embassy to Rome and probably to Florence (*ibid.*, pp. 111–2 and 165–6). Two of Enrico's brothers, Filippo and Guido, acted jointly with him in the embassy and the defence of Carnaiola. The 'Giovanni di Bartolomeo' who was 'conestabile militum' in 1216 (*ibid.*, p. 74) may have been yet another brother.

It is clear that in the first half of the century the Filippeschi were less numerous than the Monaldeschi and played a far less conspicuous part in the political life of the commune. In this period only six of them are mentioned in extant documents, against fifteen Monaldeschi; and Enrico alone had a career that could compare in length and distinction with those of his principal Monaldeschi contemporaries. No family could approach the Monaldeschi in wealth and influence. Although the comparison relates to a later period, and the wealth of both families lay primarily in agricultural land, it is noteworthy that in 1292 Monaldeschi property within Orvieto (which far outstripped that of any other family) was valued at four times the property of the Filippeschi (Pardi, *Catasto, passim*).

One cannot leave the Guelf and Ghibelline families without a reference to the survival of their struggle in the rival theories propounded by historians to explain 'what they fought each other for'.

To the nineteenth-century historian the Ghibelline was a feudal warrior, living for preference in a mountain castle, a German by descent and reactionary by his inborn antipathy to the urban bourgeoisie; his Guelf enemy represented the 'forces of the future', a town-dweller, merchant, and democrat. To some extent the nineteenth century abolished this misconception by its own history, for at its close the contest with the German invader no longer dominated the Italian scene. Thus the socialist Salvemini in his *Magnati e Popolani a Firenze*, published in 1899, continues to judge the thirteenth century in the light of the nineteenth, but since the Risorgimento has not solved all Italy's problems the Guelfs will no longer do for his heroes. He denies the identification of Guelfism with democracy, virtually equates Guelf with Ghibelline, and conjures up a truly democratic third party, the Popolo!

Nothing suggests that the struggle between Orvieto's Ghibellines and her Guelfs was one between opposed economic interests or *Weltanschauungen*. The Filippeschi, it is true, were large landowners, and are not heard of as traders. But the Monaldeschi refuse to fit into the part assigned them. Certainly they were merchants (their 'fundicus' is first mentioned in 1247: ACO, Lib. Don., fo. 3v), but the bulk of their wealth was probably derived from their vast agricultural holdings in the contado.

The concentration of Filippeschi land is interesting. Almost all of it was situated in one area north of Orvieto, around Ficulle, Fabro and Salci (*Ephemerides*, pp. 313 and 318, etc., etc.). The property of the Monaldeschi was much more spread out. The fact that a good deal of it was situated at Bolsena and south of Orvieto (ACO, Rif. 1318, fo. 82v; Dottarelli, doc. XLII; etc.) might suggest that the Monaldeschi's pro-papal sentiments were connected with the advisability of keeping on good terms with both claimants to the Val del Lago, and a chronicler confirms the truth of this hypothesis for a rather later period.[1]

The conflict between the factions doubtless took on economic as well as political forms as vengeance and the memory of old wrongs built up a tradition of hatred which (as in 1313) was easily ignited by a spark from without. But the rivalry and pride underlying the conflict were only the equivalent within the narrow society of a town of the same pugnacity which at other times has found its outlet in wider fields.

---

[1] 'Li figlioli di messer Ormanno non si volivano impacciare con questa guerra perchè la maggior parte delle loro chastella stavano nel distretto del Patrimonio, sì che non volivano essere contra la Chiesia' (*Ephemerides*, p. 62, *ad* 1353).

THE CAREER OF CARDINAL THEODERIC
(See pp. 71-2)

CARDINAL THEODERIC of Orvieto was a personage of considerable importance during the pontificate of Boniface VIII; Boase describes him (p. 127) as 'one of Boniface's most trusted servants'. It therefore seems worth while collecting in one place the few facts that are known concerning his career.

Theoderic's father was named Giovanni di Bonaspeme (see Genealogical Table III), but his family is usually referred to as that of the 'Ranieri'. In 1275 Theoderic was Prior of S. Andrea, the municipal church of Orvieto. In this capacity he apparently met and impressed Martin IV during the latter's stay at Orvieto, for he was made a papal chaplain and a collector of papal taxes in Germany (*Reg. M. IV*, nos. 244-5, etc.). Theoderic continued to hold these offices under Honorius IV (*Reg. Hon. IV*, nos. 114-6, etc.) and Nicholas IV (*Reg. Nich. IV*, nos. 151, 2516-8). Celestine V appointed him Archbishop-elect of Palermo, but he was transferred by Boniface VIII to the see of Pisa (*Reg. B. XI, n.* 235: *Reg.B.VIII*, n. 390). In February 1297 he became a papal chamberlain, and in December of the following year a cardinal (*Reg. B. VIII*, n. 1549; Chr. Pot. 4, p. 171; Potthast n. 24752, which has 'Viterbensis' in error for 'Urbevetanus'). Thereafter the Pope showered benefices on Theoderic, on his numerous nephews, and on his brother Zampo (who became Bishop of Soana in 1302). In 1299 Cardinal Theoderic was entrusted with the organization of the military campaign against Giovanni di Ceccano in the Campagna. In June a new town, Città Papale, was founded by Boniface to replace destroyed Palestrina, and Theoderic became its first Cardinal-Bishop (Boase, p. 182). In the same year he became Rector of the Tuscan Patrimony, an office he held until late in 1300 (*Reg. B. VIII*, nos. 3417, 3905, 5549; Chr. Pot. 4, p. 172). This was the last occasion on which he was entrusted with special duties. He survived his master and died on 7 December 1306.

It is clear that Cardinal Theoderic occupied a very special position in connection with Boniface's central Italian schemes. Not only was he a sort of 'Adviser on Aldobrandeschine and Orvietan Affairs' to the pope, but he never forgot his place of birth and was always ready to press its claims on the pope and Curia. The possession of an unofficial but influential representative at the Curia was obviously of great assistance to Orvieto. Thus a mysterious payment of 600 florins made by the commune to Cardinal Theodoric in December 1298 (*C.D.*, DLXXXIV) was probably a recompense for some service rendered. It was Theodoric who urged Orvieto to attack the Countess Margherita and Guy of S. Fiora in 1299 (p. 72), and he was a witness to the signature of many of the deeds concerning Orvieto's pacification with Todi in 1300-1 (*C.D.*, pp. 376, 379, etc.). His greatest service to the commune, though it bore no fruit, was his secret intimation of the possibility of securing papal recognition for Orvietan rule over the Aldobrandeschine contado (p. 73). Another characteristic gesture was his speedy action in letting Orvieto know of the pope's return to Rome after the outrage of Anagni. The commune's cynical attack on the Aldobrandeschine lands, undertaken as soon as it knew the pope to be in trouble, must surely have been a source of dismay to Theodoric, who now saw the two masters whom he had striven to serve at war with each other. But cardinals in his day were experienced in the affairs of the world, and it is to be doubted whether his surprise was as great as his dismay. Of Theodoric's own personality nothing is known. No chronicler has given him so much as a phrase. It is clear from the nature of his own career and from those of his distinguished nephews, Ranieri and Benedetto, that there was much administrative ability in the family, but there is no information concerning any other aspect of his character.

THE ARTI

THE following is a list of the twenty-five Arti c. 1300 (from Pardi, *Comune & Signoria*, pp. 18-9).

1. Judges and notaries.	13. Pork-butchers ('pizzicagnoli').
2. Merchants.	14. Carpenters.
3. Woollen manufacturers.	15. Millers.
4. Hosiers.	16. Dealers in oil and salt.
5. Mercers.	17. Rope-makers.
6. Butchers.	18. Inn-keepers.
7. Smiths.	19. Greengrocers.
8. Tanners.	20. Barbers.
9. Tailors.	21. Manufacturers of quicklime.
10. Masons.	22. Potters.
11. Fishmongers and poulterers.	23. Tile-makers.
12. Tavern-keepers.	24. Manufacturers of mill-stones.

25. Muleteers.

By 1316 there was also a guild of goldsmiths, and in the same year the doctors were included in the Arte of judges and notaries.

BIBLIOGRAPHY

Where works are referred to in the text in an abbreviated form this is given in brackets after the title.

SOURCES

Documents

Auvray, L. (ed.). *Les Registres de Grégoire IX*, Paris, 1896-. (*Reg. G. IX*).

Caetani, G. *Regesta Chartarum* (in *Documenti dell'Archivio Caetani*), vols. I-II, 1922. (*Regesta Chartarum*).

Cecchini, G. (ed.) *Il Caleffo Vecchio del Comune di Siena*, vols. I-III, Siena, 1931-40. (*Calef. Vecch.*).

Cerlini, A. 'Carte Orvietane dell'Archivio Farnese' in *Boll. R. Dep. St. Patr. per l'Umbria*, XXXVII, 1940 and XLII, 1944.

Ciacci, G. *Gli Aldobrandeschi nella Storia e nella 'Divina Commedia*,' vol. II, Rome, 1935. (Ciacci).

Costantini, N. *Memorie Storiche di Acquapendente*, Rome, 1903. (Costantini).

Degli Azzi-Vitelleschi, G. *Le Relazioni tra la Repubblica di Firenze e l'Umbria nei secoli XIII e XIV secondo i documenti del R. Arch. di Stato di Firenze* (2 vols.), Perugia, 1904-9. (Degli Azzi).

Digard, G., Thomas, A., Faucon, M., Fawtier, R. (eds.). *Les Registres de Boniface VIII*, Paris, 1890-. (*Reg. B. VIII*).

École Française de Rome (eds.). *Les Registres de Martin IV*, Paris, 1901-. (*Reg. M. IV*).

Fumi, L. *Codice Diplomatico della Città d'Orvieto*, Florence, 1884. (*C.D.*).

Fumi, L. *Il Duomo d'Orvieto e i suoi Restauri*, Rome, 1891.

Fumi, L. *Gli Statuti di Chianciano*, Orvieto, 1874. (Fumi, *Chianciano*).

Fumi, L. *Gli Statuti e Regesti dell'Opera di S. Maria d'Orvieto*, Rome, 1891. (*Statuti . . . dell'Opera di S. Maria*).

Gay, J. (ed.), *Les Registres de Nicholas III*, Paris, 1898-. (*Reg. Nich. III*).

Grandjean, C. (ed.), *Les Registres de Benoît XI*, Paris, 1883-. (*Reg. B. XI*).

Gualterio, F. A. (ed.), *La Cronaca di F. Manente* (documents appended), Turin, 1846. (Gualterio).

Guiraud, J. (ed.), *Les Registres d'Urbain IV*, Paris, 1901—(*Reg. Urb. IV*).

Guiraud, J. (ed.), *Les Registres de Grégoire X*, Paris, 1892—(*Reg. G. X*).

Jordan, E. (ed.), *Les Registres de Clément IV*, Paris, 1893—(*Reg. Cl. IV*).

Langlois, E. (ed.), *Les Registres de Nicholas IV*, Paris, 1886-. (*Reg. Nich. IV*).

Libri dell'Entrata e dell'Uscita della Repubblica di Siena (XVII vols.), Siena, 1907-42. (*Entr. & Usc. Siena*).
Migne, J. P. (ed.), *Regesta Innocentii III* (*Patrologia Latina*, vols. 214-7), Paris, 1855.
Potthast, A. *Regesta Pontificum Romanorum*, Berlin, 1875. (Potthast).
Pressutti, P. (ed.), *Regesta Honorii Papae III*, Rome, 1888. (*Reg. Hon. III*).
Prou, M. (ed.), *Les Registres d'Honorius IV*, Paris, 1898-. (*Reg. Hon. IV*).
Regestum Clementi Papae V, Rome, 1885. (*Reg. Cl. v*).
Regestum Reformationum Comunis Perusii ab anno MCCLVI ad annum MCCC, (vol. 1 only published, 1256-60), Perugia, 1935. (*Reg. Per.*).
Theiner, A. *Codex Diplomaticus Dominii Temporalis Sanctae Sedis*, vol. I, Rome, 1861. (Theiner).
Ughelli, F. *Albero e Istoria della Famiglia dei Conti di Marsciano*, Rome, 1677. (Ughelli).
Valle, G. della. *Storia del Duomo di Orvieto*, Rome, 1791. (Della Valle).

Chronicles

In *Ephemerides Urbevetanae*, ed. Fumi, L., in *Rerum Italicarum Scriptores*, new series, Città di Castello, 1904-.' (*Ephemerides*):
(1) 'Chronica Antiqua' (also printed in Gualterio and in MGH, vol. XIX) 1161-1313. (Chr. Ant.).
(2) 'Chronica Potestatum', 1194-1224. (Chr. Pot. 1).
(3) Ditto, 1161-1276. (Chr. Pot. 2).
(4) Ditto, 1233-1260. (Chr. Pot. 3).
(5) Ditto, 1255-1322. (Chr. Pot. 4).
(The above chronicles are on the whole very reliable though the entry under many years consists of nothing but the name of the Potestà. There are some errors, especially in names—thus Chr. Pot. 1 confuses Parenzo with his brother Pietro. A version of Chr. Pot. 1-4 with many misreadings was published by G. F. Gamurrini in *Arch. St. Italiano*, s. V, 3, 1875, under the heading 'Le Cronache di Orvieto').
(6) 'Cronaca di Luca di Domenico Manente' (1174-1325 and 1375-1413). (L. Manente).
(This Italian chronicle, written in the early fifteenth century, is unreliable, especially for the twelfth century, but as the chronicler approaches his own times he becomes sounder. Nevertheless even some early passages have the appearance of being based on documents now lost, and it is here that Manente's value lies. He commits many anachronisms and can only be used with great

caution, especially on the factions (see p. 51 n.). When the documents he has used are extant they often confirm Manente, but some he misunderstood completely. He provides a plausible explanation of many of the agreements, etc., that he mentions, but this was the task he set himself to fulfil even when the history behind a document was unknown to him; at times he is clearly relying upon his imagination. The chronicle lacks the years 1325-75, but the missing part can be reconstructed from the *Historie* of Luca's nephew Cipriano, given in *Ephemerides*, pp. 415 et seq.).

(7) 'Cronaca di Francesco di Montemarte' (1333-1400).
(This fourteenth-century chronicle has some interesting references to Orvieto's quarrel with Todi over Montemarte in the thirteenth century and to the rôle of the Montemarte family in the internal dissensions of the Monaldeschi after 1321).

(8) Extracts from a lost chronicle cited in M. Monaldeschi's *Commentari Historici di Orvieto*, Venice, 1584.
(Unfortunately little has survived of this chronicle, which is very detailed in such parts as are extant; the account of the fighting of August 1313 is particularly valuable. The author has a strong pro-Guelf bias.)

OTHER ORVIETAN CHRONICLES

'Una Continuazione Orvietana della Cronaca di Martin Polono', ed. Fumi, L. in *Archivio Muratoriano*, fasc. 14, Città di Castello, 1914. (Cont. Orv. Polono).
(Certainly written at Orvieto, probably towards the middle of the fourteenth century, v. Fumi's introduction, pp. 99-111. It is partly based on earlier chronicles. It is reliable on the whole but contains several small errors such as the statement that Neri della Greca died soon after the rising of 1284. Has a strong pro-papal bias.)

La Cronaca del Vescovato Orvietano scritta dal Vescovo Ranieri, ed. Perali, P., Orvieto, 1907. (*Chr. Ranieri*).
(A very brief chronicle, invaluable for the history of Orvieto's bishops before c. 1230).

Chronique du Couvent des Prêcheurs d'Orvieto, ed. Girardin, P. M., and Viel, A. M., Rome and Viterbo, 1907. (Caccia).
(Lives of the most prominent Dominicans of Orvieto, written in the first half of the fourteenth century by a friar named Caccia. It contains much information that is of interest for the history of the commune.)

S. Pietro Parenzo. La Leggenda scritta dal Maestro Giovanni, ed. Natalini, A., Rome, 1936. (*Parenzo*).
(Also in the *Acta Sanctorum*, *ad* 21 May.) (See Chapter II.)

OTHER CHRONICLES OF PARTICULAR INTEREST FOR ORVIETO

'Brevi Annali di Perugia', 1308–, in *Arch. St. Italiano*, 16, i, 1850.
Dragomanni, F. G. (ed.), *Croniche* of G. Villani, Florence, 1844.
Duchesne, L. (ed.), Continuation of Polono in *Liber Pontificalis*, Paris, 1886-92. (*Lib. Pont.*).
Fedele, P. (ed.), 'Cronache Sanesi' in RIS, N.S., xv, 6.
Hartwig, O. (ed.), 'Sansanominis Gesta Florentinorum' in *Quellen und Forschungen zur ältesten Geschichte der Stadt Florenz*, Marburg, 1875.
Seppelt, F. X. (ed.), Stefaneschi's Life of Celestine V in *Monumenta Coelestiniana*, Paderborn, 1921.
'Vita Metrica Urbani IV' in RIS, O.S., III, 2.

SECONDARY AUTHORITIES

Antonelli, M. 'Vicende della Dominazione Pontificia nel Patrimonio di S. Pietro in Tuscia dalla Traslazione della Sede alla Restaurazione dell'Albornoz' in *Arch. Soc. Rom. St. Patr.*, xxv-vii, 1902-4. (Antonelli, 'Dominazione Pontificia')
Antonelli, M. 'Una Ribellione contro il Vicario del Patrimonio (1315-7)' in *Arch. Soc. Rom. St. Patr.*, xx, 1897. (Antonelli, 'Una Ribellione').
Boase, T. S. R. *Boniface VIII*, London, 1933. (Boase).
Bonelli, R. *Fasi Costruttive ed Organismo Architettonico del Duomo di Orvieto*, Orvieto, 1943.
Bruscalupi, G. *Monografia Storica della Contea di Pitigliano*, Florence, 1907.
Buccolini, G. 'Serie Critica dei Vescovi di Bolsena e di Orvieto' in *Boll. R. Dep. St. Patr. per l'Umbria*, xxxviii, 1941.
Caetani, G. *Domus Caietana*, vol. I, pt. I, Sancasciano Val di Pesa, 1927.
Caetani, G. *Caietanorum Genealogia*, Perugia, 1920.
Calisse, C. *I Prefetti di Vico*, Rome, 1888.
Calisse, C. 'La Costituzione del Patrimonio di S. Pietro in Tuscia' in *Arch. Soc. Rom. St. Patr.*, xv, 1892.
Ceci, G. *Todi nel Medio Evo*, Todi, 1897.
Ciacci, G. *Gli Aldobrandeschi nella Storia e nella 'Divina Commedia'*, vol. I, Rome, 1935. (Ciacci).

BIBLIOGRAPHY

Davidsohn, R. *Geschichte von Florenz*, Berlin, 1896. (Davidsohn).
Dottarelli, C. *Storia di Bolsena*, Orvieto, 1928. (Dottarelli).
Ermini, G. *La Libertà Comunale nello Stato della Chiesa* (2 vols., vol. 1 in *Arch. Soc. Rom. St. Patr.*, II, 1926; vol. II, Rome, 1927).
Ermini, G. *I Parlamenti dello Stato della Chiesa dalle Origini al Periodo Albornoziano*, Rome, 1930.
Ermini, G. 'I Rettori Provinciali dello Stato della Chiesa da Innocenzo II all'Albornoz' in *Rivista di Storia del Diritto Italiano*, IV, January-April 1931.
Ermini, G. 'Aspetti Giuridici della Sovranità Pontificia nell'Umbria nel secolo XIII' in *Boll. R. Dep. St. Patr. per l'Umbria*, XXXIV, 1937.
Falco, G. 'Sulla Formazione e la Costituzione della Signoria dei Caetani, 1283-1303'ˈin *Rivista Storica Italiana*', Turin, vol. VI (new series), July 1928.
Fumi, L. *Orvieto. Note storiche e biografiche*, Città di Castello, 1891.
Fumi, L. 'I Patarini in Orvieto' in *Arch. St. Ital.*, 3rd S., XXII, 1875.
Fumi, L. 'Notizie tratte delle più antiche Sentenze Criminali del Podestà d'Orvieto' in *Boll. R. Dep. St. Patr. per l'Umbria*, XIV, 1908.
Fumi, L. 'Di una Falsificazione contenuta nell'antico Regesto della Chiesa d'Orvieto' in *Boll. R. Dep. St. Patr. per l'Umbria*, XVI, 1910.
Jordan, E. *Les Origines de la Domination Angevine en Italie*, Paris, 1909. (Jordan).
Lisini, A. *La Contessa Palatina Margherita Aldobrandeschi Signora del Feudo di Sovana*, Siena, 1933 (and in *Boll. Senese di St. Patr.*, III, fascs. 1, 3, 4, 1932). (Lisini).
Luchaire, A. *Innocent III, Rome et l'Italie*, Paris, 1904.
Pardi, G. *Comune e Signoria a Orvieto*, Todi, n.d. (Pardi, *Comune & Signoria*).
Pardi, G. 'Serie dei supremi Magistrati e Reggitori d'Orvieto' in *Boll. R. Dep. St. Patr. per l'Umbria*, I, 1895. (Pardi, 'Supremi Magistrati').
Pardi, G. 'Podestà, Capitani e Vicari in Orvieto nei secoli XIII e XIV' in *Studi Storici*, Pisa, XVII, i, 1908. (Pardi, 'Podestà, Capitani, Vicari').
Pardi, G. *Il Catasto d'Orvieto dell'anno 1292*, Perugia, 1896 (and in *Boll. R. Dep. St. Patr. per l'Umbria*, II, 1896). (Pardi, *Catasto*).
Pardi, G. *Il Governo dei Signori Cinque in Orvieto*, Orvieto, 1894. (Pardi, *Signori 5*).
Pinzi, C. *Storia di Viterbo*, Rome, 1887-1913.
Rondoni, G. 'Orvieto nel Medio Evo' in *Arch. St. Ital.*, 4th S., XVIII, 1886, and XIX, 1887, and in *Album Poliglotto per il VI Centenario del Duomo di Orvieto*, Siena-Rome, 1891.

Schevill, F. *Siena: The Story of a Mediaeval Commune*, London, 1909.
Sora, V. 'I Conti di Anguillara' in *Arch. Soc. Rom. St. Patr.*, XXIX, 1906.
Volpe, G. *Movimenti Religiosi e Sette Ereticali nella Società Medievale Italiana*, Florence, 1926.

INDEX

INDEX

INDEX

For EU product safety concerns, contact us at Calle de José Abascal, 56–1°,
28003 Madrid, Spain or eugpsr@cambridge.org.

www.ingramcontent.com/pod-product-compliance
Ingram Content Group UK Ltd.
Pitfield, Milton Keynes, MK11 3LW, UK
UKHW010046140625
459647UK00012BB/1637